ENLIGHTENMENT MAN & MASON

VOLUME II OF
RENAISSANCE MAN & MASON

Library of Congress Control Number: 2021920909
© Piers A. Vaughan 2021.

All rights reserved. No part of this publication may be reproduced, distributed, or transmitted in any form or by any means, including photocopying, recording, or other electronic or mechanical methods, without the prior written permission of the publisher, except in the case of brief quotations embodied in critical reviews and certain other non-commercial uses permitted by copyright law. For permission requests, write to the publisher at the address below:

Rose Circle Publications
P.O. Box 854
Bayonne, NJ 07002, U.S.A.
rosecirclebooks.com

ISBN 978-1-947907-26-3

Enlightenment Man & Mason
Volume II of Renaissance Man & Mason

Piers A. Vaughan
foreword by Christopher McIntosh

Acknowledgements

I would like to thank Dr. Christopher McIntosh for his wonderful Foreword, which perfectly captures what I was trying to accomplish with this book; the members of St. John's Lodge No. 1, Ancient York Masons of New York, of which I am a proud member and who are the custodians of the Washington Inaugural Bible; to Jérôme Sirdey of the Départment du fonds ancient of the Bibliothèque municipal de Lyon, who while working from home during Covid still sent me scans of the Aigle Noir Rose-Croix rituals, enabling me to write my thesis and the last Chapter of this book – and on my birthday(!); to Jason Sheridan for his continued support and tireless understanding of a grumpy author and translator; and to Steve Adams of EsotericEditions.com for his incredible work on making a silk purse out of a messy Word document, and for providing an excellent cover to this volume.

Table of Contents

LIST OF FIGURES XI

FOREWORD XV

PREFACE XVII

THE STORY BEHIND THE MOST FAMOUS
IMAGE OF KING SOLOMON'S TEMPLE 23

    BACKGROUND 23

    A HAMBURG OPERA 25

    SCHOTT'S MODEL COMES TO LONDON 26

    A SPANISH JESUIT 28

    ENGRAVINGS OF VILLALPANDO'S IMAGE 32

    A FINAL MYSTERY 36

THE MAGICIAN, THE MYSTIC, AND THE MASON –
THE UNLIKELY ORIGIN OF THE SCOTTISH RECTIFIED RITE 43

    INTRODUCTION. 44

    A HANKERING AFTER CHIVALRY 46

    THE THREE GRAND PRINCIPALS. 49

    ENTER THE MAGICIAN. 50

    THE SOLDIER TURNED MYSTIC. 54

    THE SILK MERCHANT FROM LYON 57

    A FINAL ACT OF MAGIC –
        TRANSFORMATION OF A RITE 60

    CONCLUSION. 62

A DISCOURSE ON NUMBERS
(PART 1 – HISTORY). 67

    INTRODUCTION. 67

    EARLY BEGINNINGS. 68

> REDISCOVERY OF THE EARLY TEXTS................72
> THE ENLIGHTENMENT AND FREEMASONRY............75
> VICTORIAN NUMEROLOGY.........................79
> THE TWENTIETH CENTURY AND BEYOND.............81

Enochian, or How to Speak with Angels 87

An Introduction to Martinism and its Spiritual Relationship to Freemasonry 105

> INTRODUCTION...............................105
> A LESSON IN HISTORY........................107
> DIFFERENCES IN ENGLAND AND MAINLAND EUROPE..108
> WHAT MAKES AN ESOTERIC ORDER?..............109
> THE ORDER OF ELECT COHENS OF THE UNIVERSE..111
> THE THEOSOPHY OF THE ELECT COHENS..........112
> THE ORDER IS DEAD – LONG LIVE THE ORDER!...114
> THE MASONIC SUCCESSOR TO THE ELECT COHENS..116
> THE CHRISTIAN MYSTICAL SUCCESSOR TO THE ELECT COHENS...120
> THE FRENCH REVOLUTION INTERVENES...........121
> THE 19TH CENTURY RESURGENCE OF MYSTICISM....122
> THE RESURRECTION OF MARTINISM..............124
> THE NATURAL EBB AND FLOW OF ESOTERIC SOCIETIES...127
> CONTEMPORARY MARTINISM.....................129

The Kabbalistic Tree of Life: The Soul of the Rosicrucian Masonic Order 135

Did Louis-Claude de Saint-Martin Influence the Scottish Rectified Rite? 159

> INTRODUCTION...............................159
> ALCHEMY....................................162
> UNIQUE CHRISTIAN PERSPECTIVE...............165

Table of Contents

RESPECT FOR ERUDITION 167

CONCLUSION. 168

The Degrees of the Black Eagle Rose-Croix. 175

INTRODUCTION. 176

JEAN-BAPTISTE WILLERMOZ AND
THE HISTORICAL CONTEXT OF THE GRADES 176

SYMBOLS USED IN THE GRADES 181

THE OVERALL FORM OF THE
CHANCELLOR AND BAILIFF GRADES. 188

COMPARISON WITH THE TSCHOUDY MANUSCRIPTS. 193

CONCLUSION. 201

BIBLIOGRAPHY 203

APPENDIX A: EXAMPLES OF THREE DIFFERENT HANDWRITINGS . . 207

APPENDIX B: SAMPLE PAGES FROM WILLERMOZ MANUSCRIPT 209

APPENDIX C: COMPARISON OF HANDWRITING BETWEEN TWO
TSCHOUDY RITUAL SOURCES 211

APPENDIX D: GRADE OF APPRENTICE OR
KNIGHT OF THE BLACK EAGLE ROSE CROIX 213

    Dignities of the Order and Ceremonial. 213

    Origin of the Order of Knights of the Black Eagle 213

    Decoration of the Chapter. 215

    Dress 215

    Apron. 215

    Jewel. 215

    Gloves. 215

    Opening of the Chapter 215

    Steps. 217

    Obligation 217

    Sign 217

    Sacred Word. 217

    Password. 217

    Grip 217

    Sash 217

    Order 217

    Explanation of the Tracing Board 218

    To Close 218

    Catechism 218

APPENDIX E: GRADE OF COMPANION OR COMMANDER OF THE BLACK EAGLE ROSE CROIX 223

    Decoration of the Chapter 223

    Attire 224

    Sash 224

    Jewel 224

    Gloves 224

    Apron 225

    Password 225

    Sacred Word 225

    Sign 225

    Grip 225

    Order 225

    Explanation of the Tracing Board 226

    Opening of the Chapter 227

    To Close the Chapter 228

    Initiation 229

    The Chamber of Reflection 229

    Obligation 232

    Steps 233

    Instruction 234

APPENDIX F: GRADE OF GRAND MASTER OR COMMANDER OF THE BLACK EAGLE ROSE CROIX 237

    Introduction 237

    Ceremonial & Dignities 238

    Privileges 238

    Statutes & Regulations 240

Table of Contents

The Twelve Months of the Year 244

Solar Year 246

Decoration of the Chapter 248

Order of the Shields 248

The Throne 251

Scales of Solomon 252

Illumination 252

Places 253

Attire 253

Jewels 255

Sacred Word 255

Password 256

Sign 256

Grip 256

Coming to Order 256

Opening of the Chapter 256

To Close the Chapter 257

Initiation of a Bailiff 258

Decoration of the Chamber of Reflection 258

Introduction into the Chapter 259

Obligation 262

Address of the Orator 264

Address of the Grand Master 267

Catechism 268

Figure of the Pentacle 282

List of Figures

Figure 1: Engraving of Solomon's Temple from Baskett Bible......................... 23
Figure 2: Temple of Dendur, Metropolitan Museum NYC 24
Figure 3: Drawing of First Temple at Jerusalem 24
Figure 4: Schott's Model at Hamburg Museum... 26
Figure 5: Villalpanda's plan of Ezekiel's Temple.. 28
Figure 6: Plan of El Escorial 29
Figure 7: Villalpanda's Front Elevation of the Temple................................ 30
Figure 8: Villalpanda's Temple perched upon Great Foundations 31
Figure 9: Front elevation of El Escorial 31
Figure 10: Print from 1723 Exhibition of Schott's Model in London 32
Figure 11: John Field illustration in KJV 1660 33
Figure 12: von Erlach illustration of KST in 1725 33
Figure 13: St. George's Church, Lalibela 34
Figure 14: Detail of map showing Temple buttresses 34
Figure 15: Villalpando-Baskett illustration two-dimensional 35
Figure 16: Print from London exhibition three-dimensional 35
Figure 17: Masonic print from the early 1730s 35
Figure 18: Detail from 4th Grade Trestleboard of the Scottish Rectified Rite 37
Figure 19: Eastern Mandala with four entrances....................................... 38
Figure 20: John Dee's Watchtowers.. 39
Figure 21: King James II.. 44
Figure 22: Ramsay's Discourse 45
Figure 23: In Eminenti 47
Figure 24: 'Langues' and Regalia of the Rite of Strict Observance 48
Figure 25: Martinez de Pasqually 51
Figure 26: Magical Circle of Elus Cohen... 52
Figure 27: Baron Samedi 53
Figure 28: Saint-Martin 54
Figure 29: First Edition of 'Of Errors & Truth' 55
Figure 30: J.-B. Willermoz.. 57
Figure 31: Regalia of the highest grade of the R.E.R................................. 58

Figure 32: It still stands!. 62
Figure 33: Mesopotamian counting tokens 68
Figure 34: Development of glyphs into letters - Hebrew 'aleph' 68
Figure 35: Developing Hebrew Alphabet 69
Figure 36: Dotted aleph in heading. 69
Figure 37: SATOR acrostic 71
Figure 38: Cornelius Agrippa. 73
Figure 39: John Dee 73
Figure 40: Magic Square from Kircher's Œdipus Egyptiacus (1652). 74
Figure 41: An 18th Century Lodge Meeting 76
Figure 42: The Pentagram 78
Figure 43: The Magus by F. Barrett. 79
Figure 44: S.R.I.A 80
Figure 45: 8th Card of Major Arcana 81
Figure 46: Margaret Peeke 82
Figure 47: 'Sepharial'. 82
Figure 48: Richard Cavendish 82
Figure 49: Dr. John Dee 87
Figure 50: Part of Corpus Hermeticum. 89
Figure 51: Gabriel's Story, from season 13 episode 18 of Supernatural 90
Figure 52: The Great Chain of Being 91
Figure 53: Passing the River Code 92
Figure 54: Masonic Pigpen code 92
Figure 55: Enochian alphabet. 93
Figure 57: Trimethius' Code (part) 93
Figure 56: Lingua ignota 93
Figure 58: Some of Dee's paraphernalia at the British Museum 94
Figure 59: Water Tablet 96
Figure 60: The Enochian Alphabet. 97
Figure 61: Causabon's damning book 98
Figure 62: William Wynn Westcott, Supreme Magus of the S.R.I.A. 98
Figure 63: Extract from the Book of 2,400 Divine and Angelic Names 100
Figure 64: First Council of Nicea 106
Figure 65: Nag Hammadi library. 106

List of Figures

Figure 66: Plaque 107
Figure 67: Santiago de Compostela 107
Figure 68: King George I 108
Figure 69: The Age of Enlightenment 109
Figure 70: Chevalier Andrew Ramsay 110
Figure 71: Silhouette of Martinès de Pasqually 111
Figure 72: Pasqually's Treatise 112
Figure 73: Notebook of Prunelle de Lière with Elus Cohen magic circles 113
Figure 74: Willermoz' Diploma as Réau-Croix 115
Figure 75: Meeting of the R.E.R. in France in the 1930s 117
Figure 76: Meliora Præsumo 117
Figure 77: Silhouette of J.-B. Willermoz 119
Figure 78: Louis-Claude de Saint-Martin 121
Figure 79: Rosicrucian Cross from the Golden Dawn 123
Figure 80: Robert Ambelain 123
Figure 81: Dr. Gérard Encausse, or 'Papus' 124
Figure 82: Papus in his Martinist 'cabinet' 125
Figure 83: First edition of l'Initiation 126
Figure 84: Constant Chevillon 127
Figure 85: Philippe Encausse 129
Figure 86: The fundamental symbol of Martinism 130
Figure 87: Depiction of the Tree of Life according to Arthur Edward Waite 135
Figure 88: Creation (lightning bolt) and the Rosicrucian Grades 137
Figure 89: The Hebrew Alphabet 140
Figure 90: Gregorian Chant 141
Figure 91: Elo Mikhael Gabriel ve-Raphael = 701 142
Figure 92: Rose upon the Rosicrucian Cross 143
Figure 93: Elohim creating Adam (Blake) 144
Figure 94: Ain Soph 145
Figure 95: The Tree of Life 146
Figure 96: Wisdom, Strength and Beauty 148
Figure 97: Lightning bolt descending the Tree of Life 149
Figure 98: Before the Fall 149
Figure 99: After the Fall 149

Figure 100: Wisdom upon a Tree... 150
Figure 101: The Way of Return, or Way of the Serpent... 152
Figure 103: The Life of Christ Projected onto the Tree of Life... 153
Figure 104: A Martinist Manifestation of the Tree of Life... 154
Figure 105: Adhuc Stat - It still stands, it still endures... 160
Figure 106: Timeline of key events... 161
Figure 107: Manuscript page in Willermoz' handwriting from Black Eagle Rose Croix... 163
Figure 108: Saint-Martin's relationship with Willermoz?... 164
Figure 109: Tracing Board depicting Hiram rising... 166
Figure 110: Meliora Præsumo... 167
Figure 111: Image of Louis-Claude de Saint-Martin... 167
Figure 112: Willermoz' General & Masonic Code for Rectified Lodges... 169
Figure 113: Behind the scenes... 170
Figure 114: Image from Manuscript... 175
Figure 115: Examples of fonds Willermoz Manuscript covers... 179
Figure 116: Mystical Figure of Solomon (McGregor Mathers' version)... 184
Figure 117: Scales of Solomon (Willermoz manuscript)... 184
Figure 118: Seal of Solomon in Heptameron... 185
Figure 119: Sigil in Triangle from Chancellor/Companion grade... 185
Figure 120: Full sigil in Solomonic hexagram from Bailiff/Master grade... 185
Figure 121: Scales of Thales from Willermoz Catechism... 187
Figure 122: Sigil of Phul from Armadel... 187
Figure 123: List of Angels and Sigils from Willermoz' third grade... 192
Figure 124: 'Adonai' from the Willermoz ritual... 192
Figure 125: Instructions to the third grade - Willermoz MS... 207
Figure 126: Instructions to the third grade - Tschoudy MS... 207
Figure 127: Instructions to the third grade Unknown MS... 207
Figure 128: Early Tracing Board of Black Eagle Rose Croix... 211
Figure 129: Later regalia for Black Eagle Rose Croix... 211
Figure 130: Early regalia for Black Eagle Rose Croix... 226
Figure 131: Later image of apron, chronologically. Note the 'I' on the flap... 253
Figure 132: Collection circa 1762... 254
Figure 133: Tschoudy Tracing Board... 263

Foreword

eaders of the first volume of Piers Vaughan's earlier book, *Renaissance Man and Mason* (published in 2016), will have been eagerly awaiting this volume, presented as a sequel. They will not be disappointed. Like the earlier book, this is a miscellany of texts based on talks given by the author, and is marked by the same deep erudition, fascinating insights and clear, engaging style.

The collection covers a wide range of subjects from King Solomon's Temple to numerology and from the Kabbalah to the Rosicrucian movement. But, if there is a predominant theme running through the book, it is the notion of the loss of something precious at some time in the past, and the attempt to regain it, whether it be a sacred object, a long-lost wisdom or a primal state of perfection.

This theme is already present in the first contribution, dealing with the subject of King Solomon's Temple. Destroyed, rebuilt and then finally demolished in Roman times, it has over time taken on a powerful mystique that is shared by Jews, Christians and Freemasons alike. For the Freemason the Temple is a reminder of a vanished architectural splendor and the loss of certain profound secrets of the Mason's craft. Moreover, in the Masonic system of moral and spiritual development based on the symbolism of architecture and building, the Temple serves as a supreme model.

Piers shows how the design of the Temple, as it was imagined by various authors and artists, passed into Masonic lore and influenced the design of certain buildings such as the Escorial palace of Philip II of Spain, begun in 1563. This piece of information reminded me of another monarch, namely James the VI of Scotland (later James I of England), whose Chapel Royal at Stirling Castle, built in 1594, shows a striking similarity to contemporary depictions of the Temple as well as signs of having doubled as a Masonic Lodge. There is some evidence that King James himself was a Freemason. Certainly his reign was a key period in the development of what we now call speculative Masonry. And, significantly, he strove to present himself as a Scottish Solomon.

Enlightenment Man & Mason

The name of Scotland later became one to conjure with in higher degree Masonic circles, as the author describes, thanks in large measure to Jacobite emigrants to France. Hence the emergence there and elsewhere in Europe of rites invoking the Scottish mystique, such as the Scottish Rectified Rite or Chevaliers Bienfaisants de la Cité Sainte, one of the higher degree Masonic orders that sprang up in the latter part of the 18th century, with their chivalric grades and elaborate rituals. In the world of these orders we find again the theme of humanity's loss in the distant past of a more perfect and exalted state of being, which the initiate aspires to regain through a process of "reintegration," a word used by Martinez de Pasqually, founder of the Order of the Elect Cohens, in his book *Traité de la réintegration des êtres*. As Piers points out, these notions are redolent of Gnosticism with its belief that the world is a kind of prison in which our souls are trapped, cut off from the true divine realm from which they came. This world view pervades the writings of Pasqually's follower Louis-Claude de Saint-Martin, whose ideas, along with those of Pasqually, gave rise to the movement known as Martinism. Two chapters of this book are devoted to the seminal influence of Saint-Martin and Martinism.

The same Gnostic stream is evident in the Rosicrucian tradition which features especially in two of Piers Vaughan's chapters: one on the Kabbalah in Rosicrucian Masonry and the other on the Black Eagle Rose Croix, a rite with alchemical elements, founded by Jean-Baptiste Willermoz in the 1760s. Again in Willermoz we find the theme of loss and rediscovery, as Piers points out. Willermoz "saw the existing structure of the Catholic faith as not providing what he desired so earnestly: a return to a primitive and esoteric Christianity he envisaged, framed by esoteric belief and Ritual rather than conventional dogma". Even the chapter on numerology, and its application in many different esoteric traditions, touches on the theme of loss when Piers writes that we need to "restore the primitive dignity of numbers".

The book is enriched by an abundance of well-chosen illustrations. One of the images, which was used in the German rite of the Strict Observance, is a broken column, a motif often found in Masonic iconography and emblematic of the notion of a lost perfection and the striving of the Mason to regain it. Perhaps more than any of the other illustrations, it encapsulates the essential *Leitmotiv* of this book.

Christopher McIntosh

Preface

Back in 2016 I produced a book which I hoped would both appeal to and answer some of the questions being asked by newer members of the Craft. Enticed by advertisements, and by the extraordinary level of interest generated by books like Dan Brown's *The Lost Symbol* and movies like *National Treasure*, the level of inquiries and actual initiations was increasing considerably.

For those who joined erudite Lodges and what are called 'Traditional Observance' Lodges, expectations usually matched the experience, with quality rituals well executed in a civilized environment and venue, always with a good lecture, and followed by profound and extensive debates over fine liquor and cigars. They were the lucky ones.

The rest found themselves members of aging and tired groups, where their questions about symbolism and secret, esoteric knowledge – the very things which had attracted them in the first place – were met with ignorance or even ridicule. After all, why waste time with education? Clams don't bake themselves!

It was with those poor souls in mind, lost in a cultural wilderness, that I wrote my book *Renaissance Man and Mason*. If they couldn't get their 'fix' in their local Lodge, at least they could keep up their education through reading, and be reassured that yes, there *are* secrets in Masonry! I carefully kept the Chapters, or talks, short, mostly no more than a dozen or so pages long. Each could be read in one sitting, then pondered. I hoped that such a 'sampler' approach would lead the readership to an interest in the great writers of the past and encourage them to go more deeply into subjects I had introduced to them. By introducing that jargon which is often a barrier to understanding, I hoped that they would find such books less intimidating. Finally, I hoped that they would not become discouraged, and realize that there were many, many Masons out there with similar interests to them, and that it was worth persevering in the Gentle Craft. I also made sure the book was twenty-two chapters long and wondered if anyone would spot this 'Easter Egg': that the number of chapters equaled the total number of Hebrew Letters or the cards of the Major Arcana.

I was not disappointed! Indeed, I was surprised and gratified at how many worked this out. I was also very pleased by the number of Masons who came up to me at talks, Masonicons and social events to thank me for the book and to tell me how much it had helped them.

But most of all I was astonished by the number of different ways people were using the book. Of course, many of them were obtaining it and reading it to feel a bond with all those Freemasons who shared similar interests in history, symbolism and meaning. But I also discovered that the book was selling well abroad, which I hadn't even thought about when I wrote it. In the States readers were being ever more creative. I lost count of the number of Masonic Book Clubs which had decided my book was an ideal size for their members to read a Chapter a week, or a month, and come together to discuss it. There were Masons who gave the book as a gift to friends; one Grand Lodge even purchased a number to give to its Officers. Some even gave them to their wives, perhaps in the hope that their spouses would assume their husbands were engaged in worthy aims and not simply getting drunk with their buddies. Finally, I remember selling one copy to an elderly lady at the Masonic Home in Utica, New York: she was curious to know more about Freemasonry and felt it would be far more interesting to read about what we studied, than simply picking up a recruitment brochure.

Five years later, I have still been writing, translating, travelling, giving talks, and living up to the injunction to 'make a daily advance in masonic knowledge'. It's high time for a second book. This time the format is a little different. I felt that I had already done the book with small, digestible chapters. For those who had completed that book it was time for deeper materials, a longer and more thoughtful focus on specific topics. It was also important that these be linked, so that there was an opportunity to reinforce ideas and messages, instead of offering a 'potluck' of stories. And so, this book was born as a series of interlinked papers leading to one conclusion.

The focus of this book is predominantly the Age of Enlightenment, and so the title *Enlightenment Man & Mason* immediately sprang to mind. The Enlightenment was a mixed bag for Freemasons. On the one hand they loved to see progress in all the fields of the Arts and Sciences, the expansion across the globe, and learning about new cultures and mythologies. But on the other, the replacement of the old ways by so-called modern science was leading to an agnostic – or even atheistic – trend which went completely against the landmarks of Masonry. While some, for example, the Encyclopedists, embraced this new approach, many, while not exactly clinging to a Church which they saw as corrupt and overly influential behemoth, still believed in the faith of their youth, and reacted with horror at the thought of an atheistic society, devoid of all ethical and moral pointers.

A major focus of this book will be that counter-Enlightenment movement which sought to preserve the old ways and religion and attempted to curb the greater excesses of this new wave. Therefore, most of the papers focus on that period, particularly in France and mainland Europe, where these forces played out during the 18th and early 19th centuries. Although the first paper could be said to focus on England and the United States, to be honest there was little happening there in terms of this extraordinary war being carried out behind the scenes.

In this book you will find eight papers (and yes, that is another important number in the numerical theosophy of Martinès de Pasqually, Louis-Claude de Saint-Martin and Jean-Baptiste Willermoz, all of whom you will come to know very well by the end of this book). For them, the number '8' stood for perfection, the descent of the one who was both Man and Spirit; since the number '4' represented Man, being the number of the elements and the vivifying power (and yes, I didn't miscount: for these masons there were only 3 elements, as we shall see); and therefore '8' represented both Man and Spirit which joined with Man to become the ultimate expression of God's power: the Repairer.

The papers range from a look at a curious diagram in the King James Bibles to a series of papers about Orders founded by his Jacobite successors in France. We will meet our three protagonists mentioned above, and spend some time exploring numerical systems, including theirs. Much of this surrounds the formation of the Scottish Rectified Rite, or Knights Beneficent of the Holy City, an Order which, had the French Revolution not intervened, had a real chance of becoming the only – or at least the major – Masonic Order practiced in Europe.

We also examine one related Order which, while outside the family of Freemasonry, is nevertheless closely linked both spiritually and in terms of its founders, and that is Martinism. While little is openly written about this Order (Saint-Martin its founder said: 'I never wanted to make any noise', and its focus is on *silence* and remaining *unknown* – a lesson some more modern manifestations of this Christian mystical path appear to have forgotten), we are certainly able to explore some of its similarities with Masonry.

We also explore how Saint-Martin, and though him Martinism, must have influenced the Scottish Rectified Rite, and helped to transform what had been little more than another nice little set of rituals with fancy costumes and moral lessons into a blueprint for salvation itself.

Much of the Order's symbolism, like Masonry in general, is based on the Tree of Life, so there is a refresher course on this important symbol, ending with an exploration of how the Tree of Life also features in Martinism. And since these protagonists were focused on communicating with angelic forces, a paper on the Enochian or Angelical Language of John Dee explores why this might have been the case. In this manner we begin to get inside the minds of these masons in order to better understand their world view, and what made them tick.

The book ends with a first ever publication of translations, with commentary, on the Order of the Black Eagle Rose Croix, the last ritual written by Willermoz just prior to his joining the Elus Cohen and then creating the Scottish Rectified Rite. In referring to it we can understand the deep yearning for esoteric meaning in Masonry which he was seeking, in this instance through alchemical symbolism.

While some symbols and comments will appear more than once in different papers, you must remember that this both helps to fix certain ideas in the mind and reinforces the messages. On a mundane level, too, these papers were never delivered together, so from a practical standpoint some repetition is inevitable. I hope you find these papers as interesting and useful as many of you found those in *Renaissance Man & Mason*!

Piers A. Vaughan
Autumnal Equinox 2021

The Story Behind the Most Famous Image of King Solomon's Temple

A Celestial Archetype

The Story Behind the Most Famous Image of King Solomon's Temple

t was while visiting the Henry Coil Masonic Library and Museum at the Grand Lodge of California that I noticed an image of Schott's realization of King Solomon's Temple proudly displayed on the wall. I was very familiar with it, since it is one of the major prints in the George Washington Inaugural Bible, in the proud possession of my Lodge, St. John's № 1 of New York City. Seeing it reminded me of a question which has nagged at me ever since I first saw it nearly thirty years ago: why does it look more like a Palladian creation of the late seventeenth century than a primitive structure built by tribal nomad thousands of years ago?

It was time to do some research!

Figure 1: Engraving of Solomon's Temple from Baskett Bible

Background

One of the most striking images among the 103 steel engravings of maps and scenes in the George Washington Inaugural Bible, printed in London by Mark Baskett in 1767, is the image of the Temple of King Solomon. It is an elaborate image, and very striking, reminiscent of an opulent 17th Century Baroque palace, and quite out of place given the true origins of the First Temple. However, the beauty of the image was truly revealed in 2003 when the Bible required extensive restoration.

One hundred years earlier an attempt had been made to preserve the most important pages and images in the Bible, which had begun to suffer the wear and tear of over one hundred and fifty years of use, not least in being handled by the many people who wished to catch a glimpse of *the* Bible and see *the* page used by Washington at his inauguration. Unfortunately for the Bible, state of the art preservation techniques at that time consisted of slavering glue over the unfortunate pages, then applying a thin transparent layer of silk to protect them. So, the challenge was: how to remove the silk without destroying the underlying page in the process. The North-East Document Conservation Center (NEDCC), who was undertaking the restoration, wanted to have a way to experiment prior to committing their processes to this unique Bible. Fortunately, we had a spare copy, indeed a Mark Baskett Bible of the same date, which only differed in that it also contained the Book of Common Prayer and engravings by a different artist. However, one of the images which had deteriorated greatly in the Washington Bible was the picture of King Solomon's Temple, and this was also present in the other copy. The NEDCC was therefore able to subject the picture to the various restorative processes prior to using them on the Washington Bible.

Thus, this particular page was thrust into the spotlight for all of us, and I began to wonder why this unlikely image seemed so widespread as a representation of King Solomon's Temple.

But not only was this image of the Temple at Jerusalem a staple in King James Bibles; it can also be seen hanging as a print in many of the engravings of early English Masonic meetings and table lodges, too. The images may be small and details lacking, but the tell-tale façade, the five towers and the colonnades on either side are always present, even if in abridged form. But let us begin with the Bible illustration.

Figure 2: Temple of Dendur, Metropolitan Museum NYC

Figure 3: Drawing of First Temple at Jerusalem

We should remember the circumstances surrounding the building of the First Temple (*sans* the various controversies about whether it even existed). Taking the accounts in the Books of Kings and Chronicles[1] at face value, this was the first permanent building erected by a nomadic group of tribes, which up till then had worshipped their god in a tabernacle, or temporary shelter made of poles, ropes and cloth. It was placed atop a mountain, Mount Moriah, as if to be closer to the god in whose honor it was built. Although there was no one present who had lived in captivity in Egypt, there must nevertheless have been stories handed down of the immense temples built to honor their gods.

---

[1] Primarily I Kings Chs 6 to 8; 2 Chron. Chs 2 to 5.

The Most Famous Image of King Solomon's Temple

It is evident that at least some of these features were incorporated into the First Temple at Jerusalem. We have an outer courtyard as a means of separating the profane from the sacred space, and vessels for purifying oneself prior to entering the outer courts of the Temple itself. At the entrance were two great pylons, but now cast as pillars, through which one had to pass in order to gain entrance. The interior was richly decorated, and divided into several chambers, some of which could only be accessed by the Temple priests; and one room was accessible only to the High Priest. The Holy of Holies contained the Ark of the Covenant, which was not dissimilar in style to the arks and the effigies of gods regularly carried in public processions through the streets, upon two poles, by the Egyptian priests.[2]

Despite the hyperbolic descriptions of the Temple in the Old Testament, we must nevertheless not lose sight of the fact that, in a land where most people lived in temporary structures, it would not have taken much of a permanent building to arouse feelings of pride, stability and awe in this formerly nomadic people. Tales are often exaggerated, and added to the fact that we are still not completely certain about the true size of ancient weights and measures, we should be cautious in our interpretation of how elaborate this edifice was.

The Second Temple, rebuilt by Zerubbabel following the return from exile in Babylon was, we know, a shadow of the first; and the Bible tells us that, while the younger Jews marveled at the building (which is a way was odd, since they had grown up in Babylon – one of the most advanced cities in the world at the time, which boasted many splendid temples and palaces, and the incomparable Hanging Gardens), the elders who remembered the former Temple sat in silence and wept.[3]

This temple was extended and largely rebuilt during the reign of King Herod at the time of the Roman occupation. This temple did not survive the Roman siege of Jerusalem in 70 C.E.

However, it is the Third Temple, the one of Ezekiel's Vision[4], that will come to occupy our thoughts more completely as we contemplate the image in the Washington Bible.

A Hamburg Opera

Sometimes, threads come together seemingly at random, and conspire to move history in a particular direction. Gerhard Schott (1641 – 1702) was a lawyer and adviser in Hamburg. In 1677, having an interest in music and as a friend of the librettist Christian Heinrich Postel, he was persuaded by Christian Albrecht von

---

[2] Noegel, Scott B., "The Egyptian Origin of the Ark of the Covenant", pp. 223 – 242 from *Israel's Exodus in Transdisciplinary Perspective*, Quantitative Methods in the Humanities and Social Sciences, © Springer International Publishing Switzerland 2015.

[3] Ezra 3:12.

[4] Ezekiel, Chs 40 to 42.

Schleswig-Holstein-Gottorf to found the first public opera in Germany. To ensure his venture was not censored by the local clergy, who saw the erection of an opera house as damaging to morality, he ensured that early performances at the opera house had a religious flavor. The inaugural performance was of a Biblical Songspiel, quickly followed by an opera in two parts, entitled "The Destruction of Jerusalem" which covered the taking of Jerusalem and the destruction of the Temple by Nebuchadnezzar. The libretto was written by his friend Postel and the music by Kapellmeister Conradi, and for which he commissioned a wooden model in 1680.[5]

Why a model?

A letter from Dr. Hagedorn in the Hamburg Records Office, dated October 20, 1899, says that the general public were not at all impressed with the set used for the opera, expecting something far grander, since many tracts of the time claimed that the Temple was an architectural masterpiece. This inspired Schott to commission this creation of a model in wood, which took approximately six years to execute at enormous cost, depicting the Temple in all its believed finery, including the personnel, the sacrifices, and the ceremonials. This was housed in a separate building behind the opera house.

Figure 4: Schott's Model at Hamburg Museum
(by An-d - Own work, CC BY-SA 3.0, https://commons.wikimedia.org/w/index.php?curid=26153827)

The opera itself appears to have been a somewhat tedious affair, given the fact that both Parts were comprised of three Acts and a Prologue. No doubt the libretto would have fared better had it been orchestrated by a later composer to the Hamburg opera, George Frederic Handel, who arrived at the age of 19 to take up the position of second violinist in 1703.

Schott's Model comes to London

Following his death in 1702, his family had some difficulty selling the artefact, due to its high price because of the amount of work which had gone into its construction. Indeed, it appears that a transaction was not completed until around

---

[5] Goldhill, Simon, *The Temple of Jerusalem*, pub. Profile Books, London, 2004, p. 140.

The Most Famous Image of King Solomon's Temple

1717, when either a Gentleman from England[6], or an agent of Frederick Augustus I King of Poland[7], acquired it, depending on the source you read (of course, it is possible that the Englishman had been the king's agent). We do know that, following its exhibition in London in 1723 and possibly up to 1730 it was moved to Dresden to form part of an exhibition of Jewish ceremonial art, and following this it had several owners before being acquired by the Hamburg Museum in 1910.[8]

As an aside, accounts differ as to its size. Some say the model was 3 meters in length and width (around 10 feet), and this is certainly the size of the model now displayed in Hamburg Museum. However, other descriptions state its size as being 13 feet high and 80 feet around, or 20 feet on each side. However, unless two were built, the chances are the one currently on display in Hamburg Museum is the original one, and that is definitely 3 meters square. And yet the Daily Courant newspaper in London, on March 3, 1729, described the model as: "To be seen at the Royal Exchange every day, the Model of the Temple of Solomon, with all its Porches, Walls, Gates, Chambers and Holy Vessels... Within the Model are 2,000 Chambers and Windows, and Pillars 7000; the Model is 13 feet high and 80 feet round..." It is difficult to believe that the newspaper more than tripled the size of the model without anyone writing into them to complain! So perhaps there *were* two models doing the rounds. Perhaps the original, later displayed in London in 1723, and ending up in Hamburg was 3 meters across; while a larger one was made for the 1729 exhibition, based on the original design. It matters not to our tale, since it is the design which is important, and not the size.

Masonic scholarship takes over at this point. It has been suggested by many scholars that the initial appearance of the model in the London Royal Exchange made it a catalyst for much of the symbolism of the Third Degree[9]. We must remember that it is believed that only two Degrees existed at the inception of the Premier Grand Lodge in 1717, and that the Third Degree did not come into existence until the early to mid-1720s. Two theories exist about this Third Degree: either the first two were shortened and the Third Degree was extracted from them to form an independent Degree; or the Third Degree was invented, as it were, from scratch.

Given the immense interest that the exhibition of Schott's Model generated, especially among the educated classes – and we will come back to this point shortly – it is certainly not a stretch that a significant number of Freemasons based in London were also among the many visitors, and that the physical sight of a symbol so

---

[6] Rylands, W.H., in *Ars Quatuor Coronati*, Vol XIII for year 1900, pp. 24-25.
[7] Wikipedia Contributors, "*Hamburg Temple Model*", Wikipedia the Free Encyclopedia, 1 Oct., 2015: https://en.wikipedia.org/w/index.php?title=Hamburg_temple_model&action=history
   Note: While 6 sources are cited, they are not attached the specific facts, so while the body text cites this purchase, the fact is not linked to a specific citation.
[8] Ibid.
[9] Morrison, Tessa, *Isaac Newton and Solomon's Temple: a Fifty Year Study*, Avello Publishing Company, Issue 1 Volume 3, 2013.

important to the Masons, whether operative or speculative, would certainly have led to many an interesting discussion in the taverns following such a visit.

However, there was one piece in the jigsaw missing, and that was: did Schott imagine this extraordinarily modern-looking Temple himself, or did he base his design upon an earlier description? Up till now, most Masons who look at the Schott model as a possible catalyst for the third degree have limited themselves to assuming the model in itself was sufficient to spark this exercise. It was then that I found another thread, which led from an original design to Schott's model. This part of the story was to be found among books on architecture.

A Spanish Jesuit

Juan Bautista Villalpando was born in 1552 in Córdova, Spain. From an early age he exhibited a strong interest in architecture, which he married to his intense faith; and at the age of 23 he became a Jesuit, also studying architecture and geometry under Juan de Herrera, architect to King Philip II.[10]

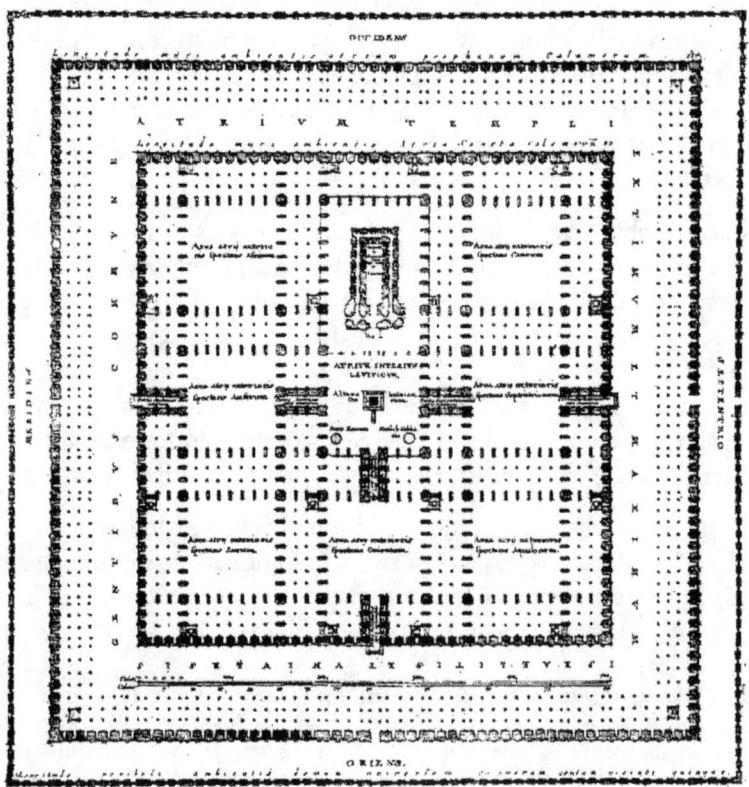

Figure 5: Villalpanda's plan of Ezekiel's Temple

---

[10] Kravtsov, Sergey R. (2005). *"Juan Buatista Villalpando and Sacred Architecture in the Seventeenth Century"*, Journal of the Society of Architectural Historians. 3: 312–339.

The Most Famous Image of King Solomon's Temple

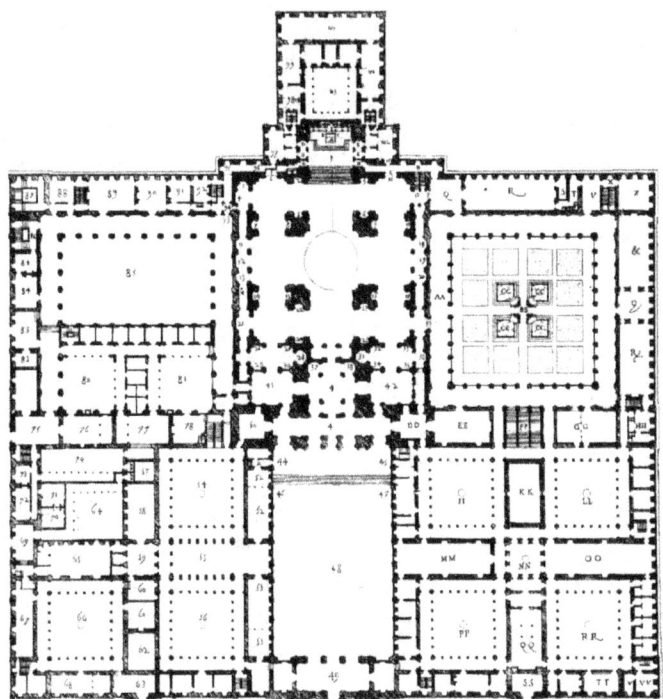

Figure 6: Plan of El Escorial

Very early on he became obsessed with the book of Ezekiel in the Old Testament, in particular his vision of the Temple of Jerusalem, and co-authored a book entitled "Commentary on Ezekiel" with Jerónimo del Prado. Despite the latter's untimely death following the publication of the first of three volumes, Villalpando went on to complete the other two.[11] Despite the publications being sponsored by Philip II of Spain, Villalpando was accused of heresy by the Inquisition for his extraordinary interpretations of the vision; but was subsequently found innocent, with the pope taking a personal interest in his work.

He believed the design of the Temple was based upon geometry and drawn in an orthographic projection. This is a way of showing a three-dimensional object in a series of two-dimensional images on paper, usually a front, side and top view; a form we commonly call a blueprint. He likened this ability to see all sides simultaneously to God's vision. He went on to propose a link between Vitruvius' famous book on Classical Greek Orders of Architecture, *De architectura*, and King Solomon's Temple, suggesting that the Temple was built first, and therefore all Classical architecture derived from this perfect original form. This meant that all architecture was divinely inspired and reconciled pagan Classical architecture with God's design.

---

[11] Villalpando, Juan Bautista & Prado, Jerónimo del, Hieronymi Pradi Et Ioannis Baptistae Villapandi E Societate Iesv in Ezechielem Explanationes Et Apparatus Verbis AC Templi Hierosolymitani: (Latin Edition), Wentworth Press, 2016 (paperback reissue).

His ideas extended further, and he entered the realms of Hermetics by suggesting that the Temple was an archetype, with Ezekiel's vision being that of the perfect Temple in heavenly Jerusalem, as later described by St. John in his Book of Revelation. He also saw in the Temple an image of the microcosm, or man. After all, if we imagine God to be the Grand Architect of all things, His design will be seen across all His creations, in the Universe, the Temple, and in Man.

Given that all design is driven by geometry, there was a Sacred Geometry common to the Temple and to Man which we should seek to understand. And incidentally this was a task which Sir Isaac Newton – an avid reader of Villalpando – pursued with great enthusiasm: and on his death, his work which included an extensive chapter on the geometry and history of the Temple, *The Chronology of Ancient Kingdoms Amended* was posthumously published in 1728, adding to the excitement generated by Schott's model in London.

Villapando's works were eagerly read by the intelligentsia of Europe, who found avenues of study and philosophical debate in his clever synthesis of divine inspiration, biblical and classical design, and esoteric indications of a link between man, Temple and God; a synthesis which led to all kinds of symbolic interpretations, and which was most certainly one of the many inputs to the Third Degree.

Indeed, his floorplans, with their grids and squares, were adopted by many architects, particularly in the layouts of monasteries, and even featured in many churches and synagogues of the Baroque era. Their simplicity was later to influence even the layout of planned cities.

However, it is his realization of the Temple of Ezekiel in pictorial form which really set the scene for centuries to come. It is an extraordinary piece of work. Firstly, it is unbelievably extravagant in scope, given that the First Temple, as we stated earlier, must have been a pretty simple affair.

Figure 7: Villalpanda's Front Elevation of the Temple

However, we must remember that Villalpando was not really reconstructing Solomon's Temple, but the ideal blueprint seen by Ezekiel. Secondly, it is extraordinarily Classical in design, and completely unlike anything we might expect a primitive nomadic tribe to build, especially since their only experience of permanent structures would have been those in Egypt. However, we must remember that Villalpando was attempting to forge a link between pagan and Judaic architecture by suggesting that the neo-Classical Greek architecture of the Renaissance era was valid, since it took its roots from the Temple at Jerusalem, which would therefore would have been envisaged as being in a Classical style.

Figure 8: Villalpanda's Temple perched upon Great Foundations

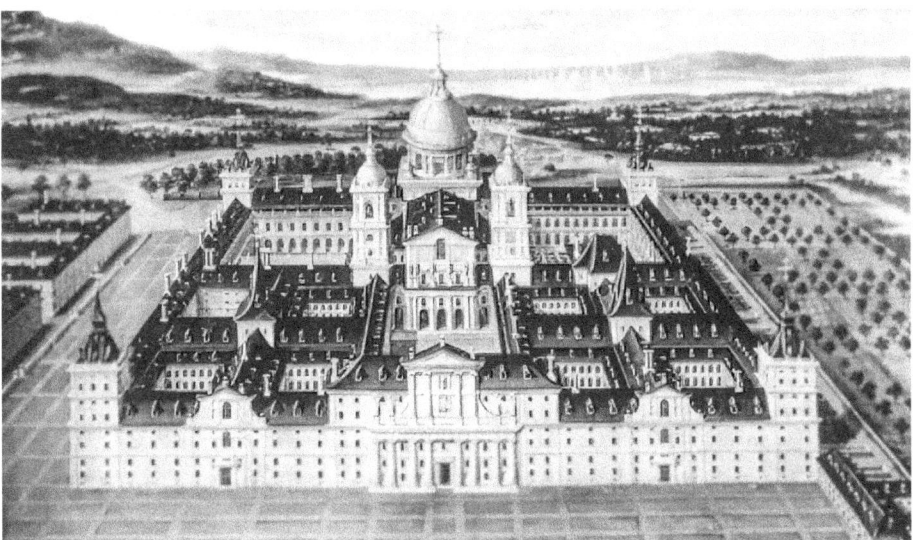

Figure 9: Front elevation of El Escorial

As an aside, his calculations from Ezekiel's vision extended to a need for the foundations on which the Temple rested to be of a massive size – so great indeed that they dwarfed the Temple itself!

There is even a strong indication that his designs heavily influenced the design of the opulent palace of Philip II, El Escorial, begun in 1563, which would hardly be surprising given the fact that Villalpando had studied under the King's architect, and the King himself had sponsored the Jesuit priest's hefty tome on Ezekiel's vision of the Temple. Indeed, if we look at an image of the palace, we can detect many similarities with the floorplans and the elevation as depicted by Villalpando.

What is particularly interesting is that, far from eliciting howls of outrage or mirth (except from the Inquisition, that is), Villalpando's image of King Solomon's Temple became so widely accepted it found its way into Bibles; Schott's model; academic treatises by Newton and others; palaces, churches and monasteries; prints and engravings; just about everything from buildings to beermats.

Engravings of Villalpando's Image

Perhaps the two most well-known manifestations of Villalpando's design, as made famous by Schott, are in the Baskett version of the King James Bible and the prints sold at the exhibitions of Schott's model in London (of which the Henry Coil Masonic Museum & Library in the Grand Lodge of California, San Francisco has a copy; and I saw another on the internet for auction with a recommended price of some $21,000–$28,000 – not bad for a print which originally sold for 5 shillings!).

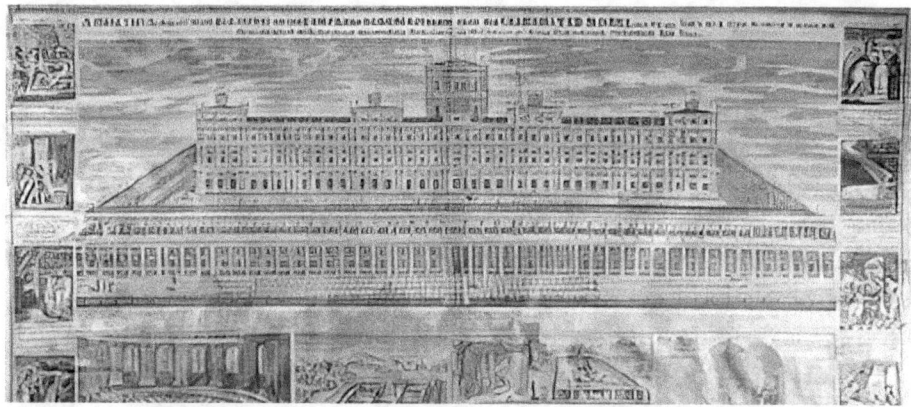

Figure 10: Print from 1723 Exhibition of Schott's Model in London (Courtesy of Henry Coil Masonic Museum & Library, San Francisco)

However, the image had been appearing in the King James Bible from at least 1660. In John Field's version of the Bible we find the following engraving, familiar to all of us by now.

If you look closely, you can see that the solution to the problem of how to deal with the extremely deep foundations was to bury them, literally, in a deep pit, which must have been huge! Bridges carried the faithful across to the Temple from the rest of Jerusalem. This theme was repeated in Fischer von Erlach's interpretation dated 1725, which gives us a cross-sectional view of the pit.

The Most Famous Image of King Solomon's Temple

Figure 11: John Field illustration in KJV 1660

Figure 12: von Erlach illustration in 1725

Indeed, it is reminiscent in appearance to the granite-hewn churches built in the 12th Century under the orders of King Lalibela in Ethiopia. While the similarity is coincidental, and clearly King Solomon's Temple was envisaged as an edifice and not a *bas relief* carved from rock, it is hard to ignore the similarities in the story. When King Lalibela came to power he sought the support of the Ethiopian Orthodox Church by building these churches, having as his goal the creation of a New Jerusalem, having allegedly visited the old city in his youth. It is astonishing, then, to find the King ordering the creation of churches built in pits, some three hundred years before Villalpando put quill to parchment.

Figure 13: St. George's Church, Lalibela

However, the approach did raise one awkward question: surely the purpose of building the Temple was to place it on top of a mountain – Mount Moriah – to be closer to heaven; not buried in the ground?

By the time of the Mark Baskett engraving of the Temple, the image of Villalpando-Schott used was the one from the exhibition, which ignored the foundations entirely. However, they were not entirely omitted, as we can see from this detail from the City of Jerusalem from a 1757 Mark Baskett print run of the Bible below. The Temple at the top may have lost its buttresses; but the tiny image in the map still shows traces of the original design at the bottom.

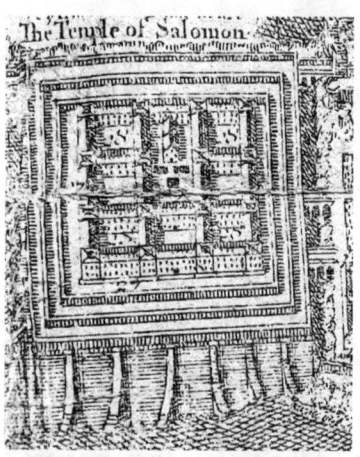

Figure 14: Detail of map showing Temple buttresses

It is worth noting in passing that the image in the King James Bible is a flat, straight-on view, while the one in the surviving prints from the exhibition are from a higher viewpoint, providing a more three-dimensional image. This is no doubt to emphasize that fact the Schott's model was indeed three-dimensional; while the Bible adhered more closely to Villalpando's concept of orthographic projection.

Figure 15: Villalpando-Baskett illustration two-dimensional (compare to Baskett Bible version – identical design but clearly redrawn)

Figure 16: Print from London exhibition three-dimensional

The proliferation of this image, together with the prints in circulation from the exhibition, no doubt led to many Lodges procuring one for themselves, and in prints from the era we can often see proudly displayed on the wall what was probably one of the prints purchased at the London exhibition of Schott's model; or perhaps from purveyors like Richard Ware of Ludgate Hill, London, who were not above selling overrun copies of the engraving for their Bibles to make some extra money!

Figure 17: Masonic print from the early 1730s

An image was now indelibly fixed in the minds of most Europeans. For at least 150 years, King Solomon's Temple would conjure up the image of a Classical Renaissance palace, not unlike El Escorial. And this image was to spread to the Colonies in America, since before the Revolutionary War it was forbidden to print Bibles locally, and all copies had to be obtained from Europe, the two most common being the Geneva Bible and the King James Bible, which still carried the Villalpando-Schott image of the Temple.

A Final Mystery

By joining together two threads, one from the study of architecture and one from Masonic scholarship, we have traced how a Jesuit priest in the 16th Century devised an extraordinary image of King Solomon's Temple which endured the attacks of the Inquisition and went on to become a pattern for future buildings, churches, monasteries and quite probably much of El Escorial. In addition, the work provided an excuse for architects to incorporate all the Classical styles of architecture into any building whatever, safe in the knowledge that they were doing God's work. We have also seen how his theories of God as Architect opened the doors for much philosophical speculation about the macrocosm and microcosm, and the role of sacred geometry in all creation. And finally, this image of the Temple became the standard for several generations of Christians, from the most erudite bishop to the humble family at home, teaching their children to read using the only book they possessed, the King James Bible with its illustration of the Temple at Jerusalem. But one mystery remains. Indeed, it is the very issue raised by the Inquisition when it challenged Villalpando's interpretation of the Holy Scriptures.

Surely this elaborate palace erected to God bears no resemblance whatsoever either to the description of King Solomon's Temple found in Kings and Chronicles; or to the reality of what the nomadic tribe would have been able to build, given that the descriptions in Kings and Chronicles were probably a gross exaggeration in the first place!

And this, ironically, is why this drawing lends itself so well to Masonry!

A concept common to the Kabbalah, Classical Philosophy and even Psychology is that of the Archetype. Let us use the Kabbalah for now, since the other two fields really differ only in terminology. The Kabbalists envisaged four successive worlds of emanation from the Ain Soph (or Divine Architect in our example). These were the worlds of Emanation, Creation, Formation and Action. Put simply, the first stage is an idea, a pure concept issued from the mind of God. This in turn begins to develop into a creation, as yet without a shape or form, but now with a definite purpose. Now this purpose become an archetype, or in

The Most Famous Image of King Solomon's Temple

Classical thought the 'perfect example' of a thing: to us, the blueprint. Finally, this blueprint is realized in the physical world through action.

Figure 18: Detail from 4th Grade Trestleboard of the Scottish Rectified Rite

In a way, the descriptions of the Temple in the Old and New Testaments are in reverse order. Consider the Holy Temple and City of Jerusalem as described in Revelations. This in a way is the highest form of the Temple, closest to the thought of God. Reading the description, we find this city has four walls as a perfect square, with twelve gates arranged in the middle of the four sides, as one large gate flanked by two smaller. The center is a mountain on which stands the Lamb bearing a banner with a cross upon it. If this is the celestial Eden, then perhaps the central cross now represents the four life-giving rivers of Pishon, Gihon, Hiddekel and Euphrates?

Incidentally, for those who understand certain 19th century mystical and Masonic schools of theosophy, it is worth recalling Ezekiel's reference to Eden in Chapter 28, where the 'Son of Man' is told by God to speak against the King of Tyre, who is described as the 'seal of perfection', adorned with precious stones from the day of his creation, and placed in the garden of Eden upon the central holy mountain by God himself as a guardian cherub. But the king sinned through wickedness and violence. So, he was driven out of the garden and thrown down to the earth, where now he is consumed by God's fire. And tradition tells us another was put in his place… This should be extremely familiar to anyone with some knowledge of the teachings of Louis-Claude de Saint-Martin or Martinez de Pasqually.

As a further aside while considering the concept of archetypes, if, as some believe, all religions initially had the same purpose, but being expressed variously in the languages and cultures of each tribe or nation took separate paths, until their differences appear to be greater than their similarities, it might be worth noting some commonalities in this image of heaven. Without going into detail, we should be struck by the fact that many religions center on a mountain, usually with the goal of ascending to its summit, such as Mount Moriah and Mount Zion, Mount Abiegnus of the Rosicrucians, and Mount Meru of the Hindus and Buddhists. Again, the perfect square with four main gates at the four quarters, and the importance of the number 'four' (rivers, elements, quarters) lead us to note the similarities between the vision of Revelations with the Mandalas of the Eastern traditions, and closer to home, of John Dee's image of the Four Watchtowers in his Enochian scrying work with Edward Kelley in the late 16th Century. Indeed, it often leads one to wonder whether certain images fell into the hands of each of these groups; or whether they were all led to see the same archetype, from which they drew their own culturally-tinted versions? But back to the main topic.

Figure 19: Eastern Mandala with four entrances

The Most Famous Image of King Solomon's Temple

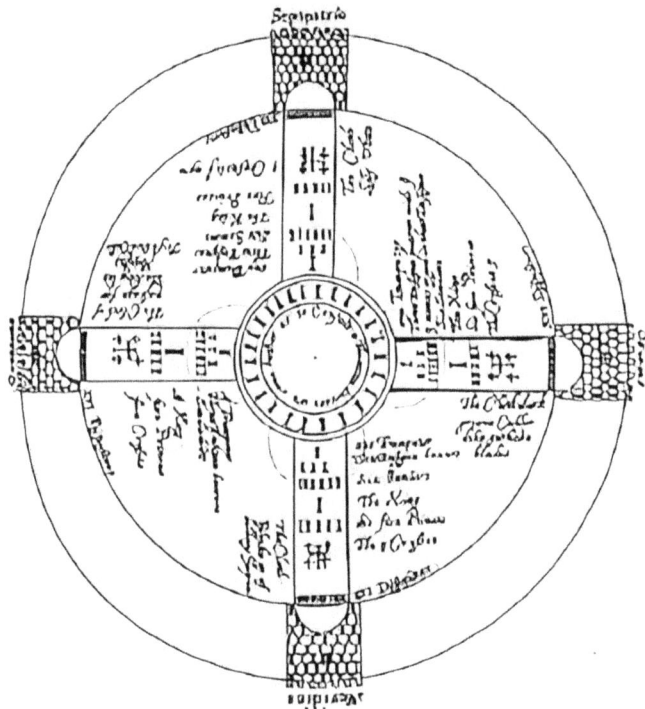

Figure 20: John Dee's Watchtowers

This is the Temple which Ezekiel sees in his vision, and he tries to describe it in words, thereby giving Form to that which God created. It is the blueprint of perfection which Ezekiel gives us, which some extremists believe will bring about the End of Days if this Temple is actually built; while we can also recognize the blueprint given to David to pass to Solomon his son to bring to fruition by building Temple at Jerusalem. However, perfection is impossible to achieve by man, and Solomon could only do his best to imitate that perfection. Through action he created what was but a poor reflection of the *archetypal temple* on earth, and since it represented the microcosm, it was indeed fitting that it was an imperfect reproduction of perfection, since man is not yet perfected, and the divine spark is not yet ready to reunite with the Source.

While it is strange that the general public tacitly accepted the diagram of God's perfect Temple as being a true representation of King Solomon's Temple in all these illustrations without a murmur, perhaps we can begin to understand why this diagram occupied the greatest minds of the age for one hundred and fifty years; and why speculative Masons were drawn so strongly to this image as the ultimate enigma, the final analogy, the lost symbol on which to base their Order.

The Magician, the Mystic, & the Mason

The Unlikely Origin of the Scottish Rectified Rite

The Magician, the Mystic, and the Mason –
The Unlikely Origin of the Scottish Rectified Rite

Perit ut Vivat

"The true soul of Freemasonry must be depicted not according to the men enrolled
under its banner, but rather according to the Tradition it claims to hold."
CONSTANT CHEVILLON

 have long carried a torch for this extraordinary Rite, ever since I was invited to become a member in Belgium back in the late 1990s. To me it is, quite simply, one of the most perfect series of ceremonies ever written. Far more than a simple series of rituals which teach morality or good behavior, it is literally a blueprint for reintegration with God for those who have eyes to see. When I hear Masons say that 'there are no secrets in Masonry', my mind immediately returns to these astonishing Rites, and all I can do is smile.

It is in homage to those great and fearless men who created this opus that I dedicate this paper, in the hope that they, the Passed Masters, will not judge too harshly those who have since sought to turn it into a dining club, an excuse to feel elite or 'special', or have even used it as a vehicle to pursue the most unmasonic and unchristian attacks of those who would follow the true path...

Introduction

This is a story about a ritual which *almost* became the standard Masonic Ritual for much of the world.

One question many people looking in at Freemasonry from outside is: why are there so many different variations, so many different rituals, so many different bodies in an Order which claims to be universal? Wouldn't we expect to see a small number of common rites practiced throughout the world, to emphasize the universality of this Order? After all, until a couple of hundred years ago the syllabus in all Universities had been nearly identical, drawing on the Seven Liberal Arts and Sciences, and most religions make use of a small body of common rituals.

The proliferation of Masonic rituals can be attributed to three basic sources: political differences, legendary differences, and regional invention. Of course, it can be argued that there are many other influences which led to this explosion in rituals, but we will limit ourselves to these three factors here. This also explains the origin of a word commonly heard in Freemasonry – rectification – which simply means that somebody took an existing ritual and believed that they could improve on it.

Firstly, there is no denying that, when a country takes over an invention from another country, it will try to impose its own gloss, its own flavor on it. This is even more important when those countries are at war, or at least regard each other with deep suspicion.

Figure 21: King James II

Such was the case in the 17th Century with King James II of England, Ireland and Scotland, who had been deposed in the Glorious Revolution as the last Catholic King. He fled to France and established his court just outside of Paris. Since this meant that England was now committed to Protestantism, the new society called Freemasonry took on very different flavors in England and France.

In England, when the Grand Lodge was formed in 1717, great pains were taken to prove its loyalty to the Hanoverian throne, for there is no doubt that Freemasonry was seen by a suspicious public as being potentially allied to the Catholic cause.

Meanwhile, the Stuarts, realizing the political advantage of claiming Grand Mastership of an Order which would rally the French aristocracy to a common interest while recognizing their premiership, were only too happy to issue patents and charters both to form Lodges, and to individuals giving them authority to do this. The supporters of James II and his successors were called 'Jacobites' meaning they followed James; and because of his title as James VII of Scotland, the charters issued were called 'Écossais' or 'Scottish' charters. It is worth stating up front that there is no connection at all between Scotland and these charters, or any Rite bearing the name 'Scottish', other than the fact that they were issued by the exiled King of Scotland in France. In a way, if the Rite generally practiced in the United States should be called the American Rite, the rites which came from France should properly be called the French Rites. But that will never happen!

Secondly, this also led to variations concerning the origins of Freemasonry. In England the traditions ranged from prosaic, including the great builders of the Gothic cathedrals and the Mystery Plays of old; to the fanciful, including tracing the origin of the Order to Adam, as he wore an apron according to Genesis 3:7!

In France, however, a rather nobler origin was envisaged, which was finally stated in a speech called the Discourse of Chevalier Ramsay, an ardent Jacobite. In this well-known speech he claimed a Chivalric origin for Freemasonry. Now, although he did not expressly indicate the Templars, back-stories were not long in coming, arguing that following the destruction of the Knights Templar by Philippe le Bel of France in 1307, and the papal bull *Vox in excelso* issued by Clement V in 1312 formally dissolving the Order, a small band of Templar knights had fled to Scotland under the protection of the monarch, Robert the Bruce, and had infiltrated Masonry, introducing their secrets and rituals into this body. Towards the end of his speech, Ramsay said: "From the British Isles the Royal Art is now repassing into France, under the reign of the most amiable of Kings, whose humanity animates all his virtues...", implying that the seat of that Chivalric and Crusading Order had now returned into France, and adding further authority to the charters now being issued by James II's son, the Old Pretender or James Stuart – 'pretender' in this case meaning 'claimant to the British Throne'.

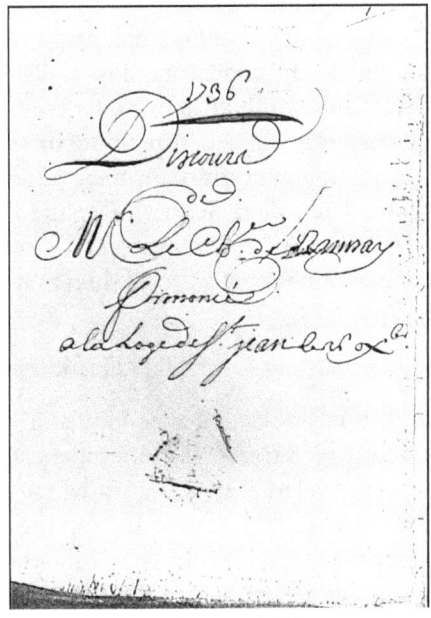

Figure 22: *Ramsay's Discourse*

Thirdly, it is human nature to take something and try to improve on it, or even create anew. How else would we explain the explosion of rites which proliferated in England, mainland Europe and even the Americas during this time? If seemed as if anyone who could write would try their hand at creating new rituals based on history, chivalry, biblical or ancient civilizations; even Hermeticism; Rosicrucianism or Alchemy.

No subject was taboo, no ritual too involved and no regalia too elaborate. There was something to satisfy anyone's sense of vanity.

It is to avoid drowning in this morass of rituals that we will confine our focus specifically to three, all of which mutually impacted one another, and leave the history of the rest to other scholars and authors. The three which impact the thread we are following are the Rite of Strict Observance, the Order of Elect Cohen of the Universe, and the Scottish Rectified Rite. Before we embark on a study of any of these, let me once again stress that the Scottish Rectified Rite has nothing *whatsoever* to do with the Ancient Accepted Scottish Rite, and that its name merely means that it was a Rite which was vaguely connected with a charter issued by the House of Stuart, and that it used an existing ritual which was then heavily redacted, changing its meaning considerably while retaining its overall shape. And that ritual came in fact from Germany!

I will permit myself a small aside when I point out that, in the early 1900s, a gifted Mason and profession cellist, Eduard Blitz attempted to introduce the Scottish Rectified Rite into the United States, but after a few years returned the charter to Europe, complaining bitterly that the Southern Masonic Jurisdiction were doing everything in their power to thwart his efforts, not understanding that a Rite called 'Scottish Rectified' wasn't attempting to claim is was a *better* version of the Ancient Accepted Scottish Rite. We can only assume that Masonic scholarship wasn't as good then as it is now!

A Hankering After Chivalry

History books and anecdotal stories love to remind us that Freemasonry is an Order which treats all its members equally, telling us about popes and monarchs who marveled at meetings in which the Lord of the manor would sit quietly in the pews while the farmhand ran the meeting; or of the workmen and aristocrats alike wearing white gloves to hide the callouses which would, at a glance, distinguish them from one another. Nor are we immune in the United States, as proud Masons from Oyster Bay in New York recount the story of President Teddy Roosevelt attending his local Matinecock Lodge, telling the secret service contingent to wait outside, since he felt safer among his Brethren than anywhere else.

The reality was somewhat different in mainland Europe. While England attempted to live up to this ideal, in France, Germany and other countries Freemasonry was much more the plaything of the wealthy or those who aspired to be, who had the time and money to indulge in this diversion. Lodges and Chapters were predominantly composed of the middle classes – the bourgeoisie – who were only too keen to join an organization which gave them unfettered access to the aristocracy and decision-makers of the time and allowed them to meet in secret to discuss any subject they wished, without the interference of the Crown or the Church.

The Magician, the Mystic, and the Mason

This goes a long way to explain why Pope Clement XII issued his bull *In eminenti* in 1738, banning Roman Catholics from joining Freemasonry. Although the Stuarts were Catholic they had no issue with admitting Protestants to Freemasonry; and similarly, Protestant Florence was admitting both Catholics and atheists. Although the bull was couched in religious terms, the intent was clearly political in nature, and as well as preventing Catholics and Protestants from having a place where they could explore their differences freely, Masonic ideas such as one man one vote, and the importance of universal education were also terrifying concepts to countries run by Church and King.

We saw earlier that, while Chevalier Ramsay extolled the virtues of a Freemasonry founded on Chivalry in France, it was in fact in Germany that the first major Order to embrace these ideals came into existence. There are two simple reasons for this. Firstly, Germany had a far more military vein running through it, holding still a fond remembrance of the Order of Teutonic Knights, and in an eerie reflection of words used some two hundred years later, an oath of 'Strict Observance' which expressly meant unquestioningly obeying the orders of all superior officers. Secondly, while it was unlikely that either the Pope or Louis XV of France would be so bold as to try to have members arrested, Germany, being predominantly Protestant, was still a safer place to house an Order which maintained the clauses of Templar Revenge of seeking the death of the King of France and the Pope for their ancestors' involvement in the Order's demise, and to find and restore the imagined Templar treasures!

Figure 23: In Eminenti

The Order of Strict Observance, then, claimed Templar roots, and was based on a system of six Grades, composed of the Entered Apprentice, Fellowcraft (or Companion) and Master Mason Degrees (which firmly therefore established it as a Masonic, rather than purely chivalric, Order), which were followed by a Grade of Scots Master, which alluded to the translation of the Templar Order to Scotland. Finally, two further Grades – Novice and Knight – were available to the aristocracy, while commoners could only be received as Lay Brothers, for a high fee. Founded by Baron von Hund in 1751, it was a recreation of the Templar Order, even to his naming the *langues*, or Tongues dividing Europe into nine Provinces.

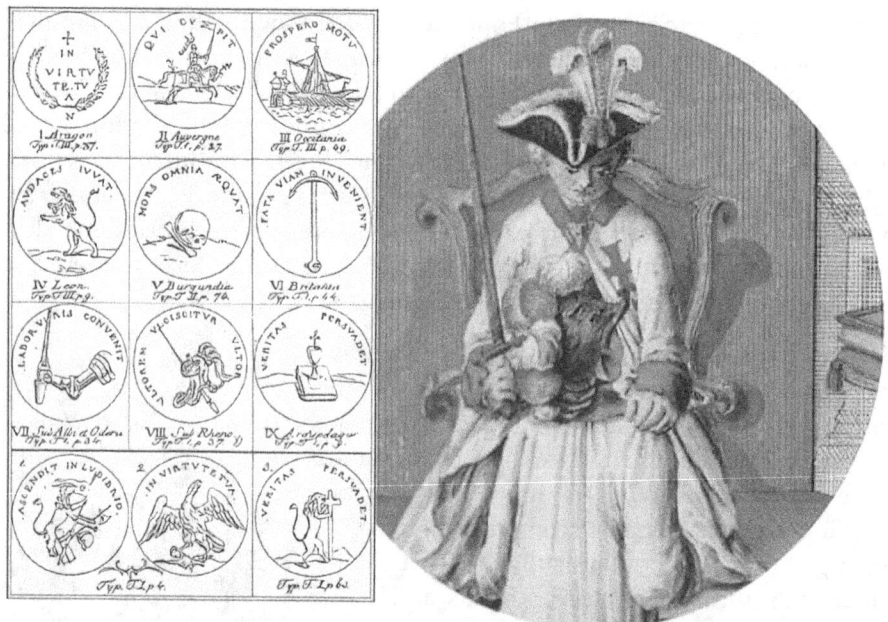

Figure 24: 'Langues' and Regalia of the Rite of Strict Observance

The Knights were given high-sounding Latin mottoes, and soon the aristocracy were expressing interest, culminating in the recruitment of several German princes, becoming almost the only Masonic obedience in Germany, and spreading into Italy, Holland, Switzerland, Russia and eventually a corner of France, as we shall see later.

One of its attractions was the mysterious idea that it was controlled by 'Unknown Superiors', which also implied secret or occult knowledge hidden within the Order which would be imparted to those worthy to receive it. Indeed, an Order of Clerics grew up alongside the Strict Observance, claiming great secrets which were, however, never forthcoming. Following two Conventions in 1775 and 1776 aimed at sorting out the identity of the Unknown Superiors and the great secrets of Templary, a charlatan names the Baron von Gugumos convinced an audience desperate for anything esoteric that he had the true transmission from the Orthodox Patriarch in Cyprus, and that for a large fee he would reinitiate them and sell them regalia. Promising to go to Cyprus to obtain all the missing secrets while they built a suitable altar for him, he walked out the door, never to be seen again...with their money. By the end of 1777, with no Unknown Superior named – while many theories suggest he was in fact Bonnie Prince Charlie, though he himself denied this – no secrets uncovered, and the death of Baron von Hund in October of that year, the Rite of Strict Observance was reaching the end of its life.

This fact was about to be exploited by one of the most cunning Masons of the 18th Century!

The Three Grand Principals

Before embarking on the life and teachings of our first protagonist, Martinez de Pasqually, it is time to admit that the anglophone world has access to only a fraction of the scholarship and source materials available to French-speaking scholars. Entire bookstores in France are given over to the Scottish Rectified Rite, the Order of Elus Cohen, Martinez de Pasqually, Jean-Baptiste Willermoz and Louis-Claude de Saint-Martin. Scholars have expended rivers of ink both on the history of these people and their Orders, and the symbolism and theosophy of what they teach. There are several organizations solely devoted to the study and dissemination of authoritative papers on the teachings of Pasqually alone. And every year sees another twenty or thirty books published on these subjects as new interpretations are made, or new source materials come to light. And all this, sadly, is in French! I make this point to emphasize the enormous importance this subject plays in the *Zeitgeist* of European Masonry – and the extraordinary lack of knowledge about this in England and the United States – and also to admit that, even with my extensive reading on the subject, I can do no more than paint a very imperfect picture of the full story.

That said, to avoid becoming lost in what is in fact a relatively straightforward story, I will begin by providing the summary, and by doing so will provide what I hope is a straightforward flow of facts, before departing down the tributaries which feed this great river.

As we saw, by 1778 the Strict Observance was close to death, and its credibility was waning fast. However, it was going to be saved for posterity in a most unusual manner.

Pasqually was an extraordinary man who had invented both a bizarre and fascinating form of gnostic theology based on his unique interpretation of the Holy Bible, which extended to the introduction of theurgical Masonic practices in order to obtain certain signs. Put simply, his Masons practiced magic! Into this Order came Willermoz, a renowned Mason, and Saint-Martin, a young and enthusiastic man from the military. The Order itself didn't survive for long, mainly due to a lack of written instructions and the early death of its charismatic founder. However, the flame of his teachings remained bright in his two proteges, both of whom were to enshrine them for posterity in their writings and rituals. Saint-Martin, although he moved away from theurgy into mystical Christianity, used his popularity as an author to preserve Pasqually's theosophy; while Willermoz used the unfortunate demise of the Rite of Strict Observance to safeguard Pasqually's teachings within the system of Grades. Indeed, his plan was to make this the only Masonic Order on mainland Europe. And if it hadn't been for the French Revolution some seven years later, this might have been the reality for all Freemasons today.

In fact, if we look at the Swedish Rite, which drew its roots from very similar sources, and which is now practiced across Norway, Sweden, Denmark and Iceland, we can see a glimpse of what world Freemasonry might have looked like if it had avoided the pan-European meltdowns of the late 18th and early 19th Centuries. Indeed, walking around the Grand Lodge of Norway in Oslo a few years ago, I felt as if I had been mysteriously transported into a physical realization of the Tracing Boards – or educational plans and diagrams – of the Scottish Rectified Rite. While the Swedish Rite was in formation throughout the second half of the 18th Century, it took the genius of Duke Karl, who was head of the Strict Observance for two years and who became King Charles XII of Sweden, to undertake its final transformation into a cohesive and spiritual system which so closely resembles the Scottish Rectified Rite, and which today reigns as the sole Masonic system in several Nordic countries.

The Scottish Rectified Rite, or *Knights Beneficent of the Holy City*, which it was also called, was a noble and ambitious plan, and even if we know the outcome – that the French Revolution prevented it from taking place – we can nevertheless admire the way in which three men of genius came to influence one another and create perhaps one of the noblest systems in all of Freemasonry.

Indeed, the Order itself did survive, as an elite invitational body in some countries, but more widely available in others – at least in the past few years. In this manner, it has lasted and lived up to the motto of its First Grade, *Adhuc stat*, or *It still endures*. And of its protagonists, Martinez de Pasqually will be forever linked to his Order of Elus Cohen; Jean-Baptiste Willermoz to the creation of the Scottish Rectified Rite; and Louis-Claude de Saint-Martin with the extraordinary Order of mystical Christianity which, in Pasqually's and his honor, is called Martinism.

However, given that all these people, and their Rites, have been the subject of so many books, I will limit myself here to the briefest thumbnail of each.

Enter the Magician

Martinez de Pasqually, who appears to have had a number of different combination of names, which even he appears to have varied from signature to signature, was probably born in Grenoble sometime between 1710 and 1727. Fortunately, we can be a little more certain of his death, which was on September 20, 1774 in Haiti, then St. Domingue. Almost immediately the questions begin. Some have conjectured that he was a Jewish convert to Catholicism, or his father was an Ashkenazic Jew from Spain – or Portugal – who converted prior to Don Martinez' birth. Whatever the truth, he was most certainly Catholic for the duration of the period of his life which concerns us here, although some of his beliefs and rituals certainly point to a more eclectic upbringing than would be traditionally found in a purely Catholic household. We might believe he was self-taught, and yet his writing style, which we find in his extraordinary *Treatise*, does not demonstrate a particularly strong command of French vocabulary or grammatical construction. So, any education he received was probably verbal, and possibly in a language other than French.

We learn that Pasqually's father received a warrant from Charles Stuart in 1738 to establish Masonic Lodges, and that this right was hereditary, with Pasqually using the same warrant to found Lodges. There is no real reason to dispute this authority, since during his time as Grand Master of his Order nobody saw fit to challenge his right, even though his work brought him into conflict with other early Scottish Rite Lodges in Bordeaux, who accused him of poaching members and distorting their rites. It is interesting, however, to note the same claim to authority as that claimed by the Rite of Strict Observance, which was from its 'Unknown Superiors', specifically *Eques a Penne Rubra*, or *Knight of the Red Feather*, who it was claimed was the same Charles Stuart, or the Old Pretender.

Figure 25: Martinez de Pasqually

After a couple of false starts, around 1765 he founded a very peculiar form of Freemasonry called the *Ordre des Chevaliers Maçons Élus Coëns de l'Univers* (*Knight Masons Elect Cohen of the Universe*, which we'll abbreviate to the usual 'Elus Cohen'). The system had ten Grades, of which the first six were broadly Masonic; while the last four were distinctly magical in nature, requiring the Mason not only to receive a form of 'ordination', but to perform regular rituals which were a combination of traditional Catholic prayers and offices, and a series of theurgical Operations involving the drawing of magic circles, the burning of incense and recitation of spells and strange names, and observing the air following these ceremonies for signs of what he termed '*La Chose*', in English '*The Thing*', which by means of flashes, cracking sounds, passes and especially sigils, indicated that the ritual had been effective. But effective in what way? Pasqually based his system on a peculiarly gnostic interpretation of the Bible, which he finally had written down in 1775, and passed round his most senior members, those of the tenth Grade called the *Réau Croix*.

We will see both Willermoz and Saint-Martin join his Order, and Saint-Martin himself writing down the *Treatise on the Reintegration of Beings into their Primitive Estate*, the title of his extraordinary exegesis, as Pasqually dictated it. In this he described man as being created by God to watch over his Kingdom and especially over the evil spirits which he had imprisoned on Earth. However, these spirits persuaded man that, being created from God's breath, while all other created beings were born of a father and mother, he was as powerful as God and, like Him, capable of creation. In his pride man attempted to create *Heva*, or the prototype Eve, but in failing only managed to entrap his own glorious body in a coating of red mud, thereby joining the spiritual part to the material part.

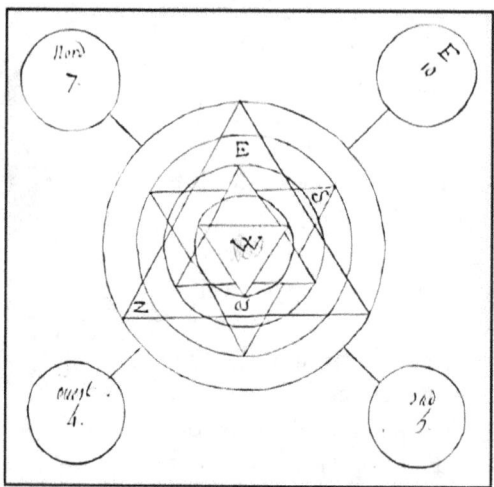

Figure 26: Magical Circle of Elus Cohen

God intervened to complete *Heva's* creation, but in punishment for his wickedness banished man to the very Earth over which he was meant to be in charge and deprived him of his primitive – or original – rights; yet He taught him how, through a series of Operations or Magical Practices, he could seek the Path of Return and once more be reinvested with his primitive rights. In his absence another was sent to take his place, and this was Heli, or Elias, whom Saint-Martin later referred to as the Repairer, the Christ.

If the Repairer was then the Grand High Priest, Man himself was nevertheless an Elect Cohen or Priest, who looked to the day when, once again, he would be able to worship perpetually in the Holies of Holies, instead of being only able to glimpse the reflection of God's glory but one instant a year. The observations the Initiate made following each Operation, then, was to seek signs of 'La Chose', to indicate that he was indeed on the right path.

The reason all this theosophy fit so well with Masonry was the fact that Pasqually based his entire system on symbols and especially numbers, particularly the passage in The Wisdom of Solomon, Chapter 11 verse 20: "…but thou hast ordered all things in measure and number and weight." Given that measure and weight did not feature particularly in the Trivium and Quadrivium taught in Universities at that time, Pasqually – and later Saint-Martin – focused almost obsessively on the correlation of numbers with Creation, as Sir Isaac Newton had done similarly with regard to the measurements of King Solomon's Temple just under a century earlier. And any mason knows the emphasis placed on numbers, particularly 3, 5, 7 and 9, in Freemasonry. A read of Pasqually's *Treatise* or Saint-Martin's book *Of Errors & Truth* will show the importance of numbers in their eyes, and just how much they believed God used them in the act of Creation.

However, while the theosophy was enough to engage Saint-Martin for the rest of his life, and to persuade Willermoz to remodel the Strict Observance around it, the Order itself was doomed almost from the start. All the Operations, a lifestyle of fasting and extensive times in prayer proved too much for many of its members. The infrequency of Pasqually's communications with his Temples, together with the lack of rubrics and instructions, all proved too much for all but the most devoted disciples. Finally, his departure in 1772 to take up an inheritance in Haiti and his death there in 1774 led to the Order passing from memory shortly thereafter.

But, like the Order of the Temple, the body might be dead, but the spirit lived on, in Masonry and in Mystical Christianity. Indeed, 1774 could be said to have been a signal year for the Order, for although it was already dying, along with its founder in Haiti, Saint-Martin was writing his first book under the pseudonym of the 'Unknown Philosopher', which would be proclaimed as one of the greatest books on Masonic philosophy of the age. He remained an adherent to the theosophical vision of his Master, while distancing himself from the complex theurgical practices and rituals, asking him: "But Master, is all this truly necessary to know God?" In the meantime, in the same year Willermoz was preparing to bring the Order of Strict Observance to Lyon, his hometown, seeing in it a possible means of saving Pasqually's teachings in a Masonic vehicle more suited to his high vision than the collection of seemingly random rituals culled from the early Scottish Rite in Bordeaux.

For now, we may imagine Pasqually's ghost living on in Haitian culture, for surely it is possible that the locals, seeing this tall, gaunt, white-faced man standing in crossroads and graveyards, dressed in a top hat or tricorn and long cloak, drawing circles and magical sigils in the soil with his silver-topped cane, might have given rise to the more recent Loa in the Haitian Vodou pantheon: Baron Samedi, also known as Baron Cimitière and Baron La Croix; and whose Christian syncretic equivalent, coincidentally, is *Saint-Martin* de Porres. There is no proof of this, but it is indeed a very wishful thought! Incidentally, the Vodoun system of tying body and soul together is not so far away from his theosophy, where spiritual man is tied or linked to a tangible, material body, from which he seeks to free himself.

Figure 27: Baron Samedi

The Soldier Turned Mystic

Louis-Claude de Saint-Martin's early life is of little consequence to the story. He was born into minor aristocracy in Amboise on January 18, 1743. History recounts that he was a sickly child, and it appears that his mother died early, for he was very closely attached to his step-mother. His father wanted him to be an attorney, but after passing the requisite examinations he found the position unchallenging, preferring rather to go into the army, which his apparently indulgent father didn't prevent, and through the influence of the Duc de Choiseul he secured a commission in the regiment at Foix, in the South-West of France, near Bordeaux. Mercifully for him, this was a rare period of peace in France, and he was able to pursue his reading of spiritual topics in relative tranquility.

Figure 28: Saint-Martin

Martinez de Pasqually had married the daughter of a former major in that regiment, and through this connection and the membership of some of his military friends in his Order, Saint-Martin was received into the Order of Elus Cohen in the latter part of 1768, at the age of 24. It is worth noting that, according to Waite, Saint-Martin wrote these words either on the eve of the Revolution or shortly thereafter: "It is to Martines de Pasqually that I owe my introduction to the higher truths." Given his spiritual journey over the coming twenty-one years, it is important to note that, whatever direction he later took, his respect for his first Master never waned. By 1770, Saint-Martin had left the army to become Pasqually's personal secretary. Now we know he didn't have much money – no doubt his father wasn't prepared to support him in a third change of career – and he wasn't truly independently wealthy until the publication of his first book, *Of Errors & Truth*, which both sealed his fame and guaranteed a steady income. Nor was Pasqually efficient at husbanding funds. Therefore, it can only be left to the imagination how they survived during these early years.

So, given that Pasqually left for St. Domingue two years later, Saint-Martin would have jumped at the chance to go to Lyon to build on a long and fruitful correspondence with his friend Willermoz, which resulted in the publication of his first book, *Of Errors & Truth*, in 1775 by Willermoz' Masonic Brothers and friends, the Frères Périsse. Now his financial situation was secure, and he was also acknowledged a philosopher by his followers (though the deists at the time, including Voltaire, were less than complimentary of his writings. On being given a copy, according to David Bates in his academic paper, Voltaire remarked: "I don't believe anyone has ever printed anything more absurd."). He followed this book with a second, *Tableau Naturel*, in 1782.

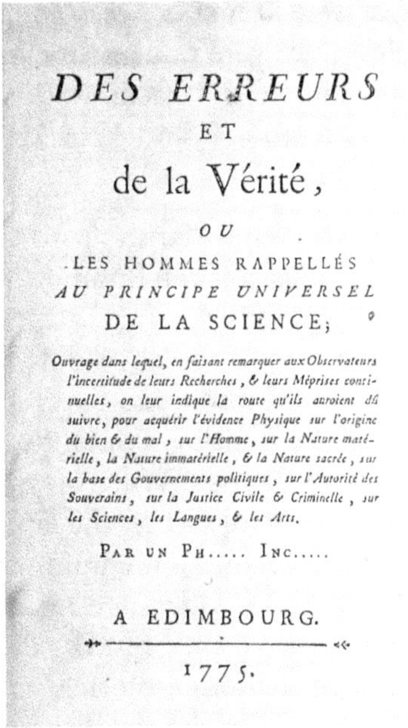

DES ERREURS

ET

de la Vérité,

OU

LES HOMMES RAPPELLÉS

AU PRINCIPE UNIVERSEL

DE LA SCIENCE;

Ouvrage dans lequel, en faisant remarquer aux Observateurs l'incertitude de leurs Recherches, & leurs Méprises continuelles, on leur indique la route qu'ils auroient dû suivre, pour acquérir l'évidence Physique sur l'origine du bien & du mal, sur l'Homme, sur la Nature matérielle, la Nature immatérielle, & la Nature sacrée, sur la base des Gouvernements politiques, sur l'Autorité des Souverains, sur la Justice Civile & Criminelle, sur les Sciences, les Langues, & les Arts.

PAR UN PH..... INC.....

A EDIMBOURG.

1775.

Figure 29: First Edition of 'Of Errors & Truth'

Here, and in his later writings, Saint-Martin was to turn the process which Pasqually had called Reintegration into a series of steps. Firstly, unconscious people, performing their daily tasks like automatons, and barely aware of their surroundings, were called 'Men of the Stream'. We have only to observe people walking along sidewalks, on trains, in cafes, glued to their tiny smartphone screens to see exactly what he meant in modern times! None of these people are even aware that there is a real world full of sights, sounds and experiences surrounding them. They would rather take a photograph of a beautiful meal and post it on Facebook than put the phone down and give their undivided attention to the work of art which the chef had just created for their sensual pleasure.

Once a person had awoken, and realized there was more to life and the universe filled with more powers and forces than were ever dreamed of in our philosophy, to misquote Shakespeare, we leave this 'Forest of Errors' and become Men – and Women – of Desire, now seeking the Path which will lead us back along the way of our prevarication, and which leads to our Reintegration into our Original or Primitive Estate. Our desire will transform us into a New Man, and finally, if we accomplish our goal, into Spirit-Man, who will finally part company with the material flesh which has cloaked us for so long, and once more we will be clothed in the Glorious Body, that incorporeal form in which we came into existence.

There can be no denying that this Order, and the Strict Observance and Rectified Rites which followed, are Christian. But it is noteworthy that, while English Freemasonry began as Christian – indeed both it and even the American Rite retain many Christian symbols such as a veneration for the Holy Saints John and quotations from the New Testament in their rituals – it changed into one which accepted people of all religions, first by chance and later by design as its Empire spread across the globe; whereas the Elus Cohen was distinctly gnostic in outlook, and its approach to Christianity was unorthodox enough to cause extreme concern in any priest of the time who happened across it, unless they were similarly inclined as, for example, Dom Pernety, a Benedictine who admired the teachings of Swedenborg, and who founded the Illuminati of Avignon in 1779; and Abbé Pierre Fournié, the last-known personal disciple of Pasqually.

However, Saint-Martin's path led to different quarries, and later he discovered the writings of Jakob Böhme, the 17th Century German Christian mystic, which added to his vision of mystical Christianity and, while he never ceased to admire his first Master, took him down other avenues which ended with him resigning from all his Masonic and mystical Orders in order to devote himself to contemplation and writing. For all that he still maintained a friendly correspondence with Jean-Baptiste Willermoz, and on another occasion spent time with him in Lyon, notably when the latter had become involved in a form of automatic writing involving a medium who allegedly channeled an entity called *l'Agent Inconnu* or the 'Unknown Agent', which was confusingly similar to *La Chose* or to the many 'Agents' cited by Pasqually and Saint-Martin in their books, and led Papus, the famous esotericist of late 19th Century Paris, to claim that Saint-Martin wrote his books under the pseudonym of *Philosophe Inconnu* or 'Unknown Philosopher' while influenced by this *Agent Inconnu*. Arthur Edward Waite later pointed out that this was impossible since the *Agent Inconnu* didn't appear till seven years after he had completed his second book. Ultimately, it appears both Saint-Martin and Willermoz were unimpressed by the medium's messages from the *Agent Inconnu*, as Saint-Martin departed again almost immediately, and shortly thereafter Willermoz burned most of the received writings.

When the French Revolution began Saint-Martin, being a minor aristocrat, was arrested and questioned, but his inquisitors found him hard to understand and, finding it difficult to tell whether his obtuse writing supported or condemned kingly rule and aristocracy in general, they released him to become a teacher at Alnay, where he died peacefully at the age of sixty on October 13, 1803, only four and a half years after the start of the Revolution.

While his books, and the later ones influenced as much by Böhme as Pasqually, may seem Christian in nature – and we must remember that he is attempting to counter the deist and even atheist movements of his time, disparagingly referring to them as 'the Observers' – he is hardly countering their arguments with orthodox theology, and indeed his first book earned a place of the infamous Roman Catholic *Index Librum Prohibitorum*, or banned book list! This may be because it was published by a known Mason rather than for dubious theology, but since the *Index* doesn't need to give reasons, we may never know.

His contribution to the Scottish Rectified Rite may only appear tangential, but we must remember that not only were his early works considered seminal in Masonic philosophy, but also his long period of work as Pasqually's secretary and his years of correspondence and discussion with Willermoz on precisely the nature of the *Treatise* made his contribution to the renaissance of the Strict Observance under Willermoz a strong force indeed, and he is invariably listed as one of the three great influencers of that Rite. Indeed, a later paper in this book considers some evidence that he was indeed influential in that direction. One might end with the comment that it is rather extraordinary that, given his influence on mainstream Masonic thinking for so long, his most influential books have never been translated into English until now. However, they are not the easiest read, and weren't to readers in the 18th Century either! But the result is well worth the time spent.

The Silk Merchant from Lyon

Jean-Baptiste Willermoz was one of twelve children born into a bourgeois family in Lyon on July 10, 1730. Showing an interest in Freemasonry at an early age, he joined at age 20 and was Master of his Lodge two years later.

Over the years Willermoz gained a great expertise in writing new, mystical rituals for the Craft, including an early version of the Rose Croix, believed by Brig. A.C.F. Jackson, the renowned English Masonic scholar, to be the earliest known version of the Ancient Accepted Scottish Rite ritual, as well as the Knight of the Black Eagle Rose Croix which was quite a different ritual, with its deeply alchemical imagery, no doubt encouraged by his brother, Dr. Jacques Willermoz who was studying alchemy in Marseilles at that time. Other rituals included Grand Scottish Trinity, Founder or Sacrificer, Sovereign Templar Grand Elect, and Knight of the Sun.

Figure 30: J.-B. Willermoz

Similarly, he had assembled his friends to form a number of Lodges. He had financial expertise from his businesses manufacturing silk and working in silver, was well travelled, and had a network of contacts both in the Masonic and business worlds which extended across France, Germany and beyond. He was on friendly terms with aristocrats and Masonic leaders alike (he even met with Cagliostro in Lyon on at least one occasion, although he was apparently unimpressed by the latter's Rite of Memphis).

It was with this background that he encountered a disciple of Pasqually while on a visit to Paris, and not long after joined the Order of Elus Cohen in 1768. He dutifully followed his Master's instructions, such as they were, but it was not until much later that he finally achieved success in obtaining the 'passes' necessary to receive the final Grade of *Réau Croix*. Nevertheless, his devotion to Pasqually's teachings long after the Master left French shores, together with his extensive communications and sojourns with his long-standing friend and fellow disciple, Saint-Martin, helped to shape his beliefs and his understanding of Pasqually often-obtuse system. Although he drifted apart from his friend Saint-Martin in later years, as Louis-Claude divested himself of all attachment to Masonry, nevertheless their friendship had a lasting effect on his approach to his masterwork, the Scottish Rectified Rite.

Figure 31: Regalia of the highest grade of the R.E.R.

Now, Jean-Marc Vivenza, an acknowledged scholar in this area, takes a markedly more cynical view of Willermoz' motives in joining the Rite of Strict Observance than his predecessors. The usual view was that Willermoz simply liked to join interesting things, and the Rite of Strict Observance proved too exciting to pass up, leading him to write requesting a Charter. However, it's notable that he did this in 1773, around the same time that Saint-Martin was staying with him to write his first book. Remember that, by now Pasqually had left for St. Domingue (Haiti) and was not expected to return, and the Order of Elus Cohen was already fraying; and probably daily Willermoz was sitting with his two close friends, the Périsse brothers who were Masonic Brothers as well as local publishers, and Saint-Martin, who would have been developing his views on Pasqually's *Treatise* and which no doubt sparked lively discussions in their social gatherings.

Vivenza, therefore suggests that Willermoz had a long-term plan to save Pasqually's teachings. Now, Pasqually had grafted his theurgic system onto a collection of Scottish Rite rituals which were not necessarily the best vehicle for a progressive system for the development of a form of theurgic chivalry, culminating in Reintegration into the First Estate. We know little about Pasqually's original rituals (the only remnants remaining to us appear to be the 9th Grade which looks very like the Order of the Red Cross, some Catechisms, the Treatise itself, and a few snippets; and while some modern groups claim to have more, until they submit them to the scrutiny of experts in handwriting, period materials and contextual exegesis, I cannot include them in the corpus of his work), and despite some brave attempts, most notably by Robert Ambelain, to reconstruct them, these are guesswork at best. However, even a casual look at even the Francken (1783) or Baylot (1764) manuscripts which contain some of the earliest known rituals remind us that the Scottish Rite is not a completely progressive and unified system of Grades. Given this, one may imagine how the structure of the chivalric Grades of the Strict Observance, moving from the Old to the New Testament, and cumulative in nature, would appeal to Willermoz as a perfect vehicle for his vision.

Therefore, Vivenza believes that Willermoz, seeing the imminent demise of the Strict Observance, determined to press it into service, and made sure his group became members a mere four years before the Convent of Gaules held in Lyon in 1778, which was no coincidence since it meant that it was hosted by the Prefecture of Auvergne, over which Willermoz had control, where they began to question the very foundations of the Strict Observance, including its structure, the existence of the 'Unknown Superiors', and its adherence to the Templar Vengeance rites. From this Conference a number of key decisions were taken, including the abolition of any assumed connection to higher powers or shadowy leaders, the removal of any declaration of vengeance and its substitution with the traditional Masonic injunction to follow and respect the laws and leadership of the country, the recognition of a Masonic element and a chivalric element to the Rite, and the renaming of the Chivalric Order as the Knights Beneficent of the Holy City of Jerusalem, to be under the Scottish Rectified Rite as the new name of the Order. All this was captured in a new Code of Conduct for the Order. But perhaps the boldest change of all was the fact that henceforth *anybody* could potentially be admitted to spiritual knighthood, for the upper echelons of the Order were no longer based on earthly privilege, but instead on spiritual development.

With this in place, all Willermoz now had to do was to take his new Order onto the National and even the international stage, and persuade the leaders of Masonry that firstly, this should become the one true form of Freemasonry; and secondly, that Willermoz should be allowed to rewrite the rituals to fit in with the new ethos.

So, in 1782 the famous Convent of Wilhelmsbad took place and with the support of most of the French delegates and the Princes of Germany, Willermoz got his wish. Incidentally, the biggest loser at this Convent were the Illuminati, but that would be the subject of another paper, and incidentally, if you go onto any Conspiracy Theory website, you'll be told that the Illuminati won. After all, it would be boring to admit they went home with nothing, and died as an Order shortly thereafter…

Perhaps the best support for Vivenza's theory of Willermoz being quite a schemer lies in Willermoz' own words, when he wrote of the Strict Observance that he had been inspired by *La Chose* after the Convent of Gaules, which in his case seems to have provided him with counsel rather than proofs: "I am daring to develop a plan for it to be less in my country, and as one of its guides, to make use of the 'lights' that I had received elsewhere…."

A Final Act of Magic – Transformation of a Rite

And now comes the true magic in the progress of the Rite of Strict Observance – its transformation into perhaps the most, beautiful, the most symbolic, and the most perfect Rite ever known in Freemasonry.

Willermoz' cunning planning, his expertise in writing Masonic ritual had paid off. He now had free range to do what he wanted with these rituals.

As so it was that, although the final hand which created these rituals was that of Jean-Baptiste Willermoz, it was most assuredly the theosophy and teachings of his Master, Martinez de Pasqually, that he was inserting so expertly, showing his expertise born from decades of writing and enacting Masonic rituals, and which perhaps reflected so some extent his handiwork as a purveyor of finest silks. For indeed it seems that his skill was in producing that silk purse from what, if not a pig's ear, was certainly little more than a Chivalric whimsy until then. And with what attention he performed the work! Recalling his conversations, too, with his friend Saint-Martin, some twenty years after the deaths of both his mentor and his friend he was still at work polishing and rectifying these masterpieces. Indeed, despite the French Revolution, despite the hardships of the Siege of Lyon, the loss of his brother to Madame Guillotine, he was to work on that Rite until his death at the grand old age of 94 in 1824, intent on making it the most perfect vehicle for what he believed was no less than a revelation from God.

Time prevents me from going into detail about these sublime rituals. However, I can say that, unlike most Masonic Rites, which are often a collection of quaint rituals more or less collected together into a story, these recount nothing less than the entire history of Man, from his Creation, through his Prevarication, his Fall, and the means to regain his former splendor and be Reintegrated into his former glory. But further, it doesn't just recount the story: hidden within the rituals are the means to *accomplish* this.

The first three Masonic Grades tell the story of the terrible Fall of Mankind and relates the stories of the Old Testament from the point of view of the Treatise; while the fourth, the Master and Perfect Master of St. Andrew is a pivot Degree, showing man the image of Hiram as the resurrected Christ, and inviting him to allow this avatar to possess his body and lead him to redemption.

For Hiram is now nothing less than the Repairer, and the light to lead man along the Path. This pivot Grade also shows him a glimpse of the celestial Jerusalem, with his promise of restoration, as we move from the Old to the New Testament, and the substitution of the Old Law, the Old Covenant with the New Law, the New Covenant. The Squire Novice brings him to the very portal of the City, and the Knight Beneficent of the Holy City into its precincts, to enjoy his primitive state of perfection.

Yet while these six Grades lead man through the complete story of Pasqually's theosophy, there were two more secret Grades, those of Profès and Grand Profès which were only open – and known – to those who had the capacity to understand the full story. In those Grades the initiates, for now they were truly initiates of Pasqually's system, received two lectures which essentially summarized Pasqually's *Treatise*: and Willermoz' desire to preserve the teachings in perpetuity was accomplished.

This leads us to one important question: was the Profession theurgical? As someone who has been studying this question for over twenty years, I have to say that I believe it was (and *should* be). There is no empirical proof since no records were made of their meetings. However, I find it very hard to believe that they didn't practice the old rituals, seeing that Willermoz was assembling the same friends around him who had run the Cohen Temple in Lyon for many years, who had joined him and his Alchemist brother in their several Masonic creations, and who had read and discussed the teachings of Pasqually and Saint-Martin, as well as performed the rituals of the Elus Cohen, we are told with success. For all these reasons, it seems entirely possible to me that, whatever happened later, when the city was besieged, and the sacred Order taken to Switzerland by his nephew, no doubt with few rubric instructions, at this time what these Brothers did in their Professed meetings in Lyon was to discuss the Treatise and perform theurgical Operations!

Yet, for the rest of the members, since Willermoz left the *structure* of the Strict Observance intact, what purpose would there be in taking over that respected Order if it didn't house the foundation, the structure in which to preserve Pasqually's teachings? And lest you think I am simply making this up, let me leave you with one example of how Willermoz transformed Baron von Hund's Rite, while retaining the external structure.

In the first Grade of the Strict Observance, the new Entered Apprentice is shown an image, that of a broken column, associated with the destroyed first Temple at Jerusalem. Yet they are later told that this broken column represents the Templar Order, whose head, Jacques de Molay, was cruelly burned at the stake, yet still stands, *Adhuc Stat*, propagated in secrecy and ready to rise again.

In the Scottish Rectified Rite we are shown the same image and the same Latin motto, but now we are told instead that the broken column represents man in his fallen state, separated from his primitive home, and separated from the First Principle with created him. Now instead he is told that, rather than needing to rebuild the column and the Temple to restore the terrestrial Templar Order, his purpose in life is to restore the balance between him and his Source, so that he may begin his journey towards reintegration by rebuilding the broken link between him and his Creator and reestablish himself once more as the true intermediary between God and the Universe.

Figure 32: It still stands!

Conclusion

This has been a very thorough exploration of the origins of the Scottish Rectified Rite. We have seen how the proliferation in Orders and Grades in Europe following the expulsion of the Catholic king from England gave rise to a desire to create a single Order into which all Freemasons would seek admission. We have seen how initially it looked possible that the Rite of Strict Observance would fulfil this need, but that while it was built on a strong foundation, its structure was effectively empty of meaning, and it also perpetuated the hereditary distinction between the aristocracy and commoners, offering no alternative to daily life.

We saw how an unlikely prophet created an unstable Masonic Order based on his gnostic and unorthodox interpretation of the Biblical story, into which came two extraordinary people, one a spiritual philosopher and the other a career Freemason. The mutual influence of these three men brought about a seismic shift in how Freemasonry was to be viewed: no longer as a collection of moral stories with fancy costumes, but rather a curriculum for spiritual enlightenment and even an alternative road to the Church – then seen as barren and corrupt – in accomplishing a personal identification with the Repairer and following the Path of Return to the Author of All Things.

This led to a daring plan to take over an Order which was beginning to lose its way, and through a series of pan-European Masonic Convocations to use its structure to build a cohesive system of symbolism and education which could be followed by *any* Mason to achieve spiritual enlightenment, overseen by a small number of Professed leaders who would guide this Order with a benign and benevolent eye; while its adherents would practice all the Cardinal and Theological Virtues to bring about a society ruled by a synarchy.

Freemasonry might have looked very different today if this had been accomplished. A new Order had been established, it had the support of the most influential Masons in Europe, and within a few years it is quite possible that all other mainland European Rites would have been absorbed into it.

But it was not to be.

At the very moment of its triumph the French Revolution burst upon the scene and carried everything before it, Church, Monarchy, Freemasonry; and by the time it was over, it would take many years to start to put the pieces back together once more.

Nowadays, this Order is beginning to retake its rightful place, at least in a few countries where Rectified Lodges are expanding; and more cynically it has also become a worthy vehicle on which Masonic scholars can build their reputations.

Perhaps one oddity in all this is the fact that there are *two* lines claimed for the Order from Willermoz: that of traditional Freemasonry, and that of Martinism, the resurrection of the teachings and ideals of Louis-Claude de Saint-Martin, whose adherents are far closer to understanding the theosophy behind the Scottish Rectified Rite than their Masonic counterparts, who are often more interested in the superficial trappings of pomp and circumstance than the profound blueprint contained in it. Perhaps our final point, then, might be that it was the non-Masonic Christian Philosopher who ultimately came to preserve the soul, the character and the purpose of this sublime Rite.

A Discourse on Numbers

(Part 1 – History)

A Discourse on Numbers
(Part 1 – History)

hy Part 1, you ask? *Well, this paper was given during a Covid-19 Zoom session of the annual meeting of the Societas Rosicruciana In Civitatibus Fœderatis, or S.R.I.C.F. in 2020. I was intending to write Part 2, to cover more practical aspects of Numerology in general, and that of Martinism, the Golden Dawn, indeed the Masonic Rosicrucians who have their own interpretation, and other systems in time for the 2021 meeting, which it was hoped would be in person. But time got away from me, and I add this paper in the hope that, in the future, Part 2 will appear!*

Introduction

This paper is about numbers. After language, they are perhaps the most important tool to humanity. Indeed, as most of us know, in many of the early languages, letters were even used as numbers. Here we will consider something of the history of numbers, from their earliest use to how they ended up being considered so important to be the subject of the Lecture which follows our first Grade of Zelator. Most of what I will have to say you will know, though I hope it may prompt you to look at things you thought obvious or familiar in a new way. I also hope that you may even take away some new things you weren't aware of. However, I will say that, unlike some of my previous papers which had a more practical flavor, this one focuses predominantly on history. However, I hope there is sufficient information to encourage you to dive deeper into any area which piques your interest. It can all be found in the omniscient Akashic Records in the Cloud – the World Wide Web!

Numbers affect everything in our lives. After language it is the most important symbolic system. We count our calories, our birthdays, our mortgages, our air miles, our weight, our number of Facebook friends, and our calendar dates in numbers. We use them to calculate how to get to the moon and how to build an atomic reactor. We use them to catalogue our knowledge, in libraries and online. We use them to measure distances and areas, to count objects, to check weight, and even to measure the fourth dimension – time – and bring it under some semblance of control.

When I was at school in England at the age of 7, we started the day with recitals of numeric tables: firstly, the two to twelve times tables, then money (12d = 1s, 18d = 1/6d, 20d = 1/8d, 24d = 2s, etc. – that dates me![12]). In those days there were no calculators, no smart phones, no computers – even sales tills only added; they didn't tell you how much to give back to the customer! Then we moved on to measures (inches, feet, yards, chains, furlongs, miles), then weights (ounces, pounds, stones, quarters, hundredweight, tons). We were building a dexterity with numbers which would serve us for the rest of our lives. It's interesting that we started the day with numbers, measures and weights. We will return to this later.

Early Beginnings

In at least one early culture, Mesopotamia, counting tokens have been found dating from as far back as 4000 B.C. In fact, counting preceded written language in this culture, which tells us that, for one or more of the earliest civilizations, numbers had a greater value to them than writing. Over time this changed, it is believed due to the growth of religion and the need to communicate both ideas and to preserve history. Later on, we find an alphabet beginning to develop which is strongly pictorial or glyphic in nature, and in which we find the origin of written text. The fact that the initial glyphs represented things which were important to the early nomadic tribes is significant.

Figure 33: Mesopotamian counting tokens

For example, if we trace the first letter of the Hebrew alphabet, the letter Aleph, or 'A', we see it began as a glyph of the head of an Ox, which over time changed into the present-day letter. While this isn't a talk on alphabets, I cannot resist making one observation.

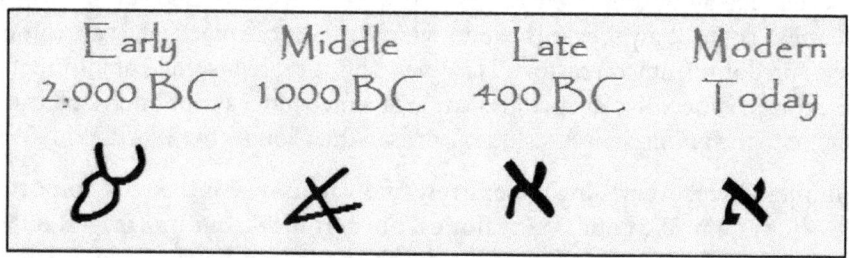

Figure 34: Development of glyphs into letters - Hebrew 'aleph'

---

[12] For younger readers who are a still scratching their heads, the old currency system in the UK had 12 pennies or pence (written as 'd' after the Roman word denarius) and 20 shillings – or 240 pence – to a pound. Hence: 12 pence = 1 shilling, 18 pence = one shilling and sixpence (one word since it was an actual coin), 20 pence = one shilling and eight pence, 24 pence = 2 shillings.

A Discourse on Numbers

Most Hebrew letters derived from pictograms which, over time, developed into their common alphabet, a process which usually becomes fixed when a sufficient number of people become literate, for the clear reason that it is hard to communicate between one another and across time if the alphabet keeps changing! After a time, it is hard to see the original sense of the letters of the language. However, one advantage of early languages is that each letter, as well as a sound, also had a meaning. We said above that Aleph means 'Ox'. Although it is equally hard to see the original glyph in the other letters of the current Hebrew alphabet, from the meanings we can learn about the type of lifestyle, in this instance nomadic.

Thus, there are letters which mean house, camel, ox goad, water, snake, sword, fishhook – all things which would be of paramount interest to a group of hunter-gatherers. Would we expect a fully settled civilization to be obsessed by similar things? Well, let's consider some of the Egyptian alphabet. There, among the pictograms we find the following objects: jar stand, reed leaf, basket, woven reed mat, bolt of cloth, quail chick, door bolt.

From this we can see how the alphabet of the Israelites, while it shared certain things in common with the Egyptian one, such as having no vowels and a foundation in pictograms, developed differently from the Egyptian alphabet because of the different needs driving the origin of their letters.

Aleph			
Image:	Ox Head		
Meaning:	Strong, Power, Leader		
Beyt			
Image:	Tent		
Meaning:	Family, House, In		
Gimel			
Image:	Foot		
Meaning:	Gather, Walk		
Dalet			
Image:	Door		
Meaning:	Move, Hang, Entrance		
Hey			
Image:	Man with arms raised		
Meaning:	Look, Reveal, Breath		
Vav			
Image:	Tent Peg		
Meaning:	Add, Secure, Hook		
Zayin			
Image:	Mattock (Hoe)		
Meaning:	Food, Cut, Nourish		
Hhet			
Image:	Well		
Meaning:	Outside, Divide, Half		
Tet			
Image:	Basket		
Meaning:	Surround, Contain, Mod/Clay		
Yud			
Image:	Arm and closed hand		
Meaning:	Work, Throw		
Kaph			
Image:	Open palm		
Meaning:	Bend, Open, Allow, Tame		

Figure 35: Developing Hebrew Alphabet

Another advantage of early languages is that, as well as having a sound and a meaning, they also had a numerical value, there being no separate numerical system at that time. Thus, each letter of the alphabet carried a value. Aleph was 1, Beth 2, Gimel 3 and so on. The 22-letter alphabet, together with 5 variations when letters appeared at the end of a word, allowed them to count from 1 all the way up to 999.

Incidentally, to throw a bone to the esotericists, the way of depicting 1,000 was to go back to Aleph, 1, now to the power of 3, by adding a dot above it. In the late 19th Century, the Ordre Kabbalistique de la Rose Croix adopted a similar symbol by adding an aleph with one, two or three dots to their signatures to indicate their membership.

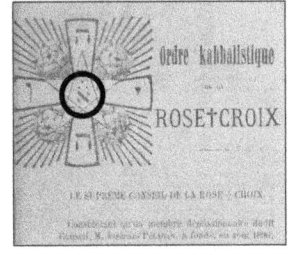

Figure 36: Dotted aleph in heading

69

The power and richness of early alphabets was that a letter had a glyph, a meaning, a number and a sound, so when you were creating a word out of these glyphs, far more was going on than simply creating a long string of phonetics out of a collection of single ones. As an example, let's take the name of the city Bethel. Firstly, 'Beth' is the second letter of the Hebrew alphabet and means 'house'; 'El' is one of the names of God. So, we now know that Bethel means 'House of God'. If we decompose 'El', we find it made up of Aleph, 'Ox' and Lamed, 'Ox goad'. The Ox was the most powerful beast known to the Israelites, and it signified Strength; and along with man, the eagle and the lion (incidentally a letter in Egyptian), it represented the epitome of power, as seen in the Merkabah, or fiery chariot, of Ezekiel. Similarly, the Ox goad, a wooden staff with a metal knife in the end, represented authority and control – for example, Moses' staff of authority, or a king's scepter. Combining power and might, we have God. If we spell it out in full, Bethel (ביתאל), the letters add to 443. Another word which sums to the same total is Betulah, or Virgin, which is a symbol of Earth; for in Christian symbolism at least, the Earth composed of its loyal members, that is, the Church, is the bride of Christ. We will see another such appropriation in a moment; but for now, let's remember that in the Torah, Bethel is both the place where Abram built an altar to the Lord, and Jacob dreamed of his famous ladder.

Nechash (Serpent)
נחש
50+8+300 = 358

Meshiach (Messiah)
משיח
40+300+10+18 = 358

To give a famous example of this technique of associating words with an identical numerical value, consider the two words, *Nechash* and *Meshiach*, both of which sum to 358. This tells us they have a connection. If I then tell you that *Nechash* means Serpent and *Meshiach* means Messiah, perhaps you may recall that Christian exegetists identify the brazen serpent hoisted up on a pole by Moses to cure the afflicted Israelites as being a harbinger of Christ raised up on a cross to save us all. But don't take their word for it: listen to the Gospel of John (well, it had to be the mystical one, didn't it!). In Chapter 3 verse 14, he says: "And as Moses lifted up the Serpent in the wilderness, even so must the Son of Man be lifted up." But of course, the Gnostics had to take it that one step further, and say it was also the same Serpent in the garden of Eden who freed man from the stupidity of ignorance. But that's a whole different lecture!

Now, numbers were clearly so important to the Hebrews that it is hardly surprising to find their extensive use in the Bible. We need look no further than the first few verses of Genesis to find the importance of the number '7' to them, for example, or therefore why the same number makes a Lodge 'perfect'! We won't dwell on this, but there is one rule to be aware of. They were really focused on the numbers from 1 – 9, so that whether they wrote 2 days or 200 years, the main gist of the number was the same, except perhaps in magnitude.

This is why, for example, we find Noah spending 40 days upon the waters, Moses wandering for 40 years in Sinai, or Jesus sojourning for 40 days in the wilderness. In their alphabet, 4 signifies a doorway or transition, 40 signifies water, and 400 signifies the end – or even a cross. In light of this, I hope you can begin to see why the use of specific numbers was so important to them.

Perhaps the verse in the Bible which underpins and emphasizes this more than any other is Wisdom 11:21, which says of God: "Thou has ordered all things in measure, and number, and weight." And in Job 28:24–25 we read: "For He looks to the ends of the earth, and sees under the whole heaven; to make the weight for the winds, and apportion the waters by measure." In other words, God used numbers for the act of Creation, which is one reason we refer to him as the Grand Geometrician in the Fellowcraft Degree.

If numbers, then, were imbued with divine powers, then it is hardly surprising that, over time, alongside the divine attributes of these sacred interpretations there grew a school of thought which ascribed independent power to numbers, and they became talismans in themselves, divorced from their roots.

In the Hebrew and early Christian faith they would appear on talismans and amulets worn to ward off evil powers or to attract good spirits. While some included biblical quotations or images, many would include what are known as magic squares, filled either with letters of words. One known to most Christians from those times which use words is SATOR AREPO TENET OPERA ROTAS, which reads the same across and down; or the famous ABRADACABRA within a triangle and adding one letter at a time. This apparently meaningless word is believed by many scholars to derive from Aramaic, meaning

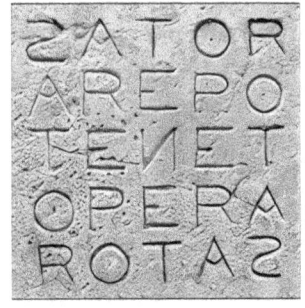

Figure 37: SATOR acrostic

"I will create as I speak", an extraordinary reflection of God's act of Creation, and which asserts man's role in the Universe as the microcosm, containing within himself the ability to create which, according to many philosophies, is his birthright as the *imago dei*, or image of God, and which of course he performs all the time – at least in the material world. Similarly, in other parallel societies of the time, such as Ancient Greece or Rome, we see numbers playing an increasing role in augury. For example, augurs would count the number of birds flying overhead and draw conclusions from that for everything from the outcome of a war to the health of a king. Incidentally, this superstition has carried through to our own times in the famous children's rhyme about magpies. While you may know the modern version, one going back to 1780 in England went: "One for sorrow, two for mirth, three for a funeral, four for a birth." This resurgence of superstition will come back to haunt us from the Victorian times onwards.

The importance of numbers was carried forward on the wings of the emergent Christian faith, as we see in the seven churches in Asia (or *Assiah*), the seven Seals of the Great Book of Revelation, the seven Sacraments, the seven Gifts of the Holy Spirit, the seven candles on the altar in presence of a bishop (at least in Catholic Churches), and so on. The number seven has become indelibly linked with perfection.

However, perhaps on the back of the more superstitious application of numbers, as the years progressed through the Dark Ages number became more intertwined with esoteric symbology, and despite the fact that numbers didn't come into their own as a separate system from letters – for until the 14th Century most educated people continued to count using Roman letters, which ironically we use up to the present time as in the movie house MCM, meaning 1900, to give just one example, or on most cornerstones, incidentally – people saw sigils in the 'I's, the 'V's, the 'X's, the 'L', the 'C's and the 'M's of Roman counting. The biggest leap came when the Hindu-Arabic numbering system came to the West, and even now we call numbers 'Arabic'. Then letters and numbers were finally divorced from one another, and even Latin texts would include Arabic numbering. Of course, the downside of this was that the link between words and numbers (or creation) was irretrievably lost, and now letters stood for nothing but sounds. I will leave it to the reader to decide whether this was a step forward or a step backward.

Rediscovery of the Early Texts

The end of the Middle Ages and the beginning of the Renaissance saw an explosion in erudition. The end of the Middle Ages did not come quietly, and the relative stability – albeit harsh for most – which Europe had known for nearly a thousand years was now challenged successively by plague and famine, endless wars, and the Western Schism which destroyed the unity of the Roman Church: all of which threw the continent into seemingly unending upheaval.

A Discourse on Numbers

The Renaissance ushered in an era of humanism, and in particular an age of culture and scholarship, brought about by the rediscovery of Classical Greek philosophy. Among them, they rediscovered Protagoras, who said that "Man is the measure of all things." This refocus of the quotation in the Book of Wisdom set many on a path which differed from the passive route of their forebears. Platonic philosophy was teaching them that there were three stages in creation: thought, will and action. This is how God created the heavens, the macrocosm; and in the microcosm, this is how man created on earth.

And what an outpouring there was: fine art, beautiful music, advances in architecture through the rediscovery of concrete, and writing. Man no longer needed to be a passive observer of Creation: he could affect it! If man was the measure of all things, then he had a connection with everything, and he could use that connection to influence anything. Thus, we see an explosion of interest in Astrology, Alchemy and Theurgy. In all of these, the use of numbers was paramount: for hadn't God created all through the use of measure, and numbers, and weight?

Figure 38: Cornelius Agrippa

Figure 39: John Dee

This was the age of John Dee and Cornelius Agrippa, and their fascination with codes, numerology and angelic alphabets. Dee was also a spy and well-versed in creating complex calculations and numerology, using the skills for both very practical inventions and the extraordinarily complex Enochian tablets for communicating with and summoning angelic forces. I was struck by a comment by Jason Louv in his monumental book *John Dee and the Empire of Angels*, in which he mentioned Dee's 'Mathematicall Praeface' to the publication of Henry Billingsley's translation of Euclid's Elements of Geometry in 1570, of which Louv says: "The preface argued for the central importance of math (still viewed with suspicion by the public) to the sciences. The preface also elaborated many of Dee's previous ideas from the *Propaedeumata* and *Monas*, suggesting that mathematics itself is a Hermetic pursuit, for it allows the mathematician to understand the thoughts of God and the method by which He had created and operates the Universe. This was a vision of God as grand governor and 'Grand Architect of the Universe', as the Freemasons would later put it."

In the meantime, among the many grimoires and books devoted to spells to control all parts of Creation, the *Second Book of Occult Philosophy* by Henry Cornelius Agrippa, one the books considered by many to be the foundation of Western Occultism, was almost entirely devoted to the magic of numbers. He discusses the powers and virtues of numbers, citing examples from the Bible, but now also from early Greek, Latin and other texts, with a heavy emphasis on Kabbalah, before going on to discuss the planets, and providing the magic squares of each (to those unfamiliar with magic squares, they are squares of numbers, the sum of each row, column and diagonal amounting to the same total). He goes on to discuss mathematics in the context of geometry, then harmony and music, then ends with the celestial bodies. I hope this is beginning to sound familiar to any Mason; for of course he is outlining a mystical version of the Quadrivium, or the last four of the Seven Liberal Arts and Sciences!

Figure 40: Magic Square from Kircher's Œdipus Egyptiacus (1652)

Finally, he turns inwards to the microcosm, the Book of Man, and in it reads the proportions, measure and harmony of man's body. Incidentally, despite all this glorious extolling of the sublimity of numbers, even Agrippa isn't above throwing in a rather more mundane use: the title of Chapter 44 is "Of Lottery, when, and whence the virtue of divining is incident to it." Yes, the lottery was around even then, and people were even then trying to find superstitious ways to beat the system!

In the Universities the Seven Liberal Arts and Sciences were taught, as every good Mason knows. We can trace their origins as far back as Plato, who wrote about most of them in his book The Republic, although in present form they are mostly associated with Martianus Capella. They went on to form the backbone of the education system for nearly a thousand years. The Liberal Arts were divided into the Trivium or threefold path (Grammar, Logic, Rhetoric) and then, when this was completed, the Quadrivium or fourfold path (Geometry,

Arithmetic, Music and Astronomy). The Trivium taught one to spell and put together sentences, then how to argue a point, and finally how to deliver this in a logical argument to other people. Armed with these communication skills, the Quadrivium then expanded one's education into space, numbers, number in time and finally numbers in time and space.

In passing, the Art of Memory, that great aid allegedly invented by the Ancient Greek Simonides which flourished at this time, where people used their 'memory palaces' to remember and store anything from academic sources to three-hour long sermons delivered from memory, and which of course later found an honorable mention as the Middle Chamber Lecture in Freemasonry, also made use of objects containing numbers in the 'palace' to remember lists of things. This was not unlike the use of the Christian Kabbalistic Tree of Life, where each Sephira was used to remember an ever-increasing list of associations, such as perfumes, planets, angels, names of God, colors, animals, plants, etc. I'm sure there was more than one 'memory palace' in which you would find, on a wall in some room, a rendition of the Ten Commandments or the Tree of Life waiting to have associations made with each of its numbers. This Art would reappear in much degraded form in the 20th Century, as we shall see later.

The Enlightenment and Freemasonry

Now, as we have seen the Book of Wisdom provided a powerful justification for the exploration of the Quadrivium during the Middle Ages, and the Renaissance interpretation led to the belief that, by using the mathematical disciplines of mathematics, geometry, music and astronomy, the human mind was demonstrating its likeness to the Divine Mind. And as we have also seen, the natural outcome of this was man seeing a greater role for himself in the Universe than merely that of passive observer; and, whether it was through scientific exploration or magical ceremony, there was an imperative to understand and control. We continue to see this in the 17th century, with Sir Isaac Newton obsessively studying the measurements of the Temple to try to understand its mysteries, and thereby gain a deeper knowledge of God.

And for our purposes, the earliest Freemasons were embarking on a similar quest, as we see them imbuing the rituals we still use with deeply significant numbers, and stories based on measure, and number, and weight, including the Tower of Babel, Noah's Ark, and of course Solomon's Temple. In context, we see the fruition of a story begun in the Middle Ages. For these were not merely tales to be told or simple plays to be performed: these came out of the notion that, by understanding God's methodology, we, too could become like God. And if God created by numbers, so by understanding numbers and their corollaries, such as geometry, harmony and how the heavens operated, we could seek to lift the corner of the veil of God's process, and perhaps even participate in it or affect it ourselves. We need not discuss the importance of numbers such as 3, 4, 7, and 12 in Masonry, and how the importance of these is equaled only by their importance in the Bible.

However, the two worlds of rational thought and esoteric thought collided head-on, especially in France. Why England, and for that matter the United States, were to be such late developers in this manifestation is something not easily answered. Perhaps it was simply due to the geography of the English Channel and the Atlantic Ocean; or perhaps because of the Anglo-Saxon mentality; or again because of some deep-seated puritanical aversion to the mystical? Be that as it may, we will have to wait until the mid 1800s to see a true resurgence of the mystical appreciation of numbers in these countries. But the fire which was soon to be lit in France would burn across Europe, engulfing Germany, Italy, Denmark, Russia and Sweden.

Figure 41: An 18th Century Lodge Meeting

The Age of Enlightenment was in full swing in the early 18th Century. Traditional Hanoverian Freemasonry had been imported into France from England, and the Modernists were pouring scorn on the ignorance of the ancient philosophers. The Encyclopedists were using their massive project to rewrite both history and understanding. Science was chasing the last vestiges of superstition out of the closets. The Church was viewed with disdain as an antiquated, inefficient and corrupt body. And yet, we must remember that all this referred to only ten percent of the population. In France, most of the other ninety percent were farmers, who lived their lives surrounded by the same folklore and superstitions as their forebears dating back to the Dark Ages – a state of affairs which persisted even until the end of the 19th Century, as we can find in the writings of Dr. Gérard Encausse, or Papus. France wore a sophisticated veneer, but peel back the IKEA laminate, and underneath was the chipboard of an almost medieval society. While there certainly was a court, the vast majority of French aristocracy was by no means socially and emotionally divorced from the farmers and tenants who worked their lands (any more than they were in England, incidentally). There was a burgeoning bourgeoisie, or middle class, who came from among those very peasants and who longed to rub shoulders with the aristocracy both for financial and social ends.

Now throw Freemasonry into this mix, with the opportunity for the Middle Classes to sit in Lodge with nobility (and peasants for that matter – remember the meaning of the white gloves?). Suddenly there was a reason for men from different walks of life to meet on common ground, share common experiences and share common mythologies. While the aristocracy yearned for relevance and a link with the past; the commoners expected to find something magical and transformational in this new endeavor.

In a way Ramsay's Discourse provided the flame to ignite the aristocracy's desires by providing a putative link with the Knights of yore, which almost immediately became identified as the Knights Templar – an immediate 'hit' because of the symbolism of the Third Degree. But that also opened the floodgates to all the 'baggage' which the Templars brought. Hadn't they been destroyed because of their unorthodox beliefs? Didn't they practice magic? Hadn't they been immolated because they possessed great secrets? All this unlocked the Pandora's Box which contained both the superstitions which the lower classes had never shed, as well as memories of the Hermetic, Alchemical Astrological and Theurgical currents, and the relatively recent excitement over the Rosicrucians. In a society which was now composed of snobbish intellectuals who sneered at such beliefs, where better to pursue them than behind the respectable – and secretively tiled doors – of Freemasonry? Most of this took place under the veil of what became known as 'Écossais' or 'Scottish' Masonry, and it's important to realize that this kind of Freemasonry, living uncomfortably alongside 'regular' Georgian Masonry, since it gave its loyalty – symbolically at least – to the overthrown House of Stuart, provided a haven for all those ostracized or cast adrift by a society which now extolled Enlightenment principles. Here is brief quote from René le Forestier, who wrote on this very subject in 1928:

"But if the flirtation Écossais Freemasonry had with mysticism and occultism was not altogether central, it no less defines the role it played in the customs of all Freemasonry in the 18th Century. Lodges became the refuge of "Men of Desire"… (to) all the contemporary Occultists, whatever their nationality wore the symbolic apron, and … all the esoteric groups attracted their largest numbers of recruits from among the Masons, to whom they advertised themselves as the representatives of the true Masonic tradition and the custodians of its ultimate secret. …If answering to the appeal which Écossais Masonry makes to us from behind the façade, we pass behind the scenes, and in the shadows we perceive a completely new world. There we make out alchemists and theurgists, visionaries and casters of horoscopes, ecstatics and exorcists…"

The importance of this was that, while in the profane world advances in mathematics were giving rise to the discovery of logarithms, calculus, analytical geometry, polynomials and algebraic equations, here in the sanctuary of the Lodge, Chapter or Temple, the biblical numbers found in the rituals were reestablishing links with the Kabbalah, Magical Squares and Numerology.

Figure 42: The Pentagram

Now the number 3 could, in addition to how many can 'hold' a Lodge, refer to the three main stages of Alchemical transformation; 5 could also refer to the joining of the 'fifth element' with the four traditional elements, a mystical interpretation both of the act of man's creation by God and a representation of the descent of the Holy Spirit into Jesus the man; and 7 could represent the planets, perfection (again, remember what makes a Lodge 'perfect'), and the power which allows Netzach, the seventh Sephira on the Tree of Life to achieve Victory through the use of the seventh letter of the Hebrew alphabet, Zayin (ז), or the flaming Sword – for the letters of early Hebrew are often referred to as 'fire letters', or the 'angelic' alphabet.

Perhaps none took this to a logical conclusion more than Martinès de Pasqually, founder of the Order of Elus Cohen, a theurgical Order based overtly on early Scottish Rite Masonry (indeed, since both he and Morin were based in Bordeaux, and later both found themselves in what is now Haiti, scholars have long debated if there was any cross-transference between them), who built a whole theosophical interpretation of numbers into his quasi-gnostic system, later promulgated by Louis-Claude de Saint-Martin. While a more detailed examination of this fascinating system will be saved for a later time, details of it can be found in Saint-Martin's books, and if one notes that the numbers 7 and 8 represent the descent of the Holy Spirit into the temporal, and the number of Christ respectively (who replaced Man in the center following his Fall), it should come as no surprise that Jean-Baptiste Willermoz, the prominent Lyonnais Mason who was a student of Pasqually and a friend of Saint-Martin, who created the Rectified Rite or Knights Beneficent of the Holy City, should have added two secret Grades to the 6 visible ones of the Order, a 7th and 8th, which mirrored Pasqually's Order in putting a person in contact with their personal angelic guide, and symbolically establishing them as what Saint-Martin termed a Man-God. Saint-Martin wrote an entire book devoted to Numbers, which was published posthumously.[13]

Victorian Numerology

Time requires us to move forward to the 19th Century, where, a century later, England finally catches up!

In the mid-Victorian times, there was a reactive emergence of interest in the occult, perhaps due to the over-regimentation of life, which was one unfortunate side-effect of industrialization. Darwin was promoting evolution, and while scientific discoveries and applications were exploding at an exponential rate, this appeared to be to the detriment of the ethereal dimension of life. Children's books began to focus on fantasies, and this was when we see the publication of Alice's Adventures in Wonderland, The Wonderful Wizard of Oz, and Treasure Island. Adult fiction wasn't far behind, with Bram Stoker's Dracula, Mary Shelley's Frankenstein, and Bulwer Lytton's Zanoni. On the esoteric front, more and more books appeared in print, perhaps commencing with Francis Barrett's monumental book The Magus, first published in 1801.

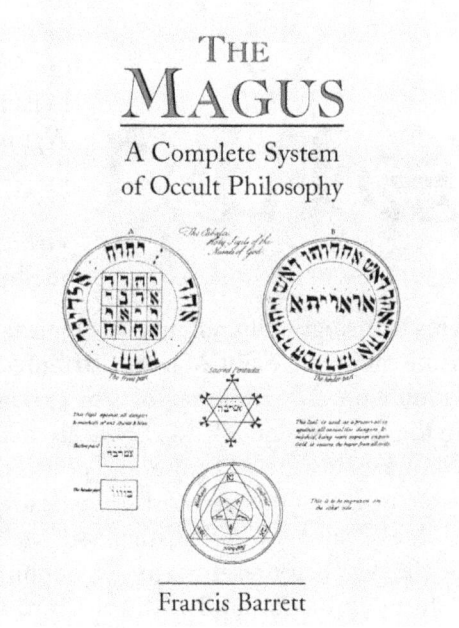

Figure 43: The Magus by F. Barrett

---

[13] This book, together with *Of Errors & Truth* and *Natural Table*, are available on amazon.com published by Rose Circle Publications.

In 1865, Robert Wentworth Little founded the Societas Rosicruciana in Anglia (S.R.I.A.), while a few years later some of its members went on to create perhaps the most famous magical society of all time: the Hermetic Order of the Golden Dawn (H.O.G.D.). The activity was just as frenzied on the other side of the Atlantic, where Rosicrucian Masonic Societies took off as well, as did the Golden Dawn; while their home-grown contributions included the Theosophical Society, various Rosicrucian Orders, the Church of Christ Scientist, and the many strange orders of the 'burned-over' district of Northern New York State.

Figure 44: S.R.I.A

Among this resurgence of esoteric interest, we find a similar resurgence of interest in the power of Numbers. As mentioned earlier, numbers were considered so important it became the subject of the first lecture the newly admitted Zelator heard on joining the S.R.I.A., a practice reflected in the other Masonic Rosicrucian bodies as well. William Wynn Westcott, onetime Supreme Magus of the S.R.I.A. wrote a book on them, entitled *Numbers – Their Occult Power and Mystic Virtues*, which goes to show the weight he attributed to their esoteric importance.

Unsurprisingly, different numerological systems attribute different values to the same number. Saint-Martin attributed the number '4' to man, while the 'doubly-powerful number' of 8, or 2 x 4, was the number which identified Christ. In the S.R.I.A. and S.R.I.C.F., we are told that "8 designates the primitive law of Nature, being the first cube, and points out that all men are born equal. It is also esteemed the number most to be desired, being the number of Justice." In the Golden Dawn, a Kabbalistically-driven system like the Masonic Rosicrucian Societates, 8 represents the 8th Sephira on the Tree of Life, Hod, meaning 'Glory', and associated with the Third Grade of Practicus. The lecture in this Grade in the S.R.I.A. concerns itself with Alchemy. It is an interesting read, and appropriate to its historical context, begins by reminding us that Alchemy is both practical and spiritual, before going into a lengthy defense of it by showing how much chemistry has been derived from it. Finally, it discusses the modern resurgence of interest among Victorian writers and practitioners, ending with the words: "it seems manifest that the writings of many medieval European Alchymists enshrine a doctrine at once exalted, fascinating in formulation, eloquent in language, and worthy of serious study." And this lecture was originally given to leaders of industry, the church and business in the Victorian age, when scientific progress had never been so all-consuming!

On the continent we see a parallel resurgence of interest in the occult, beginning with Eliphas Lévi and continued through the likes of Dr. Gérard Encausse or Papus, Paul Sédir, Joséphin Péladan and many others. Papus himself, in the footsteps of Saint-Martin, wrote an entire book on Numbers (curiously, also published posthumously). Comparing his interpretation of the number '8' we find it accords with that of Westcott more strongly than that of Saint-Martin, for he attributes it to the eighth card of the Major Arcana of the Tarot: Justice. It was no doubt the same reason that the SRIA lecture associates the number '8' with Justice. We have to remember how influential Lévi's Tarot Deck was at that time, and this is where we find Justice in his deck. However, for those familiar with Tarot asking themselves: "How can this be?", we must remember that it was Arthur Edward Waite who switched the cards of Justice and Strength, so that now Justice is the 11th card and Strength the 8th. This all took place some years after these lectures and books were written. Whether one agrees with this switch or not, it has influenced just about every deck since the Rider-Waite deck first appeared. The end of the 19th century saw even more erudite books discussing the esoteric importance of numbers.

Figure 45: 8th Card of Major Arcana

The Twentieth Century and Beyond

The 19th century ended, and as we often see following all the centennial fever which so often seems to stir up a resurgence of interest in the esoteric, things started to go back to sleep. Books on popular Numerology were reduced to cheap advertisements on the back pages of magazines such as *Star of the Magi* run by Margaret B. Peeke, who herself was a prominent esotericist and wrote a book on Numbers. There were still occasional flashes of genius, such as Sepharial, or Walter Gorn-Old, an influential English author in the fields of astrology and numerology and one of the founders of the Theosophical Society, who in 1913 published *The Kabala of Numbers* discussing the relationship between Astrology and Numbers. Another worthy tome was *Occult Geometry and Hermetic Science of Motion and Number* by A.S. Raleigh, published in 1924, which the author said: "interprets and explains symbols, Nature's universal language, which shows how God geometrizes to produce the Universe and Man, and that in understanding himself Man understands the big Universe."

Figure 46: Margaret Peeke

Figure 47: 'Sepharial'

Figure 48: Richard Cavendish

But for the main part, the high science of numbers and their relationship to Creation was reduced to little more than parlor tricks. The sublime thoughts of Jakob Boehme in his tract *How a Man May Find Himself and So Finding Come to All Mysteries Even to the Ninth Number, Yet No Higher*, was reduced to finding one's lucky number in a fortune cookie.

The art of Theosophical Addition and Subtraction, used prominently in the Kabbalah and in Saint-Martin's numerological system, was now no more than numbering the 26 letters of the alphabet in order to get a total score for your name, then reducing it to a single number to use in betting shops. The sublime Art of Memory was now used by Mentalists to wow audiences by their feats of memory in theater shows (does anyone remember the book *Thirteen Steps to Mentalism* published in 1961 by Tony Corinda, and ever since considered a foundational book for every would-be performer?). We even find Numerology featured in those exploitative compendium books on 'Magick' which were so popular in the 1960s and 1970s, born as much out of a desire to shock parents as to manifest a perhaps more genuine interest in making one's own way on a spiritual path, and beginning to explore alternatives to Mom and Dad's weakly-held religion. While most were simply cheap in thought and production values, some have withstood the test of time as veritable primers on a wide range of esoteric subjects. Two which stand out are *The Black Arts* by Richard Cavendish from 1967, and *The Encyclopedia of Ancient and Forbidden Knowledge* by Bruce King, under his more mysterious nom-de-plume Zolar, published in 1971. Both are by accomplished and recognized authors on the subject. Don't be put off by the titles: the Ciceros will tell you how a publishing house can switch titles to be more, er, attention-seeking, sometimes without even informing the author!

We need to restore the primitive dignity of these numbers!

Perhaps we might see that numbers should be more properly used in three different ways. Firstly, as a means for man to understand everything that surrounds him in his environment. In a microcosmic way, if God ordered the Universe by number, weight and measure, man may attempt to categorize it using the same units. Secondly, as a means for man to make use of this information to affect his environment, either physically or on a low plane of spirituality, using what is commonly referred to as Numerology. This spiritual attempt at God's plan could be extended to the works of magic (Dee and Agrippa, etc.), alchemy, theurgy and prophecy. Finally, we have a sublime use of numbers to better understand God's plan and man's role within it, without trying to change it, but to use the information to grow in wisdom and understanding, and become better attuned to self-improvement and, hopefully, reintegration.

We could call these three approaches Numerical Science, Numerology and Numerical Theosophy.

And finally, as the ancient injunction to Alchemists called upon them ever to seek the Spiritual Path and avoid becoming mere 'puffers', so I would respectfully ask you to seek the true symbolic significance in numbers to learn to grow in spiritual knowledge and to understand God's plan. So let us strive to ascend, rather than descend!

Enochian

How to Speak with Angels

Enochian, or How to Speak with Angels

his paper was given at the first Mid-Atlantic Esotericon held in 2019. Since the idea was to break away from the traditional Masonicon mold, and as I am often asked to be the 'shock jock' for such events, I was asked to give a lecture as far away from traditional Masonic talks as possible. This is what they got! As you can see from my initial words, I drew a short straw and got the first slot of the day, and believe me, a lecture on Enochian is probably not the easiest way to begin a day of talks. But it did the trick, and a number of people even reported experiencing odd sensations when I recited the Enochian formula...

Figure 49: Dr. John Dee

I don't know what this timeslot is called. I know the first one after lunch is known as the 'graveyard shift': I guess that makes me the 'warm-up act'! Either way, I am in a difficult position: I have a mere forty minutes to try to convey some key ideas about John Dee's remarkable system of angelic communication to an audience who, no doubt, ranges from experts far more knowledgeable than me, to those who have never heard of Enochian. So, I will not be talking about the detailed life of John Dee or his political ambitions, or very much about his chronological history at all. Similarly, I will not be giving a slavish list of all the documents and paraphernalia assembled by Edward Kelley and John

Dee during their experiments with angelic communication. You can find that in any of the many, many books now available on Amazon on the subject, ranging from scholarly treatises to practical 'How To' manuals. Rather, I will focus on why he did it, what we can learn from it, and how it was preserved by Freemasons up to the present day, when it has enjoyed a strong resurgence of interest, as evidenced by regular uses of Enochian in the television series *Supernatural*, including a summoning of Raphael by Castiel in Series 5 Episode 3.

Although this is an 'Esotericon', and not a 'Magicon' or 'Theurgicon', I promise you that I will give you an example of that angelic tongue and how it perhaps sounds, given that we have only an outline of how it would have been pronounced in Dee's time since the English language sounded very different then; and I will admit to being strongly influenced by the Hermetic Order of the Gold Dawn system of Enochian, meaning that I can, at best, speak a dialect of the pure tongue, and perhaps sound to the angels how a Glaswegian sounds to a person who speaks the Queen's English!

How did an obscure language decrypted by an Elizabethan mage, and almost lost to humanity until someone found some documents in a false drawer years after his death, preserving what was left after a kitchen maid had used a significant amount for kindling, end up being featured in a very popular television program for young adults?

Most people are aware of the fact that John Dee was truly what we would call a Renaissance man who lived in England in the 1500s and who served under Queen Elizabeth I. He was a scholar, a mathematician, an astronomer and astrologer, a chemist and an alchemist. He invented codes and was occasionally a spy both in England and in Europe for the crown. At one time he was a Catholic priest (to avoid persecution by Queen Mary, also known as 'Bloody Mary'), yet happily became Protestant under Queen Elizabeth. He was known as a magician and mistrusted by many. Educated at Cambridge he possessed a library in his home at Mortlake which was over double the size of the combined libraries of Oxford and Cambridge at the time, and yet he died despised and in penury under King James I. However, for us, his crowning achievement was the bringing to light of the angelic tongue, commonly – though inaccurately – called Enochian. To understand this extraordinary language, its origin and purpose, we need to understand the times in which John Dee lived. This is where we shall begin our journey. We shall look at where it might have come from, and what its true function was. We shall consider the means by which they obtained it, and what John Dee thought he was going to accomplish. We will consider its contents – briefly – and how it nearly died with him. We will see how it survived almost exclusively through the good office of Freemasons through the generations, until it came to its great reinvention in Victorian times. We will briefly compare the beliefs of Dee and the angelic language with modern esoteric currents and consider their similarities, asking ourselves the question whether this is, perhaps, a proof of the claim of many esoteric societies: that there is only one truth which continues untrammeled throughout the history of man, manifesting in different generations according to his needs and ability to understand. Now we are at a time where both scholars and esotericists have gone back to what remains of the original manuscripts and increased our understanding of Dee's system many times over.

The Kabbalah tells us that God created the Universe with a word (sometimes his Name, and sometimes through the *logos*), and that the true pronunciation of His name, which was lost following the sack of Jerusalem in the reign of Zedekiah, would bring about its end. A similar theory exists concerning the Enochian Calls of Dee, where the Universe was believed to have been created by angelic forces and could be similarly brought to an end by their recital. Indeed, this was said to have been the motivation behind Aleister Crowley when he famously recited the Thirty Calls of the Aethyrs in North Africa. However, what is astonishing is that by undertaking this apparent act of wantonness, Crowley might in fact have been doing exactly what Dee had hoped to do in the first place!

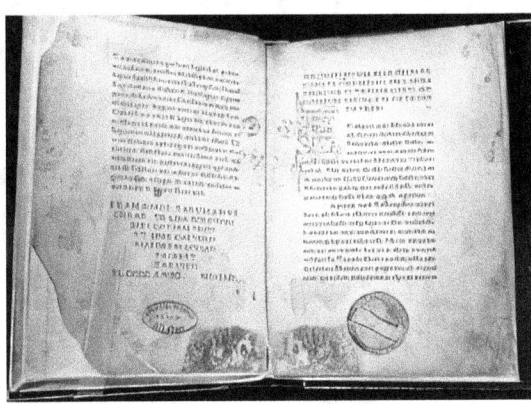

Figure 50: Part of Corpus Hermeticum

To understand why, we will return to the Renaissance. John Dee lived in what the Confucian curse calls 'interesting times.' He was born in 1527 and died in 1608. This was the age during which Constantinople fell to the Turks in 1453 leading to a wave of scholars fleeing with critical documents from ancient Greece to Italy, together with the important *Corpus Hermeticum*; Michelangelo carved David in 1504; Martin Luther nailed the ninety-five theses to the door of the Cathedral of Mainz in 1517; and Henry VII split from Rome in 1534. During this time scholars were not so much looking forward with excitement to the future, but instead enthusiastically delving into the past to see if it gave any sense about what was happening in their world. Change was all around them: religion was splintering, new virgin territories being discovered, advances in science and navigation came daily, the earth was no longer the center of the universe but rotated around the sun. The advent of printing presses and the availability of books to the upper classes who could read them, as well as documents in the vernacular, or local languages, rather than in the traditional Latin, brought a mixed blessing: on the one hand texts hitherto unavailable to the public were now available, but on the other hand, they were now read by people lacking the scholarly skills to understand their nuances, and everything was read in a literal sense, rather like the Fundamentalists of our modern era, who either through reasons of education or the cynical desire for control have no sense of nuance, historicity or exegesis. All this led to a feeling that the world was coming to an end.

Figure 51: Gabriel's Story, from season 13 episode 18 of Supernatural, by Kripke Enterprises

We should also remember that this was a time when everyone believed that the natural and supernatural worlds existed side by side, and both were equally real to them. After all, all three of the religions known to the Western World at this time were permeated with angelic visitations, and they therefore sincerely believed that the revealing of history and the future came from the mouths of God's messengers. Was it surprising, therefore, that some would seek to communicate directly with these messengers to obtain information on a more intimate basis, either for personal gain or for more altruistic reasons? Of course, the very idea of magic was considered largely demonic, so those who practiced it could take one of three directions. Either they could find a wealthy patron to shield them from their enemies; or they could hide behind the veneer of religion and claim that everything they did came with the approbation of the divine powers, and that they took great lengths to exclude any demonic influences; or they could appeal to science and say that they were merely pushing the boundaries of mathematics and astronomy to gain insight into God's wonderful creation. John Dee did all three.

As a Hermeticist, he believed that man, far from being nothing more than a link in the great Chain of Being, which assigned all beings, from God, archangels, angels, man and beasts to their assigned place in the universal hierarchy, could rise up the chain to commune with angels and all the beings above him, and even cooperate in the Great Plan, extending to the acceleration of the End Times, when the New Jerusalem would descend and everything would be set aright. Thus, the Hermetic scholar had to work both upon himself, and then to repair all of Nature by precipitating the Second Coming. This idea was taken up two centuries later by Martinez de Pasqually in France in his extraordinary theurgico-masonic Order, *The Elect Cohens of the Universe*, as we shall see later. However, his experiments were always couched in context of long and pious prayers to God and his Angels and Saints in order to try to allay the suspicions of those who wished him harm, but sadly without much success. Yet there is no doubt that Dee believed firmly that he was doing God's work, and not that of any negative power. Perhaps his strength on the theurgical side was that, being a scholar and Renaissance man, he was well-versed in the grimoires, the Kabbalah, Medicine and Religion, and could bring all these currents to bear in a synthesized system reminiscent of that created by the Hermetic Order of the Golden Dawn some three hundred years later.

Figure 52: The Great Chain of Being

As a man of science – and we should remember he was a prodigious inventor, having studied with the finest academics, astronomers and mathematicians in Europe, including Brahe, Mercator and Frisius – he approached his work through a mathematical lens, seeing numbers as the basis for all creation, and therefore taking the logical viewpoint that, if God was in all of His creation, by studying the Book of Nature we might gain insight into how He operates, and thereby learn how to assist in that operation. This is also why we find so many magic squares in his work, for he was clearly comfortable working with figures; and he also understood the mechanics of Gematria, that Kabbalistic technique by which Hebrew words with an identical numeric value are linked in a spiritual manner. For example, the words for Menorah and Noon both have a value of 295, and which by theosophical addition, or $2 + 9 + 5 = 16, 1 + 6 = 7$, result in the number of perfection or completion.

Now, many of the grimoires of the time were filled with codes and alphabets, since there was a deep fascination with ciphers. No grimoire worth its salt would omit magical alphabets! And so, we find a large number in Agrippa's *Three Books of Occult Philosophy*, and Trimethius' *Steganographica* contains a series of ciphers which were to be put to more mystical use. In this case, rather than simply being a way of playing Big Chief I-Spy with the angels and demons, or at least to hide one's notes from prying eyes, the purpose of the codes was to use spirits for long-distance communications. The potential usefulness of this was not lost on Dee. Living in a dangerous and politicized world where he moved from country to country, imagine the potential of a system by which, centuries before telephones and operators, you could instead send a telepathic message to an angel who would deliver it to another person performing exactly the same ritual in another place, without the need for courier or carrier pigeons! It is a testament to the times that when Dee informed Lord Cecil of this potential for long distance communication, he was given a grant to continue his research

This perhaps points to an answer to the question often asked, which is why Dee didn't simply try to contact his Holy Guardian Angel? After all, isn't that meant to be the point of most angelic theurgy? Dee's purpose had nothing to do with personal gain or finding buried treasure (though he was not above doing this occasionally in his spare time). He was far more concerned with international politics and bringing about the End Times. The information he sought from these spiritual advisers was how to get messages from one country to another instantaneously; how to contact the genii or angels set over the various countries of the known world and exert influence over them; and most importantly, how to cooperate in the Divine Plan of accelerating the Last Judgement and man's return to his original state of blessedness.

The language required for this would need to be far more than a simple replacement cipher, where one letter of the alphabet was replaced by another, or by some sign, like the Passing the River cipher or the Pigpen cipher still used by Royal Arch Masons today: Dee would have to communicate with the angels in a language, not just letters, and in their own language as well. This was not in fact the first attempt at this.

Figure 53: Passing the River Code

Figure 54: Masonic Pigpen code

ENOCHIAN, OR HOW TO SPEAK WITH ANGELS

Some four hundred years earlier the great Christian mystic Hildegard von Bingen has created a *lingua ignota*, or unknown language, of which we only have a couple of examples, where she substitutes some words for strange new words, linking them with Latin. What is interesting about these passages is that the words are declined, that is, different endings are added depending on the case of the noun. We have no way of knowing if longer texts purely in that language existed, or even if it was spoken, but perhaps they were a means by which the nuns could communicate secretly among themselves. Its use did appear to be limited to religious or mystical functions. What has struck scholars is that the form of the letters, and for that matter the form of letters in Trimethius' *Steganographia* resemble Enochian script, at least in passing. Whether that suggests an unconscious use of them in Enochian by Kelley and Dee, or that the letters were common to the angels transmitting them to the mystic, the cryptographer and the scryer is something for the listener to decide...

If this was the man who was going to perform the experiment with the assistance

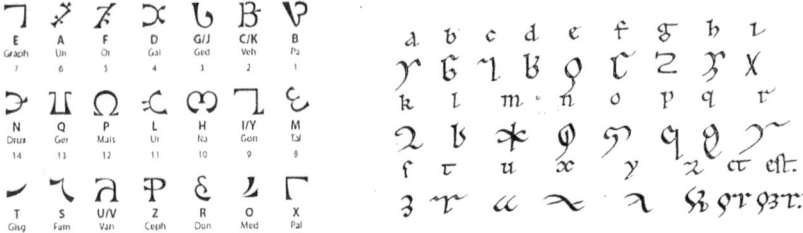

Figure 55: Enochian alphabet   *Figure 56: Lingua ignota*

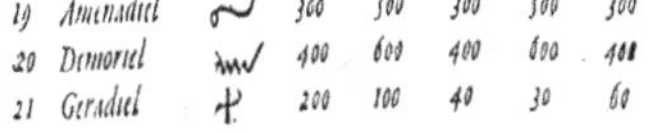

Figure 57: Trimethius' Code (part)

of a scryer, what background did he need to bring to the events? And with all due reverence to Barnabas Saul and Edward Kelley the function of the scryer is merely to recite what he sees, but it is for the scholar to interpret it. This is rather like the priests at the Oracle of Delphi, whose task it was to interpret the incomprehensible jabbering of the probably 'high' Pythia and render them in clear Greek. Familiarity with ciphers and a background in languages was obviously of help, as well as a well-grounded knowledge of the occult books of the time. A strong understanding of the books of the Bible – including those deemed apocryphal, for we know that Dee had encountered the Book of Enoch – was essential as well. A good knowledge of geography and politics wouldn't go amiss, as well as an education in Hermetic thought, given the nature of what Dee was trying to learn. Finally, his understanding of mathematics combined with his understanding of the Kabbalah would go a long way to help him untangle, codify and compartmentalize the extraordinary range of topics contained in the communications.

Incidentally, this is where the confusion over the name of the language comes from. While it had been a common assumption that the language of the angels was Hebrew, which was also called the Fire Tongue, from which you can see the immediate Christian association with Pentecost and the descent of flames enabling the cowering disciples to regain their courage and speak in tongues, this made little sense to Dee and others, who argued that this language was the one used by Adam and his successors *after* the Fall. The idea of a primal language came into being, one spoken by God, Angels and Man before the Fall, either verbally or through a form of telepathy. It was therefore logical that Enoch, the only man permitted to ascend to heaven to talk with God and his angel, *and to take down notes*, according to the Ethiopian scripture, would speak to God and the Angels in their own tongue. This is why the language came to be called Enochian. But this is strictly incorrect, since Enoch didn't invent a new language, but simply spoke the angelic tongue, which is what Dee strived to learn. However, the term 'Enochian' is now so widespread it would be swimming against the tide to insist on another name.

So, the stage was set for the Great Experiment.

Figure 58: Some of Dee's paraphernalia at the British Museum

Enochian, or How to Speak with Angels

While I don't intend to go into detail regarding the equipment, the table and the chairs, the wax tablets, the sigils and the colored cloths, the room and the incense, the one piece of equipment it is perhaps worth considering is the scrying vessel, which was sometimes an obsidian mirror but normally a crystal ball. This is a logical choice given Dee's scientific frame of mind. Dee was a student of optics. Indeed, the telescope and the microscope would come shortly after his death, which instruments allowed mankind to study the farthest reaches of the macrocosm and the tiniest cells of the microcosm. And the crystal ball similarly focused light from the Etheric or Yetziratic world, enabling man to perceive things which he was unable to see with his own unaided eyes.

As to the mindset of the two experimenters, I can offer no opinion of Edward Kelley. He is often portrayed as a rogue and a charlatan, but it is hard to determine whether this was the scientific community giving him a bad press, or due to the fact that just about every theurgist at that time had to earn a living. Even Dee was happy to draw up horoscopes for Queen Elizabeth and be paid for them – a practice continued right up to the late 20th Century in the White House, one might add. But I have absolutely no such uncertainty when it comes to the genuine intentions of John Dee. He truly believed he was working in cooperation with God and His angels to accelerate the coming of Armageddon and assisting his Nation by influencing the angelic *zeitgeists* of other countries in England's favor.

The process by which the angelic language was communicated can best be described as: choose the most inefficient manner in which you can imagine communicating anything and double it! While one might appreciate that time probably has little meaning to angels, even if those closer to us need to operate within the confines of time, they need to be aware of man's short lifespan, and for that matter his attention span. This is probably why such an experiment couldn't happen now. It's hard enough holding a teenager's attention for ten seconds. Can you imagine telling anyone they had to commit twelve to fifteen years to receiving messages one letter at a time, in a world where Twitter caps a message at 140 characters?

The process itself was relatively simple: Dee would go into his oratory and pray fervently to God, then Edward Kelley would be set up in an adjacent room scrying into the mirror or crystal, while Dee would write down everything he said as he saw it in the scrying vehicle. The system was based on a large number of enormously complicated tables of letters, 49 rows by 49 columns, where the angel of choice would point at one figure at a time with its wand, Kelley would read the letter and Dee would translate it into an Enochian letter. What was worse, the messages were provided in reverse order since the angels claimed the calls and invocations were too powerful and dangerous to be given the right way round (presumably God knew they were communicating these powerful tools to bring about the End Times, since it sounds to me more like naughty schoolchildren passing notes in class…). What is perhaps extraordinary about the process is that this was not done in a dungeon or basement, far away from prying eyes. It was performed in the midst of a bustling household, full of relatives and servants and children going about their daily business. Even odder, as the household peregrinated around Europe, all this paraphernalia was lugged with them, and set up wherever they happened to stop for a short period. This work was not performed in secret and God was not rewarding them in secret, to paraphrase Matthew 6:4!

The language itself was transmitted to them as part of a series of forty-nine calls which are contained in the *Liber Loagaeth*. Nineteen of these are Angelic Calls, and the final thirty calls were to the Aethyrs, which had a common formula and only the names needed to be changed. These are each divided into three (the last containing four) and these 91 were related to various areas of the world, by which Dee would be able to communicate with and hopefully control the destiny of those regions by means of the powers overseeing them. In this manner Dee could locate the twelve tribes of Israel, scattered during the diaspora, and by reassembling them to begin the process of the End Times. Following a litany of hierarchies which were so common to all the grimoires of the time, including Kings, Princes, Seniors and the like, finally the business at hand arrived: the alphabet.

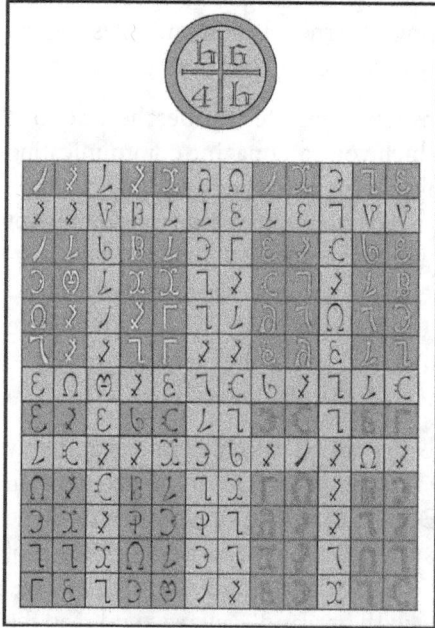

Figure 59: Water Tablet

The Great Tablet allowed one to identify the angelic hierarchies so common to the grimoires of the time. If we look at the Great Tablet, for example, it is in fact divided into four identical sections, each representing one of the four then accepted elements of Earth, Air, Water and Fire. Remember the true 'Elements' weren't discovered for over another hundred years. If we focus as an example on the Tablet of Water, we find it divided further into four subdivisions representing the equilibration of the Element, that is: Earth of Water, Air of Water, Water of Water, and Fire of Water. The Quadrant or Watchtower itself was a composite of three items: firstly, it was governed by a Calvary Cross, representing the Father, Son and Holy Ghost. Secondly, the limbs of the sub-crosses in each quarter called Calvary Crosses were surmounted by Kerubic squares which governed the quarter, just as Ezekiel's vision of the four creatures Lion, Eagle, Man and Bull were said to represent those Elements of Fire, Water, Air and Earth. Finally, Servient squares made up the remainder and were filled with lesser and servant angels.

Enochian, or How to Speak with Angels

To scry into one of these square one had first to evoke the Great Secret and Holy Names of God, before moving down to the traditional angelic hierarchy by evoking the King, Seniors and then the Angels in charge of that quarter, being the angels of Call and Command in the Calvary Cross – lest anyone think that this was sorcery – before finally asking Ezekiel's Kerubic angels to allow the person trying to communicate to get a response. The whole process was both elaborate and time consuming. But such was the importance of hierarchy, both in human and angelic worlds, that woe betide anyone who attempted to cut the process short! Even angels apparently need their egos assuaged. Finally, with all the hoops having been passed, Dee and Kelley were free to evoke their angel of choice in the scrying ball and ask their questions, which often involved stepping into the angelic world in the process known as Traveling in the Astral, to meet with their new host, test it with carefully considered trials, and when proved to be true, to be led on a spiritual journey while asking their questions.

But let's not forget that, even if you finally access an angel in Dee's system, you have to speak to it in its own tongue, Angelical (that is, Enochian). Now, when I put up a slide again of the Enochian alphabet, you'll see why it is so hard to learn. Unlike French, Spanish, Hebrew, Russian, Coptic, or any other language, there is no logic at all to the names of its letters, the way they are written and, worst of all, how they are pronounced. But perhaps this is to be expected in a race which is alien to us since not being of earth, they are in a way... aliens!

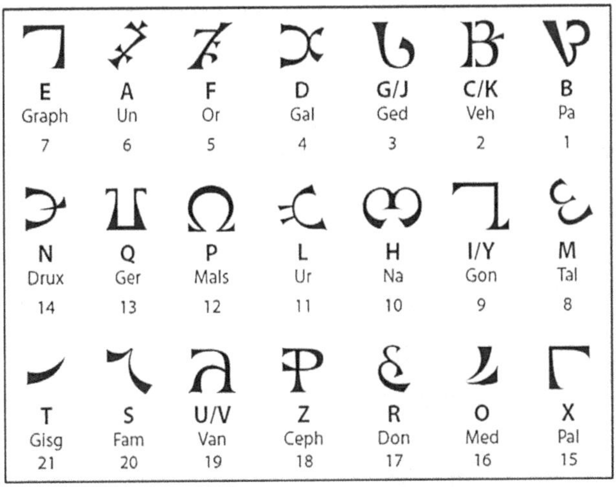

E Graph 7	A Un 6	F Or 5	D Gal 4	G/J Ged 3	C/K Veh 2	B Pa 1
N Drux 14	Q Ger 13	P Mals 12	L Ur 11	H Na 10	I/Y Gon 9	M Tal 8
T Gisg 21	S Fam 20	U/V Van 19	Z Ceph 18	R Don 17	O Med 16	X Pal 15

Figure 60: The Enochian Alphabet

While Dee died in poverty at Mortlake, his papers were initially thought to be lost. However, some ten years later the antiquarian Robert Cotton found a number of his later books and placed them in his library, and which were later sold by his son to Méric Causabon. This author published them in 1659, together with a damning commentary which led many to believe that Dee was

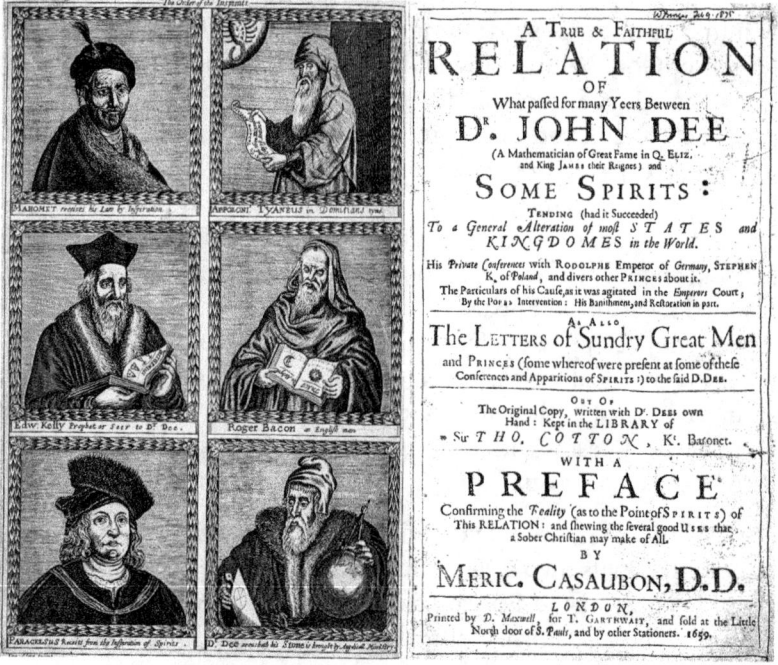

Figure 61: Causabon's damning book

quite mad. However, the earlier manuscripts had apparently been retained in a secret drawer of a desk acquired by a Mr. Jones, a confectioner, who purchased a large chest without knowing its provenance and kept it for twenty years before noticing a rattling sound when he moved it. Initially, not knowing what they were, the kitchen maid apparently used a number of these precious manuscripts as kindling, before Mr. Jones' widow, on remarrying gave what remained to her new husband, who miraculously bartered them with Elias Ashmole's servant in exchange for one of Ashmole's bound editions. Thus, in 1672, Elias Ashmole, the famous collector, antiquarian and Freemason, came into possession of much of John Dee's earliest manuscripts. This is such a starling coincidence, one wonders if the angels had a hand in it! Being the practical person that he was, he wasted no time in examining them, and we are told spent the next five years recreating Dee's angelic experiments. Sadly, we have no definitive writings on the results he obtained. These papers were later acquired by the great collector, Sir Hans Sloane, whose copious manuscripts (the collection comprises some 4,153 documents) were purchased by the Act of Parliament which saw the creation of

Figure 62: William Wynn Westcott, Supreme Magus of the S.R.I.A.

the British Museum in 1753, before making their way to the British Library in recent times. A century later, we would find two more prominent English Freemasons, William Wynn Westcott and Samuel Liddell MacGregor Mathers poring over the manuscripts of John Dee in this collection, and those in the Bodleian and Ashmolean in Oxford, as they attempted to recreate Dee's system as part of their Golden Dawn system of magic. However, not all the members were happy with a system they perceived as poorly understood, incomplete and potentially dangerous. Indeed, both Paul Foster Case and Dion Fortune omitted it from the Esoteric Schools they later founded, the Builders of the Adytum and the Society of Inner Light, respectively.

One relatively modern Order which exhibits a lot of similarities to the Enochian of John Dee is Martinism, or more accurately Martinezism. Founded by Martinez de Pasqually in the mid-1700s in France, this *Order of Elect Cohens of the Universe* made the usual claims to antiquity and to being the natural successor of the earliest manifestations of the true religion. While it has survived to our time through the more mystical Christian teachings of Louis-Claude de Saint-Martin and the Masonic Order of Knights Beneficent of the Holy City through the works of Jean-Baptiste Willermoz, the original proto-Scottish Rite Order combined a progressive series of Grades with what can be described as an esoteric way of life, incorporating a strict dietary regimen, rigorous and frequent prayers and a suite of theurgical operations which were primarily performed alone. While most of the original rituals have not survived the passage of time, despite the outrageous and so far, unprovable claims of some groups (though the search continues…), there is enough material available in manuscripts, diaries and commentaries for us to note a number of similarities with Dee's system.

Firstly, there is an apocalyptic element to the practices, in that the goal of the theurgical practices is reintegration into the Original Source, or God, firstly by working upon oneself, and then on all of mankind. While the methodology may be different, the goal is ultimately similar to that of Dee.

Secondly, the system is broadly mathematical in its approach, focusing on a theosophical meaning behind the numbers 1 through 10, and a belief that not only did God cause creation through the use of these numbers, but that, like Dee's Aethyrs, God charged in this case six Agents or Archangels to perform the act of Creation, reserving His involvement until the seventh day, when He inspected their work and blessed it. Reflecting a truth which must be very familiar by now, the system focuses closely on the words from Wisdom 11: "Thou hast ordered all things in measure, in number and weight." This agrees quite interestingly with Dee's assertion in his letter to Lord Cecil that Trimethius' book *Steganographia* concerned itself with "formal numbers, mystic weights and divine measures." Indeed, a significant part of Saint-Martin's first two books is also given over to the meaning of numbers, and in fact an entire tract is devoted to this subject alone. Saint-Martin's book *On Numbers* and his extraordinary analysis of the existence of God through the seven Liberal Arts and Sciences is not dissimilar to Dee's tract on the Monad; and clues abound both to his belief in the efficacy of alchemy of the spiritual kind (while he rails against physical alchemy), and to his belief that the objective is the Philosopher's Stone, a distinctly alchemical and Rosicrucian symbol. Surely the fact that Saint-Martin's second book, *Natural Table of the Correspondences Which Exist Between God, Man and the Universe* contains precisely twenty-two chapters is no coincidence to any Kabbalist!

Thirdly, the practices focus on summoning angelic powers, specifically to open up an ongoing channel of communication. And while the final objective appears to be to cause the appearance of a personal angel to guide the summoner, not unlike the Abramelin ritual, nevertheless the purpose is to open up this channel and to thereby gain knowledge which would otherwise be unknown to the summoner. This is realized through the sighting of a seal or sigil of the angel, which a kind of celestial reference book, the *Book of 2,400 Divine and Angelic Names*, may be used to identify the specific angel through its sigil. This is accomplished by a form of scrying, not unlike that performed by Edward Kelley, in this case by sitting in near darkness while observing a heavy cloud of incense for any sparks, letters or sigils to form in it.

The rituals are not above using extraordinary words and names which are still not completely understood, and which point to the vestiges of perhaps yet another variation of the angelic tongue. To list just a few of these names which sounds almost barbarous to our ears: Vabaham, Vaur, Viha, Vakiël, Vage, Vako, Vabam, Alim, Adiozaï – not so far in form from, for example, the King, Prince and Governors ruling Wednesday in Dee's system: Bnaspol, Blisdon, Bliigan, Barfort, Blumapo, Bernole, Bazpama – while acknowledging that Dee's system required them all to be seven letters long.

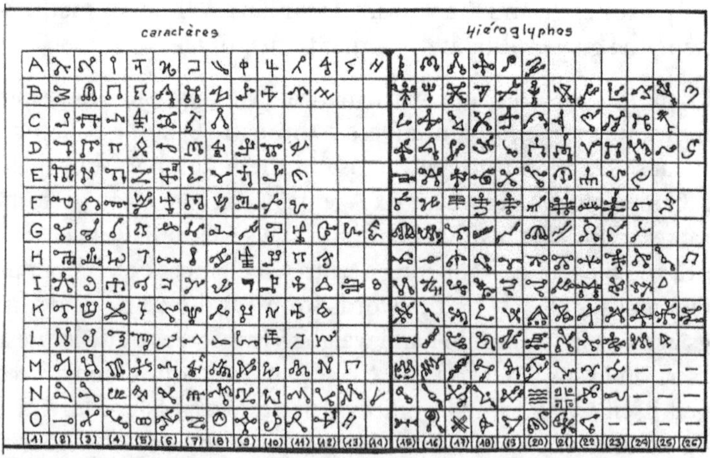

Figure 63: Extract from the Book of 2,400 Divine and Angelic Names

Enochian, or How to Speak with Angels

And finally, like the 30 Calls to the Aethyrs, many prayers of the highest Grade, that of Réau Croix, are formulaic, with gaps in the prayers and incantations to insert the relevant angelic name.

I hasten to add here that all of these are taken from original manuscripts, and not from the worthy but ultimately muddying rituals recreated by Robert Ambelain in the 1940s in Paris – a worthy undertaking which was nevertheless more born from fantasy and old grimoires than reality, while incorporating what few materials he possessed of Pasqually's system at that time.

Nevertheless, it appears we may be coming to a time when we begin to learn more about Pasqually's system. Mathieu G. Ravignat has recently written the first book to attempt to recreate Pasqually's rituals since the 1940s and using far more source materials than were available to Ambelain. Also, a friend in England believes he may have discovered some of Pasqually's lower Grade rituals in an obscure library in France. Perhaps we will one day be in possession of Pasqually's actual materials and will then be able to judge whether he was in some manner influenced by Dee's writings, or whether perhaps the angels themselves found a new conduit for their teachings some two hundred years after their original vessel has passed.

But for now, let me end by giving you a sense of how this most primitive of languages, this language which, we are told, was spoken by God, his angels and original Man, as I recite the safest Enochian invocation, that of the Hierophant when opening a Temple of the Golden Dawn, and which means: "I reign over you, saith the God of Justice, *[this is followed by three magical names on the Tablet of Union]*. Move, therefore, move and appear. Open the mysteries of creation: balance, righteousness and truth."

OL SONUF VAORSAGI GOHO IAD BALATA.
ELEXARPEH. COMANANU. TABITOM. ZODAKARA,
EKA ZODAKARE OD ZODAMERANU. ODO KIKLE
QAA PIAPE PIAMOEL OD VAOAN.

An Introduction to Martinism

and its Spiritual Relationship to Freemasonry

An Introduction to Martinism and its Spiritual Relationship to Freemasonry

his talk was given at the 'official' launch of my book, a translation of *Elementary Treatise on Practical Magic (pub. 1893) by Papus. Since he founded modern Martinism, and my other translations of Louis-Claude de Saint-Martin's book, Of Errors & Truth (pub. 1775) and Natural Table (pub. 1782) had already been published, a talk on the origins of and the revival of so-called Martinism seemed appropriate at the time. Since then I have also translated Papus' book on contemporary Martinism, entitled Martinezism, Willmozism, Martinism and Freemasonry, as well as Saint-Martin and Papus' Treatises on Numbers, titled The Numerical Theosophy of Saint-Martin and Papus.*

Introduction

In this talk we'll explore the Masonic roots of the founders of the gnostic, magical and mystical currents which gave rise to the extraordinary outpouring of Masonic ritual of the late 18th Century in France, and how this current was taken up again at the end of the 19th Century by a new generation of seekers of light, during that extraordinary period which saw the rise of the Golden Dawn, Spiritualism, the Gnostic Church, Theosophy and the Masonic Rosicrucian Bodies, alongside rapid developments in science, and how those pioneers attempted to reconcile the two streams. However, while we will examine the history and purpose of Martinism, this is not intended to be a lesson in its teachings. That must be kept for another day.

But first a few definitions. I've used the terms 'gnostic', 'magical' and 'mystical'. Let's briefly examine what we mean by these terms, which are not often heard in what we might term 'Anderson' or Anglo-Saxon Freemasonry. Gnosticism was a spiritual movement, most often associated with Christianity, but drawing from other Classical sources which existed alongside what we might now term 'Catholic' or 'Orthodox' Christianity in the Centuries immediately following the life of Jesus of Nazareth. They tended to take a far more esoteric approach to the teachings of Jesus, suggesting that there was a hidden or inner church only available to initiates, and that the Church of St. Peter was really an exoteric church.

Following the Emperor Constantine's conversion to Christianity a highly political Council called the Council of Nicea was held in what is now Turkey in 325 C.E., to determine the dogma of this new Church. However, the manner in which it was held made it next to impossible for most of the gnostic-leaning bishops (who mainly came from the North coast of Africa) to attend key votes, such as the nature of Christ, the doctrine of the Trinity and, most important, which of the many – for there were over 20 – Gospels in circulation at the time would be considered 'canonical', or official. As a result, the four Gospels we now recognize were selected, and over the following two Centuries any variations to these were ruthlessly persecuted, hunted down and destroyed, often along with their preachers. The only reason we have access to most of the so-called forbidden Gospels is thanks to a small group of monks who disagreed with that high-handed approach and buried their alternative teachings in pots near Nag Hammadi, to be rediscovered just under a century ago.

Figure 64: First Council of Nicea

As for 'magical' and 'mystical', I hope that everyone realizes 'magic' here refers to the ability to affect physical laws through the use of paranormal powers, rather than being able to do clever card tricks! Magic comes in various types and definitions, ranging from 'low', or the ability to affect minor, temporal things, to 'high' or 'theurgical', the ability to communicate with higher powers, usually angels. 'Mystical' for our purposes, refers to the ability to achieve union with divinity through self-surrender and contemplation, which is a different path to that of 'magic', in which the perpetrator is active, rather than passive, in these attempts.

Figure 65: Nag Hammadi library

An Introduction to Martinism

A Lesson in History

When the Premier Grand Lodge was founded in England 300 years ago, it was clear it didn't appear from nowhere. Earlier records, and accounts by such luminaries as Elias Ashmole tell us this. While there have been many theories about its origins, ranging from the plausible to the unlikely, it speaks to a desire to demonstrate that the Order, far from being an invention of the times, can trace its origins back to ancient history, and by doing so create a veneer both of respectability and to transcend temporary faddism.

Figure 66: Plaque

While it was largely political, European Masonry drew on longer traditions, crystallized in Chevalier Ramsay's Oration on its origins with the Templars, and the Ancient Mystery Schools of the Mediterranean and Egypt. Oddly enough, much of this lies in the name 'James'. In the New Testament James is the brother of John, and in some legends the first leader of the proto-church after Jesus, before his martyrdom by the sword passed the church to Peter. He became a popular saint and was the object of the greatest medieval pilgrimage in Europe, which ended at Santiago de Compostela (Santiago meaning St. James). In 1175, some 36 years after the Knights Templar were officially recognized by the pope, the Order of Santiago was founded to combat the Moorish invasion of the Iberian Peninsula, or Spain. We must remember that, in those days, names were not given lightly. It was not acceptable to invent a name, and the names of Saints were usually taken, leading to a child having both a birthday and a Saint's day. Indeed, even the Jewish population often sought to take names which would not draw attention to them, while maintaining their links with their faith. James, or its Latinized version, Jacobus or Jacob, is an obvious example. Thus, the last Grand Master of the Templars, Jacobus de Molay was named. And so, too, were James VI of Scotland who went on to become James I of England, and his grandson, James II.

Figure 67: Santiago de Compostela

Now, after Charles I had been executed in 1649, and the British public, tired of the puritan excess of life under the Lord Protector, Oliver Cromwell, had restored King Charles II to the throne in 1660, his son, James II, who ruled from 1685 soon worried them because of his excessively Catholic ways, and he was deposed and exiled only 3 years after inheriting the crown. He fled to France and set up court just outside Paris, from where he plotted his glorious return to Scotland, an ambition continued by his descendants, James Stuart and Bonnie Prince Charlie. From the name 'James' comes the traditional term the 'Jacobites', and the unsuccessful 'Jacobite Rebellions.'

Following the Act of Succession passed in 1701, which forbade any Catholics from taking the English throne, and following the death of the childless Queen Ann, George of Hanover was found to be the closest relative to the crown who was not Catholic, and so, in 1714, this man who could barely speak a word of English was crowned King George I of England.

Why the history lesson? Because it is critical to understanding the development of Freemasonry both in England and in Europe, both of which gave rise to many of the esoteric Orders and Societies which followed, whether by absorbing existing esoteric currents into Masonry, or by Masons founding esoteric societies.

Differences in England and Mainland Europe

Figure 68: King George I

In England, while it was very clear that Freemasonry had existed long before 1717, in that year the Premier Grand Lodge of England was founded. Why? One of the strongest theories is because the Masons had to show a complete break with their former organization, which had been strongly Stuartist, and therefore Jacobite. In order to survive the change of monarchy they had to totally reinvent themselves. Within a generation a close relative of the monarch was the Grand Master, and any pretense to earlier organizations, including Rosicrucianism, Templarism, or anything which could be seen as Catholic or interpretative – and therefore subversive – of Protestantism were expunged. For a time.

Europe was a different matter. While the former strength of the Roman Catholic Church had largely prevented rival bodies from being formed, and sovereign power had prevented groups from meeting in private to discuss matters of national importance, the arrival of the Age of Enlightenment blew most of the cobwebs away, and even the former Catholic monarch, James II, saw an opportunity in harnessing the energy of this romantic movement to his advantage. Indeed, with the weakening of the Church's stranglehold over everything and the diminishing of monarchical power, the last potential bastion against the neo-Templar movements which were springing up everywhere, had been removed. Instead of meeting in Protestant countries or in secret, many of these were now absorbed into Freemasonry, and their traditional motto or password of 'Nekam' or 'Vengeance' could be openly cried out. Vengeance against whom? The stated aim of these neo-Templars was the restoration of their honor and wealth across Europe, and also the demise or even death of the pope and the King of France, who had once presided over the destruction of the Order and the brutal extermination of its members for greed.

So, the stage was set in Europe for an explosion of Masonic Orders, which absorbed Templarism and Chivalry in general, Rosicrucian and any esoteric current they could find, including Kabbalah, Alchemy, Gnosticism, Ancient Greek and Roman Mystery Schools, and even ancient Egypt.

Figure 69: The Age of Enlightenment

Indeed, it is perhaps surprising to find that, in an Order which housed some of the keenest Enlightenment minds, currents of magic and theurgy (or angelic communication) could be found to be alive and well. Given that mainstream Freemasonry itself used some of the earliest stories from the Old Testament as its vehicles for teaching, all this fitted right in.

What Makes an Esoteric Order?

Now, to better understand the importance of these currents, we need to consider some of the key credentials which an esoteric body – including Freemasonry – need to show in order to exist and to attract members:

- A valid – or perceived – transmission from ancient times;
- Rituals which are impressive, educational and powerful;
- Secret teachings of the Order which could be studied in private;
- A belief system, be it a dogma, creed, philosophical system or outlook on man's purpose;
- Information not available to the general public or the so-called 'profane';
- Ultimately it must be 'adaptable', since absolute teachings – despite the Fundamentalist dogmas of all religious minorities – must adapt to survive changes in living standards, world view, education and man's evolution.

To this list of esoteric Orders I would add: a direct link with the Past Masters, or Passed Masters, or the presence of an 'éminence grise', often referred to as an Unknown Superior, or *Supérieur Inconnu*.

Figure 70: Chevalier Andrew Ramsay

Thus, we find the Order of Strict Observance of Baron von Hund in Germany attracting the aristocracy and monarchs alike with its claims both to direct links with the Templars and communication with 'Secret Chiefs', which appear to be somewhere between the English monarchs in exile and angelic beings.

Thus, we find Chevalier Ramsay giving his famous Oration in 1737 in France, which gave rise to the legend of Freemasonry's direct descent from the Knights Templar, their involvement in the battles of Robert the Bruce in Scotland against the English, and their founding of Freemasonry there in the 14th Century. And to quote part of his oration: "Yes, Sirs, the famous festivals of Ceres at Eleusis, of Isis in Egypt, of Minerva at Athens, or Urania among the Phoenicians, of Diana in Scythia were connected with ours. In those places mysteries were celebrated which concealed many vestiges of the ancient religion of Noah and the Patriarchs," going on to say: "At the time of the last crusades many Lodges were already erected in Germany, Italy, Spain, France, and from thence, in Scotland, because of the close alliance between the French and the Scotch (*sic*). James, Lord Steward of Scotland, was Master of a Lodge at Kilwinning, in the West of Scotland... This Lord received as Freemasons into his Lodge the Earls of Gloucester and Ulster, the one English, the other Irish."

Seeing an advantage in living up to his reputation as Grand Master of all Masons, James II and his son eagerly signed Masonic Warrants and Charters in France, and encouraged the spread of this initially chivalric fashion, seeing in it a means to obtain the loyalty, and hopefully the financial and arms-bearing support of its members. For all this, as history had shown us, the hoped-for retaking of England never took place in his lifetime, and the efforts of his son and grandson, thet Old and Young Pretenders, amounted to epic failures.

By the way, this is also where the odd term for one of the major branches of Freemasonry, the Scottish Rite, comes from. It is because the Charters being signed by James II were referred to as *Écossais* Charters (rather like the Atholl Charters of the Antients in England being named for their signers the Dukes of Atholl), and the Masonry so authorized was therefore named 'Écossais' Masonry which is French for 'Scottish'. This is why the Scottish Rite came in fact from France, and not Scotland!

An Introduction to Martinism

The Order of Elect Cohens of the Universe

However, of all the Warrants and Charters circulating in France, perhaps none were more mysterious, and which still provokes fascination and intrigue among Masons, than that allegedly awarded in 1738 to the father of a certain Martinès de Pasqually, containing the powers to establish Lodges, as well as to pass that authority on to his son.

Little is truly known about the background and origins of Martinès de Pasqually, that enigmatic Mason. In the past there has been much speculation on whether the was French or Spanish, and whether he was descended from a Jewish family. However, modern research suggests he was in fact a French Catholic, spoke French fluently but was not so good as communicating on paper, and that his occult knowledge came from study and perhaps membership in secret Orders.

Figure 71: Silhouette of Martinès de Pasqually

For twenty years, from 1754 – 1774, he ruled as Grand Sovereign over his own Order called the *Ordre des Chevaliers Maçons Élus Coëns de l'Univers*, or Order of Knight Masons Elect Cohen of the Universe, more commonly referred to as the Elus Cohen, or 'Elect Cohen'. The *Cohenim* were the priests in the Torah officially commissioned by Yahweh to officiate at religious ceremonies, and by implication to have direct communication with higher powers. He based his system on the new Scottish Rite then developing in Bordeaux, where he also had several Lodges, many with the same members as the Scottish Lodges. However, his system of somewhere between 9 and 11 Grades, was comprised of far more complicated rituals. His Order was more a way of life, requiring extensive private study, the setting up of a private oratory, following a rigorous and essentially vegetarian diet, and the recital of prayers four times a day. While the Masonic meetings were regularly held for advancement and instruction, most of the operative work was done alone. This included drawing magic circles, invoking angelic forces, and twice a year, at the Equinoxes, even summoning demonic powers in order to exorcise them. Thus, he considered this Order to be an active priesthood. Once the practitioners had received certain 'signs' from what he called 'La Chose', or the *Thing*, this allowed the members to identify their personal guardian angel, and to work with them on their individual advancement. Needless to say, this process could take many years, and was certainly not for the faint-hearted.

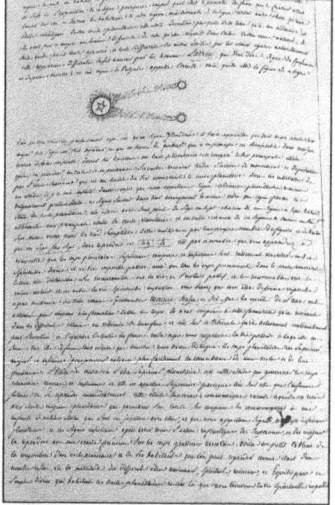

Figure 72: Pasqually's Treatise

However, what was key to this work was its context. While Masonry is not normally seen as being a religion, in the case of the Order of Elus Cohen it was as close as one could come to it. The work was based upon an extraordinary work develop-ed by Pasqually and dictated to his secretary, Louis-Claude de Saint-Martin, a work which was nothing less than a gnostic commentary on the Holy Bible. Just as entire branches of the Christian religion have been based upon on man's interpretation of the scriptures, so this extraordinary book, called the *Treatise on the Reintegration of Beings into their Primitive Estate*, was essentially a Christian *Zohar*, and, like that mysterious book which appeared in Spain around the 13th Century, was a mystical commentary on the biblical stories. Like the Kabbalah, or Hebrew mysticism, it relies heavily on numerology, and ascribes great importance to the first ten numbers, to the extent that the angelic names used in its prayers, which are largely based on the Psalms, must correspond to the numbers discovered by the member during his meditations and magical operations.

The Theosophy of the Elect Cohens

In essence, when God created the Universe, he placed what could be called angelic forces over it to govern it. But they became prideful and, to use his term, prevaricated, believing themselves to be equal to God. As punishment, God created Man to govern the prison in which he now placed them, Earth. For a while Man enjoyed his unique privileges in his Eden, being clothed in his glorious, non-corporeal body, and enjoying direct communication with his Creator. But the evil powers over which he had been set in charge worked on his pride and persuaded him that he was himself equal to God, and capable of creation. Man, or Adam, believed them, and set about working a magical operation to create another being, Heva, or Eve. But he only managed to entangle himself in the very red earth he was using to create this body, thereby confusing his immortal and incorporeal body with mud, and became a hybrid, an immortal being trapped in matter, no longer capable of direct communication with the higher powers. God completed Adam's act of creation and provided him with his mate, Eve; but as punishment for his enormous crime, he sentenced him to live in the place where once he had ruled, but now as one of the material creations which occupied it, and set another Agent, called Hély, which Saint-Martin equated with the Christ and called The Repairer, to rule in his stead, until man was able, through his own efforts, to restore himself to his primitive – or original – position of glory.

The *Treatise* also indicated that the Patriarchs of the Bible worked on their reintegration and reconciliation with God by performing 'Operations', or magical practices, which was the means by which they now had to communicate with the divine realm. This, of course, was the justification for the elaborate and complex theurgy expected of the members of his Order.

Man's purpose, therefore, was to first recognize that he was indeed an immortal being trapped in matter, to learn to rise above this and to seek the spiritual, in order to realize the ultimate goal of reintegrating both himself and everything else back into their original estate, thus restoring the original balance of the Universe which was God's creation. Later, Saint-Martin was to phrase his master's teaching in a compelling way, which is very close to the storyline of that extraordinary movie "The Matrix". He calls man ignorant of his plight, and living a daily life of routine, a 'Man of the Stream', caught up in the 'Forest of Errors'. He must awaken to his tragic situation in order to work to rise above it, when he becomes a 'Man of Desire'. As he works towards his goal and steers himself toward union with God, shedding all that does not lead to this result, he becomes a 'New Man'; and finally, in achieving his goal, he once more becomes Man-Spirit, and exchanges his material body for a glorious body, allowing his immortal soul to shine forth once more as in his first or primitive estate.

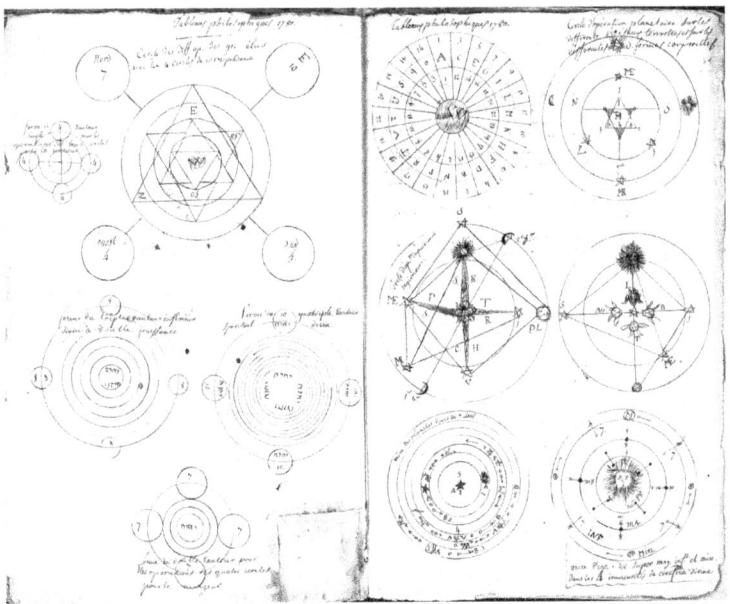

Figure 73: Notebook of Prunelle de Lière with Elus Cohen magic circles

We must remember that this was still a time when Protestant churches, on the one hand, held services lasting several hours, mostly focused on man's impotence, his inevitable sinfulness and the inevitability of Hell; while the Roman churches used Latin, and the priest mumbled to himself at the far end of the Sanctuary while his flock looked on as little more than a passive audience. This new, dangerous, thrilling, gnostic theology offered the initiate the opportunity to take his salvation into his own hands, forge his own relationships with the superior beings, provided a satisfying explanation of his present state, and offered a clear means of rising above it and saving both himself and those around him. What was not to love – except for the extraordinary commitment of time, hardship and diet?

But, as often happens in an Order founded on personality, and in which the bulk of the knowledge resides in one man alone, the Order had little chance of survival once its protagonist and founder left the French shores in 1772 to take up an inheritance in Haiti, dying there in 1774. By 1778 only eight Temples were still in operation, and in 1781 Sebastien las Casas, Grand Sovereign of the Order, ordered their closure. The Order, excepting a few small groups who probably continued to practice some of the rituals, was effectively dead.

The Order is Dead – Long Live the Order!

However, while most people who join organizations are followers, becoming rudderless when their leader leaves or dies, occasionally one or more are left behind who have the aspiration and the inspiration to continue that legacy in some form. In this Pasqually was lucky – or clever – in selecting two members who were to continue his legacy, albeit in different forms, from that time to the present day. Those two members were Louis-Claude de Saint-Martin and Jean-Baptiste Willermoz.

These two came from different backgrounds (Saint-Martin was minor aristocracy with an army commission; while Willermoz was a silk merchant) and lived in very different parts of the country (Saint-Martin in Foix, Bordeaux and Amboise – the West; Willermoz in Lyon – the South-East), which necessitated long coach drives to come together. Under normal circumstances there would be no reason for them ever to meet. Willermoz was from a large family and married, while Saint-Martin was an only child, and single. About the only thing they had in common was that they were both Freemasons, in itself an oddity since they were both raised Catholic in a predominantly Catholic country which in theory still obeyed the edicts of the pope, including the infamous ban on Freemasonry, called *In Eminenti*, which for reasons of idleness rather than policy had never really been enforced in France. Perhaps this is one of the greatest examples of that Masonic phrase which reminds us that this noble Institution brings together "men who might otherwise have remained perpetually at a distance."

An Introduction to Martinism

There is an abundance of biographies on Saint-Martin and Willermoz, so let us limit ourselves to noting that they were both avid disciples of Pasqually. Indeed, Saint-Martin even gave up his army commission to become Pasqually's personal secretary; while Willermoz devoted many years to the practices before finally obtaining his 'signs', and passing to the final Grade of *Réaux Croix* (note the name is not the same as the 18th Degree of the Ancient Accepted Scottish Rite, which is *Rose-Croix*). Willermoz was an avid Mason, having both introduced a number of Orders to Lyon, including von Hund's Rite of Strict Observance, and written a large number himself, including Black Eagle Rose Croix, Grand Écossais Trinitaire, and a number of Elect Knight Grades. In 1775, a year after Pasqually's death Saint-Martin, staying with Willermoz in Lyon, wrote his first book, *Of Errors & Truth*. He had noted a darker side to the Enlightenment, in that scientific advances were encouraging some to question the need for a God, holding that nothing which couldn't be observed could exist, leading him to call these representatives of atheism and agnosticism 'The Observers'.

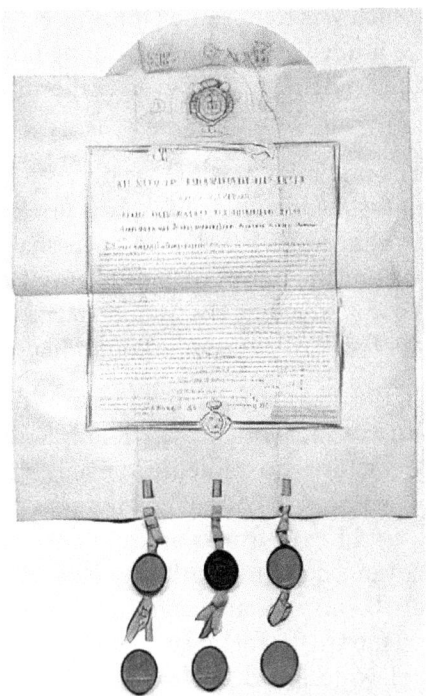

Figure 74: Willermoz' Diploma as Réau-Croix

Towards the end of his association with Pasqually and shortly before the latter went to Haiti, Saint-Martin was beginning to question the need for all the complicated paraphernalia and ritual work, called 'Operations', famously asking: "But Master, is all this truly necessary to know God?" Once Pasqually had departed in both senses of the term, Saint-Martin found himself taking a different approach, through the practice of contemplation and meditation. He never departed from his master's somewhat unorthodox theology, but he had embarked upon a new and parallel path, which he called the Cardiac Path or Way of the Heart. His books increasingly reflected this more introspective approach, and he initially wrote under the pseudonym of "Unknown Philosopher", though it appears that his identity was an open secret from the start.

Interestingly, it was during a two-year period in Lyon, while Saint-Martin and Willermoz were holding educational classes on the teachings of the Elus Cohen in Willermoz' home between 1774 and 1776, following the death of their master, that Saint-Martin read a short paper against the atheistic trends of the Enlightenment, and was encouraged by his friends to expand it into the book which was to become *Of Errors & Truth*. This book clearly hit a nerve, and was an immediate best-seller among both Masons and the Intelligentsia, earning it the grudging respect even of the anti-Masons, one of whom referred to it as the "Masonic Koran."

His first book was followed, seven years later, by another, called *Natural Table of the Relationship which exist between God, Man and the Universe*, in which he continued to develop his personal theology based upon Pasqually's original vision. The book contains twenty-two Chapters, which has led some to suggest he was reflecting the Major Arcana of the Tarot, or Book of Thoth; though to be fair the Tarot was not in common use at the time except as a diverting card game.

In the meantime, Jean-Baptiste Willermoz was continuing to develop Masonic Rituals and work with his family and friends. One of his younger brothers was an alchemist who studied in Marseilles, then a center for that kind of study. Despite the dawning of the Age of Enlightenment and the focus on science and the creation of a world apart from warfare and totalitarian regimes, science was not yet that far advanced, and in a world which was examining the circulation of the blood alongside a belief in spontaneous generation, and where experiments in electricity and gravity sat next to the four Classical Elements, a belief in magic, theurgy and alchemy was still widespread.

The Masonic Successor to the Elect Cohens

But Willermoz' greatest gift to mankind was his work before and following the Convent of Wilhelmsbad in 1782, the year that Saint-Martin published *Natural Table*. This was an International Conference which consolidated agreements made at the earlier Convent of Gaul, held in Lyon in 1778. Essentially, the Rite of Strict Observance was compelled to renounce any claim to being run by 'secret chiefs', effectively neutralizing its most compelling attraction. As the same time, a new Order based on the former was established, that of the Regime Écossaise Rectifié, also known as the 'R.E.R.' or the 'Scottish Rectified Rite', which now moved control of one of the most influential rites in Masonry out of Germany and into France. It is important to state at the outset that, the 'Scottish Rectified Rite' has no connection whatsoever with the Ancient Accepted Scottish Rite, other than the possibility that some of its rituals were penned by former members of the Elus Cohen. The reason for stating this is because in the early 20th Century, when a first attempt was made by Eduard Blitz to introduce the Regime into the United States, it was primarily the Southern Masonic Jurisdiction of the Scottish Rite which did everything in its power to prevent its adoption, under the completely erroneous belief that it was somehow setting itself up as a rival to their system!

An Introduction to Martinism

Figure 75: Meeting of the R.E.R. in France in the 1930s

This Masonic system consisted of eight Grades divided into three Bodies. It is important to realize that, while we now know the entire structure, this would have been apparent to very few outside of the Convents held in the latter part of the 18th Century, since the Second Order's existence was revealed only to those selected from the First; and the Third Order was only revealed at all to a very small minority who effectively ruled the entire Order. As a reflection of how important this Rite was – and is – in Masonry can be attested to by the fact that Willermoz spent the rest of his long life working and reworking the Grades in order to produce what is perhaps the most sublime manifestation of Freemasonry in its entire history.

The Rite is exoterically Christian. However, those who reach its Higher Grades soon come to realize that this is not the Christianity of Sunday School, and the gnostic teachings of Pasqually manifest themselves throughout the Regime. The Rite begins with the Blue Degrees of Apprentice, Companion and Master Mason, before continuing to a 'pivot' Degree of two parts called 'Master' and 'Perfect Master of St. Andrew', in a homage to the claimed roots of Chivalric or Templar Masonry in Scotland. Indeed, some of the passwords also link back both to Scotland and the Templars. This Grade resembles that of the Royal Arch in its imagery, but in this instance Hiram is not

Figure 76: Meliora Præsumo

dead, but resurrected, as he gazes towards the horizon in his cerements, the ruins of his tomb about him, reflecting the ruins of the first Temple seen at the start of the degree. The final symbol shown him of a lion sheltering from a storm beneath an outcrop, and playing with masonic implements, bears the motto 'Meliora Præsumo', or 'I hope for better things'; and indeed, it is this faith and hope which, perhaps, will bring him into the Second Order. While the existence of the Order of St. Andrew was known to Blue Lodge Masons, and indeed the members wore very different regalia and could preside over any meeting of the first three Grades, knowledge of the Second Order was known only to its members.

Once invited into the fifth Grade, an initiate became a Squire Novice, a reflection of that period of prayer and meditation expected of a knight-expectant prior to being dubbed a Knight Beneficent of the Holy City ('Chevalier Bienfaisant de la Cité Sainte', or 'C.B.C.S.' in French). But this was a spiritual knighthood rather than a warrior knighthood, having more in common with spiritual alchemy than battle. Indeed, the attentive knight would have detected many trappings of the gnostic teachings of Pasqually in these Grades, which were considered the *ne plus ultra* of French, and much of continental Masonry, at the time. And yet beyond this pinnacle of chivalric Masonry were yet two more secret Grades, those of 'Profès' and 'Grand Profès', or Professed and Grand Professed Knight. It was here that Willermoz had concealed the full teachings of Pasqually in two long lectures. It is also almost without a doubt that the earliest Professed Knights also practiced many of the rituals taught by Pasqually to his Elus Cohen, though since they kept no written record of their activities, other than the fact that they were holding meetings, we do not yet have sufficient proof to say this categorically. However, it would go against everything we know of Willermoz not to believe this was going on. For example, only a few years later, in 1783, he became interested in Magnetism, which ultimately led to what were essentially séances between 1786 to 1788, in which a medium made contact with an entity which called itself the 'Unknown Agent", or "Agent Inconnu", and which dictated a large number of teachings, before Willermoz himself finally began to have doubts as to their authenticity, and ended the meetings of what he had termed the "Society of Initiates".

However, we can never underestimate the importance of Willermoz' work, and the massive impact his Regime would have had on Masonry if it had come to fruition, and if the French Revolution had not swept its ambitions away. According to Jean-Marc Vivenza, an acclaimed scholar on the subject in France, Willermoz' ambitions for the Rite extended far beyond that of creating another interesting system of Grades.

While he, like Saint-Martin, was not overly convinced by what he saw as the excessively complicated preparations for Pasqually's theurgical operations, nevertheless he never questioned his master's theology, and his continuing belief in the ability to communicate with high powers clearly shines through both in his commitment to the Elus Cohen long after the departure of his master, and also in his later séances in attempting to communicate with the 'Unknown Agent'. Indeed, one major question has always been: why, once Pasqually had departed for Haiti in 1772, did he decide to bring his Lodge, *La Bienfaisance* (or Beneficence) over to Baron von Hund's Rite of Strict Observance in 1773? Now, we know that from 1774 – 1776 Willermoz, Saint-Martin and Jean-Jaques du Roy d'Hauterive were together in Lyon and holding meetings in Willermoz' house, where they discussed the teachings of Pasqually. These were preserved in the famous archives called *Les Leçons de Lyon*, or 'The Lessons of Lyon'[14]. As with all acts of exegesis, in the absence of their master, they continued to develop their understanding of his teachings and slowly, while not losing their gnostic foundation, these teachings were honed into a more comprehensive series of lessons. This is important, and we can see this happen both in the Lessons themselves, and in the fact that Saint-Martin's first book, *Of Errors & Truth*, which was locally published in 1775 by the Frères Périsse, one of whom at least was in all of Willermoz' Masonic bodies, also shows departures in subtle ways from Pasqually's pure teachings as laid out in his *Treatise*. This also tells us that, despite the fact that Saint-Martin and Willermoz ultimately manifested these teachings in two different ways in their life works, the underlying theology was common to them both.

Figure 77: Silhouette of J.-B. Willermoz

According to Vivenza, Willermoz loved the teachings of the Elus Cohen, but found the structure of the Order unsatisfying and unstable. The fact that most of the rituals were incomplete, and the teachings passed on by Pasqually himself only partial and in some cases incomprehensible, did not help either, for it is hard to transmit something which isn't *whole*. He found a far more satisfying and stable structure in the Order of Strict Observance. However, while the structure was sound, the purpose most certainly was not, since it was preoccupied with reestablishing the Templar Order, something irrelevant to Willermoz. Therefore, with what might seem to be a somewhat ruthless approach, he joined the Order, and within 4 years had organized the Convent of Gaul, held in Lyon, at which

---

[14] Translation available in English on amazon.com by M. R. Osborn.

all claims to Templary were formally dropped, and the Rite of Strict Observance became the Scottish Rectified Rite. As an aside, the title of the Chivalric Grade of the Order, by being changed from 'Knight Templar' to 'Knight Beneficent of the Holy City', neatly inserted the name of his personal Lodge into the title!

This was the vehicle by which Willermoz could now promulgate the teachings of the Elus Cohen. The Blue Grades built on Pasqually's theology continuing up to the Knight of the 6th Grade was now, as a spiritual equivalent of a Master Elu Cohen, a warrior against the powers of evil. As just one example, the Tracing Board of the First Grade of Apprentice, the broken column, which had been interpreted by the Strict Observance to represent the Templar Order, broken and without its leader, now became a representation of man, whose inner temple had been broken because of his prevarication, and whose celestial part had been thrown into the abyss, and on which he must work in order to rebuild, and thus restore himself to his original state of glory. In other words, the complete system of 6 Grades were much, much more than a series of rituals to teach lessons to Masons: they were a system of salvation, through which, by applying the tools given to him at each Grade, and in particular the seven cardinal and theological virtues, man could become a Man of Desire, and ultimately a New Man, accomplishing reintegration. It is no surprise, therefore, that the 7th and 8th Grades of Profession, like the Perfecti of the Cathars, provided the rulership with the unveiled truth of Pasqually's theology, and as I have suggested, quite probably theurgical operations at this level to accompany the teachings.

Remember that the Convents of Gaul, and then Wilhelmsbad in 1782, were not local affairs, but rather major Masonic Conferences attended by the leaders of most of the known European Orders of the time. The intention was to create, once and for all, a single, comprehensive system. And Willermoz was at its center, as organizer, advisor, scribe and author. Had his vision succeeded, and if the French Revolution hadn't removed this singular opportunity, this Rectified Rite might have been the face of Freemasonry throughout most of the world. Indeed, Robert Ambelain claimed in 1948, in his pamphlet *Contemporary Martinism*, that the only truly credible line of initiation from the Elus Cohen which has survived to modern times is that passed through the Profession of the Scottish Rectified Rite.

The Christian Mystical Successor to the Elect Cohens

In the meantime, Saint-Martin had been attracting quite a following with the publication of his books, and it is very clear that he had a close-knit group with whom he worked, which, unusually for the times, included a number of women. There has been considerable speculation over whether he belonged to a secret group prior to his involvement with Pasqually or following it, a group given the name of Unknown Superiors. However, unless some definitive proof turns up, this seems unlikely, since there was little spare time in his busy schedule for him to have been heavily involved in yet another group, and in any case, the term

'Unknown Superior' and 'Past' or 'Passed Masters' were, as we have seen, terms used by many Orders to attract members by claiming links with higher entities which guided and directed them. Now, since he was already giving instructions to his followers, and he was a Mason at that time, it is not a total leap of faith to conjecture that he might have had some kind of initiation ritual which he performed on the members of his inner circle.

To summarize this first flourishing of so-called Martinist ideas: if Pasqually had been the Magician or Magus, then Saint-Martin was the Mystic and Willermoz the Mason. Curiously their three different leanings brought three different approaches to the same message. And this is why the term 'Martinism' has often been used to apply to all three approaches, the Magical Elus Cohen, the Mystical Martinist Order, and the Masonic Scottish Rectified Rite. All contains the same teachings, but fitted, in a way, for different audiences.

Figure 78: Louis-Claude de Saint-Martin

The French Revolution Intervenes

However, all this was to be blown away by an extraordinary event which almost none had foreseen until it was right on top of them: the French Revolution. Saint-Martin was a minor aristocrat, so it was inevitable that he would be rounded up at one point of the terrors. However, his calm appearance, and his insistence on debating the path to God rather than worrying about his personal safety while in prison earned him the admiration of his jailers, and he was soon freed, continuing the avid study of his new hero, Jakob Boehme the German Mystic, writing more books on spiritual philosophy, and finally ending his days as a teacher in a small village in the Loire.

Willermoz survived the siege of Lyon, though his alchemically-inclined younger brother had not been so lucky, being executed during the reign of terror. He was also instrumental in safeguarding many of the Masonic and Esoteric records of that time, organizing a foray out of the besieged city to the local Lodge to rescue a large number of documents, many of which may still be read in the Fonds Willermoz in Lyon Public Library. To safeguard his precious Scottish Rectified Rite, he had his nephew carry the charter and rituals to Switzerland, with the hope that they would one day return to a France which would then be safe and free.

At this point it is perhaps interesting to note the cyclical nature of things, especially referred to as the 'fin de siècle', or end-of-century feeling. Man appears to be very open to the idea of a global ending to life, perhaps reflecting his personal fear of death and the unknown. Remembering that even the early Christian believed that the end of the world would occur within their lifetimes, when Christ was meant to come again in glory to 'judge both the quick, or living, and the dead'. A thousand years later, as the Christian calendar clicked over to four figures in the year 1000, dire predictions of world-ending catastrophes were commonplace. Indeed, the end of almost every century has been open to such claims of end-times. If they didn't take place, canny religious leaders simply moved the dates, or claimed that some magnanimous act of personal piety had saved the planet! A theme common to all of this is exclusion: the idea that only the adherent to the particular cult would be saved, an idea which has been embraced by groups as diverse as Jehovah's Witnesses with their limited seating arrangements, the Mormons who created additional scriptures to support their claims, and some groups of Evangelicals who invented an event not even found in the Scriptures called the Rapture, but which contains the now familiar theme that only they go to heaven, while everyone else goes through a whole lot of terrible suffering. Compare these brutish and selfish ideas which are wholly alien to most religions, and we can see why the concept of personal salvation, the duty to work towards the rescue of others, and the uplifting belief that every person contains a spark of the divine and can aspire to be one with and like God, and we can quickly understand why gnostic teachings such as those professed by the Elus Cohen would hold so much attraction. Indeed, one thing common to all so-called esoteric Orders, which seem to rise up and flourish at the end of each century at a time of fear and uncertainty, is that they all offer the individual the opportunity to place control into his or her own hands, be it through efficacious prayer, communication with higher powers, or even control over the Laws of Physics on our own planet.

While it is easy to pick any war to prove a point, given that mankind is so often engaged in territorial land-grabs or the confiscation of scarce resources, which, despite all protestations of moral virtue and inherent right, are really the only real reasons for going to war, if we focus on the last three cycles – or centuries – we see a repeating pattern.

The 19th Century Resurgence of Mysticism

Towards the end of the 18th Century the Western world was alive with potential and possibilities, science was advancing rapidly, yet its apparent rejection of the spiritual led to a resurgence of mystical and magical Orders. All this came crashing down towards the end of the Century in France, due to the Revolution, and in the teens of the 19th Century, due to man-made wars. Americans should remember that 1812 is not remembered in Europe because of the Anglo-American War,

An Introduction to Martinism

but rather because of Napoleon's failed attempt to invade Russia. These were followed by the Napoleonic Wars and the Hundred Days War, all of which involved most of Europe.

The end of the 19th Century saw a similar rise in scientific advancement and the Industrial era at its height, balanced by a resurgence of interest in the occult as seen in everything from the Hermetic Order of the Golden Dawn, the Theosophical Society, the rise of Masonic Rosicrucian Orders especially in England, the United States, Greece, France and Canada, Spiritualism, Faith Healing, Neo-Romanticism in art, the rise of the Independent Catholic movement and the Gnostic Church, and the veritable explosion in esoteric Orders in France. By now, due to Eastern exploration and the expansion of empires during that Century, this interest in the occult now extended to Eastern traditions as well, and we find Buddhist and Hindu practices sitting comfortably alongside Western mysticism and the Mystery Schools of Ancient Greece, Rome and Egypt, to say nothing of Scandinavian and other mythologies, too. But even as the century came to an end the seeds were already in place for the next great upheaval. By 1914 the World was once again at war, and its inhabitants had little time for the frivolous occupation of looking into one's soul and seeking higher beliefs.

Figure 79: Rosicrucian Cross from the Golden Dawn

Figure 80: Robert Ambelain

However, as before the flame of gnosis was carried forward by a brave few, and in World War II it was a French mystic, Robert Ambelain in Paris, who together with a small group of redoubtable souls in Lyon under the puppet Vichy Government which kept the spark alive, as did small groups under other totalitarian regimes in Greece, Communist Russia and Fascist Spain. In America, Israel Regardie was writing his four-volume exposé of the Stella Matutina, a later manifestation of the Golden Dawn, to the enthusiastic reception of the Supreme Magi of the English and American Masonic Rosicrucian Societies, as seen in their letters to one another even as the Blitz was going on in London. And again, we see the burgeoning of esoteric activity toward the latter part of the 1900s, with the rise of Wiccan, even the Church of Satan, and the ragtag of composite beliefs called 'New Age', together with the revival of many earlier groups ranging from the Golden Dawn to Martinism and the Elus Cohen, albeit in a modernized form to meet the expectation of a new generation.

And here we are in the middle of the 'twenties' of the 21st Century, wondering if yet another war or political differences will tear us apart, forcing us to focus on how to protect ourselves from ravaging viruses and the threat of extremism, rather than enjoying the luxury of meditating on higher things. Only time will tell.

But following our detour into the philosophy of cycles, let us return to the matter in hand.

The 'occult revival' of the 19th Century is often attributed to a French ordained deacon (though never a priest), later an author and magician, called Alphonse Louis Constant, better known as Eliphas Lévi. However, it can equally be said that similar currents of though were developing across many European countries and America – both North and South – at that time. But for our story, it is a French Doctor, Gérard Encausse, better known by his *nomen mysticum* Papus, that we must turn to for the continuation of the story of Martinism.

The Resurrection of Martinism

Obtaining his doctorate in medicine from a paper on Philosophical Anatomy and working as a hypnotist at a renowned School of Hypnotherapy in Paris, he was what we would now term a 'joiner'. He counted Maître Philippe de Lyon, a renowned contemporary mystic, and Alexandre Saint-Yves d'Alveydre among his mentors.

Figure 81: Dr. Gérard Encausse, or 'Papus'

He founded a few groups of his own and joined – and quickly left – the Golden Dawn Temple of the McGregor Mathers' in Paris, the French Theosophical Society, and the Hermetic Brotherhood, among others. Being disillusioned with conventional Catholicism he joined Jules Doinel's newly-formed Gnostic Church, based on his visions of the Cathar or Albigensian Church, which had been widespread in Languedoc in South-West France before the infamous crusades against them in 1209, which continued with persecution, wars, and the Inquisition, until the siege of Montségur in 1243 effectively ended the Cathars, whose so-called 'heresy' amounted to little more than moral disgust at the corruption of the Roman Catholic Church of the times, believing that woman held equal place in ministry, that humans are angels imprisoned in corruptible bodies, and similar beliefs which would certainly account for their attractiveness to a Martinist.

He is also known for writing a number of books on occult and magical philosophy, in both cases trying to bring a veneer of scientific respectability to the practices, as well as books on Tarot and the Kabbalah.

If this was his entire output, perhaps Papus would have been relegated to history as little more than one of the many occult revivalists of the late 19th Century who happened to write a few books at the time. However, his true claim to immortality lies in an unusual event he claims took place in 1884, when a chance encounter with another mystically-inclined French man, Augustin Chaboseau, revealed that they had both received initiation into Martinist Orders through two different chains of succession linking them back to Louis-Claude de Saint-Martin and his disciples. Papus claimed to have been given papers written by Pasqually, and the rights to the Order of Saint-Martin by Henri Delaage, and together they exchanged lines, in the manner of bishops, and then set about founding an Order to consolidate their understanding and to preserve it for posterity, which led to the formation of the Order Martiniste, or Martinist Order. Papus claimed that all he had received thought his initiation was 'three points and two letters'. The 'three points' form part of the Martinist sigil he created, and the 'two letters' are assumed to be the 'S, I', which are also incorporated into it. The story is certainly satisfying, but there is little proof to back it up. It also sounds alarmingly similar to those of the founding of most esoteric societies, from von Hund's Rite of Strict Observance with its Secret Chiefs, through the Hermetic Order of the Golden Dawn with its ciphers from Fraulein Sprengel, to the Societas Rosicruciana in Anglia of Robert Wentworth Little and his mysterious discovery of Rosicrucian rituals in a forgotten corner of the library of the United Grand Lodge of England. We find the veneer of respectability added to give gravitas and credibility to a new Body, as we noted earlier in our list of requirements for a successful new Order.

Figure 82: Papus in his Martinist 'cabinet'

The Order was structured not unlike Freemasonry, notwithstanding the fact that neither founder was a Mason, though Papus later joined the Order of Memphis-Mizraïm, and on the demise of John Yarker went on to become its Grand Hierophant. Three degrees were created, with their own rituals: Associate, Initiate and Unknown Superior. In this case the last Degree did not imply the person had passed to a higher plane, but that they should remain unknown to their contemporaries, and to remember an important quote from Saint-Martin himself: "I never wanted to make any noise." The initials 'S∴I∴' identified a Martinist, who also had secret signs and passwords of recognition, just like a Mason. In the ceremonies and in his private work in his oratory, reminiscent of the practices of the Elus Cohen, he wore a mask and a mantle, to protect himself from the attacks of unseen forces, but also to remind him of his insignificance and that his focus should be on reintegration with the Divine.

He promoted his Order with a regular magazine, *l'Initiation*, which to its credit, with a couple of gaps during the Wars, continues to be published on a moderately regular basis to this day. While the number of members was never enormous, as esoteric societies go it was one of the most successful of the time, rivalling that of the Theosophical Society and the Golden Dawn.

Figure 83: First edition of l'Initiation

However, its approach was considerably more focused on the approach of Saint-Martin in his later years, and despite Papus' interest in practical, particularly Solomonic Magic, the Order itself focused primarily on mystical Christianity, personal development, meditation and introspection, which Saint-Martin called the Way of the Heart.

The Order spread to other countries, making its way into most European lands with some success, and even into the United States under that phenomenal musician Eduard Blitz, who we remember had also tried to introduce – unsuccessfully – the Scottish Rectified Rite. Alas, despite being given a Charter by Papus, he immediately set about 'rectifying' the Order adding Degrees and creating an entire Order which he hoped to add to the Masonic stable of Degrees. However, Papus was not impressed, and removed Blitz as the Delegate to the United States, replacing him with Margaret Peeke, who was certainly a character in her own right, and who ran the Order until her death in 1908. Papus himself allegedly had designs on bringing Martinism into the Masonic fold in France. But it was not to be. He died of tuberculosis in 1916, working as a doctor in a field hospital during the First World War. In England the Golden Dawn was going through its death throes, thrust into the prurient spotlight of public opinion as the scandals of the Horos affair played out in the tabloid press; and in America the scandals surrounding faked seances and the demise of Martinism saw the esoteric revival falter and finally return to its dormant state, maintained by a handful of quiet men and women who carried the flame forward through the following decades. For there are always disciples who work in secret until it is time to bring to light the secrets which have lain buried, as Masonry teaches us.

The Natural Ebb and Flow of Esoteric Societies

Perhaps this is the time to consider another interesting fact. While esoteric Orders appear to flourish and die around the end of each Century, why is it that Freemasonry has survived almost untroubled for three Centuries? While its membership may rise and fall, and Grand Lodges may fall victim to totalitarian regimes, one of the first signs of a return to democracy has always been a resurgence in Freemasonry in a country as a core organization. Is it the message it carries? Is it the fact that it normally boasts royal or presidential patronage? Is it the network of supranational connections which maintains it through difficult times? Is it the fact that it can adapt in times of stress and warfare from being a body of free-thinking into a fraternal organization which provides friendships and fraternity to those under duress? The enduring nature of Freemasonry in the face of all attempts to kill it, while esoteric Orders rise and fall like waves on a beach is certainly worthy of meditation, or even formal study.

Indeed, even for esoteric Orders, the flame was kept alive during such times by a few. It is interesting to note that, while Freemasonry has always been seen as threatening to totalitarian regimes (think anything from the Iron Curtain, through Nazism to General Franco, and even to the Labor government in England just over a decade and a half ago, when all policemen, judges, etc. were put on a List,[15] mainly due to the bond between Brothers which is perceived as transcending National ties (despite our Obligations) – and all extremists are scared by groups of people who assemble in private to talk – Martinists were selected for even worse punishment. In Germany, under the Vichy government in occupied France, and under General Franco in Spain, while being a Mason would subject one to imprisonment, membership in Martinism was punishable by death.[16] Indeed, the Third Reich's obsession with esoteric secrets led them to take Lyon apart because of

Figure 84: Constant Chevillon

---

[15] It seems ironic and even inevitable that the main orchestrator of that persecution in the name of corruption – Tony Blair, the former Prime Minister of England – is now under investigation potential tax evasion on a massive scale...

[16] Indeed, I recall being at a Martinist event some 30 years ago in England where I met someone who had carried the flame in Spain during Franco's regime. His stories were sobering.

its esoteric heritage (but everything had been hidden before they came), and Constant Chevillon, the head of the Martinism Order there and a Gnostic Bishop was executed by Pétainist thugs in 1944.

To say that little of esoteric note occurred during the period following the First World War would be to do a number of organizations an injustice. Aleister Crowley, the Great Beast, was doing his thing in Europe, the United States and Canada, and other Orders were ticking over. Independent Catholicism was quietly breeding and spreading its tentacles as an alternative to dogmatic Christianity. AMORC was buying ad space on the back covers of comics. But it was not until the inevitable arrival of World War II that things began to move again, in anticipation of an overwhelming and dark force which threatened existence itself: Nazi Germany.

Although Switzerland had given a Charter to France to begin practicing the Scottish Rectified Rite Degrees once more, the sovereignty of the Order was not returned. Perhaps the Swiss had been surprised when Arthur Edward Waite, the well-known English author and esotericist, had asked to be received into the ranks of the C.B.C.S. in the first decade of the 20th Century, supported in this endeavor by his friend Eduard Blitz in the United States. They had made him welcome and took him through the system up to the Profession, even giving him a Charter to establish the Order in England. And although a political event prevented him from becoming Celebrant of the Metropolitan College of the S.R.I.A., which caused him to resign from the Order, he never lost contact with many of his friends, and his Orders are still considered to be the purview of this Rosicrucian Masonic Body to this day. Soon Waite, synergizing his experiences in the Golden Dawn, Martinism (which he had joined in 1897, and which he recreated himself in his personal Rectified Martinist Order) and ultimately his extraordinary Order, the Fellowship of the Rosy Cross, which he founded in 1913 and which contained a synthesis of the best of all he had learned together with his vision of the Secret Church of the Holy Grail, put him in a position to have to pick and choose among the many threads he was following.

But this interest in an Order which, frankly, had atrophied in Switzerland, being reduced to little more than an annual meeting of Helvetia Lodge, was suddenly thrown back into the spotlight by the rise of Hitler. Just as Willermoz had deposited the Order in Switzerland to avoid the French Revolution, so now Switzerland needed places to secure its sacred deposit in the event of inevitable war. It selected – or was selected – by two very different places. In 1934 it issued a Sovereign Charter to the United States, after being visited by Raymond Shute, a prominent US Politician from North Carolina; and in 1937 to the Grand Preceptory of Knights Templar of England. While Switzerland's neutrality was in fact honored, and they suffered no invasion, the Order therefore survived, carried forward in a few, but they gained a taste for the importance of the Order they had previously virtually ignored, and which had languished for nearly a century and a half in their country.

However, there was little understanding of the history or importance of the R.E.R. in England and the United States, and if anyone truly understood it, the chances are they weren't members. The reason for this was that both countries treated it like a private club. In England membership was restricted to the nine most senior members of the Grand Preceptory, while in the United States membership was restricted to a maximum of two people per State, usually Past Grand Masters or the State Heads of the Scottish Rite. And we all know how deeply these people understand Masonic heritage, symbolism and esotericism! Whether the founders had intended to work the rituals or understand the profound Christian message depends on which side of the argument you are. But it is clear that by the mid-1980s, the only time the rituals were even worked was when a new member was elected, and even them only a perfunctory version was read over the dinner table. For the second time, therefore, apart from the lines being passed on, Martinism in all its forms had suffered a second death.

The Elus Cohen was dead, having been formally closed down by its Grand Sovereign, Ivan Mosca (thought one country at least refused to acknowled his authority to do so). Martinism was reduced to a small if devoted membership, since Christian Mystical Orders were hardly the rage. And the Rectified Rite was little more than a couple of dining clubs – perhaps apart from a renewed interest in the Waite line – and an annual meeting in Switzerland.

Contemporary Martinism

Despite the tragic times, the core Order of Martinism survived, carried forward in a few faithful breasts. In Spain, Martinist groups met in secret, even though membership was punishable by death under General Franco. In the South of France, controlled by the Vichy government, the Order continued in Lyon, under Joanny Bricaud, then Constant Chevillon until his martyrdom towards the end of the Second World War. And in Paris one man who was to become a legend held meetings under the very noses of the Nazi occupiers. Robert Ambelain not only preserved the Order, but went on to write many books about it, including the story of how he kept the Order alive during the war; and even created a revised version of Pasqually's Order of Elus Cohen, despite most of the original texts having been

Figure 85: Philippe Encausse

lost. Following the end of the war, Martinism again began to stir, and by 1957, Philippe Encausse presided over the revival of his father's Ordre Martiniste.

Since then, Martinism has spread to every corner of the world, but as so often happens, in an Order in which the ego is meant to be suppressed and the practitioner remain unknown and silent in his working, the Order rapidly splintered into many groups, each claiming to be the one true successor of the line. When you think about it, this is absolute nonsense, since no currently existing Order can do more than claim a line going back to Papus or Chaboseau, and in so doing prove that they are cousins of all other valid Martinist Orders. Once again hubris and the human ability to take something pure and precious and destroy it rears its head.

Figure 86: The fundamental symbol of Martinism

This separation can clearly be seen on the internet, where, for example, an entry in Wikipedia will often deliberately leave out any reference to Martinist or other related Orders which are not directly connected to the person writing the entry. With a little close attention, it is always quite easy to see which partisan group has written the entry; and mankind, sadly, is no better informed about history for having read it. The other danger signal, which should have any prospective candidate running for the hills, is a big, brash, colorful, sexy, 'look at me!' website or Facebook page! Nothing says: 'I know little about what Martinism stands for' than a page which completely ignores the lesson of the mask and mantle, and ignores Saint-Martin's most important phrase: "I never wanted to make any noise." Like the modest guest in the parable who sits at the foot of the table, only to be seated by the host at the top of the table later on; or the alchemist who seeks the foundation of the Great Work in the lowliest of substances, it is the site which is the leanest, the quietist, which probably provides the portal to the sincerest Group of all. And that, of course, is a rule of thumb to be followed concerning any occult Order, given that the word 'occult' itself means 'hidden' and not shouted from the rooftops! And seriously, one Martinist Order has even threatened to sue another one because of a color in its Martinist Pantacle. You can't get much further away from Saint-Martin than that!

So, in our current time, Martinism has survived, mainly as a series of interconnected Orders which offer a platform of mystical, magical, theurgic, gnostic and masonic teachings. We will find a core Martinist Order, which also offers a chivalric path through the Scottish Rectified Rite, and a theurgical path through the Elus Cohen. It may well offer a more traditional Masonic one, too, since Memphis-Mizraïm has been long considered a part of this 'family' of Orders, due to Papus' involvement, and even harking back to early meetings between Willermoz and Cagliostro in Lyon, although this didn't amount to anything at that time. Given the spiritual nature of the gnostic teachings which permeate the Martinist family, there will inevitably be a Church associated with it, offering ordination to those who feel the calling, but who don't want to wear the straitjacket of formalized dogma, and see ordination as a personal route to God rather than an excuse to impose one's values on others and to proselytize. Acts of kindness and of spiritual healing are performed in secret, and the member rarely reveals his or her affiliation to anyone who is not likewise a member.

The Order is an organization which practices charity of the heart, and the only money which changes hands is when sharing costs to hire a room or make materials, for more than one organization has been expelled from the family for trying to charge for dues, or lessons, or initiations. Its approach is essentially Christian, since they are based upon the teachings of two Christian mystics: Saint-Martin and Jakob Böhme. It is a peaceful and peaceable path, a quiet place for one to examine oneself, and a support structure for those who, like Neo in The Matrix, wake up to find themselves in a hostile world and needing advice on how to proceed along the Path, now they know they can never go back. And finally, it is open to men and women, and both are able to pursue whatever paths they wish to in this mystical, gnostic landscape.

Martinism has suffered two catastrophes, and now enjoys a third period of peace. But for a third time, we are in that dangerous early period in our Century which so often has seen that war and destruction which tears away our desire to reunite with the numinous, and forces us to focus on Malkuth and the needs of the flesh. Let's all hope that, this time, we will get it right.

So, despite Martinism being an Order independent from Masonry, we can see that it probably would not have existed without it. Its roots are in the collective and independent work of three avid Freemasons, and if Masonry hadn't taken the bold step of divorcing itself from any religion at an early stage, and if the

French Revolution hadn't come when it did, the goals of the Convents of Gaul and Wilhelmsbad might have been realized, and continental Freemasonry at least might have become a single system based upon Pasqually's gnostic foundation: in which case European Masonry would, to all intents and purposes, have been Martinism! Despite this not taking place, Martinism has borrowed its structure and much of its terminology from Freemasonry, including its meeting places and its system of Grades. It has come close to being absorbed into Masonry on occasion, which might also explain the terror the Order seems to strike in the hearts of the 'good ole boys' whenever they hear it mentioned, since they see it as a potential rival to good, dues-paying members, and positively subversive in its belief in charging nothing. And of course, it is religious in its foundation, yet not aligned to any traditional form of Christianity, being gnostic in its teachings, and striving to a higher goal than that of making good men better. Fortunately, Freemasonry is not a threat to its existence, any more than attacking a person for belonging to a church would stand up in court: what happens outside of a Lodge Room is simply none of the business of Freemasonry! But in any case, as I hope we have seen, there is more than ample room for both 'under heaven and earth'.

The Kabbalistic Tree of Life

The Soul of the Rosicrucian Masonic Order

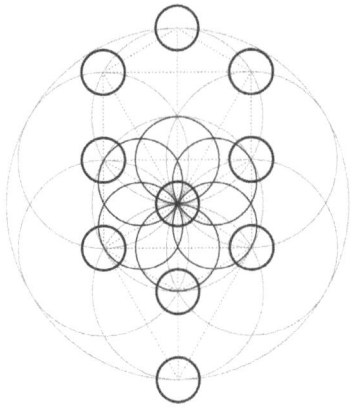

The Kabbalistic Tree of Life:
The Soul of the Rosicrucian Masonic Order

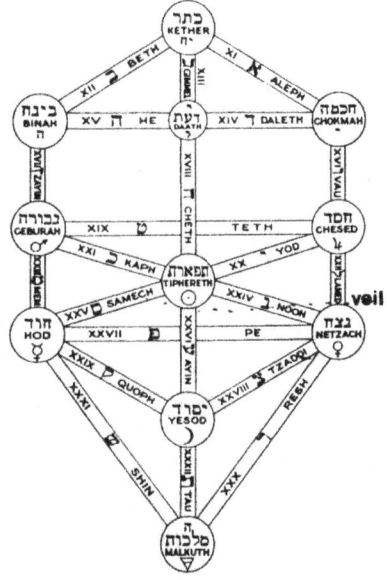

Figure 87: Depiction of the Tree of Life according to Arthur Edward Waite

 *This talk was given as an Annual Convocation of the Societas Rosicruciana in Civitatibus Fœderatis (S.R.I.C.F.) in Louisville, KY, as an introduction to the Tree of Life, as a sequel to 'The Journey in Esoteric Societies'*[17]*. This Masonic body follows the Grade system of the Rosicrucians.*

This paper is about one of the most familiar symbols in all of Western Esotericism: the Tree of Life. The Tree of Life is essential to our understanding of the Grade System of the S.R.I.C.F. as well as the S.R.I.A., S.R.I.S. and their daughter organizations, and to the Christian teachings which provide us with

---

[17] Piers A. Vaughan, *Renaissance Man & Mason*, pub. Rose Circle Publications, pp. 127 – 141.

an understanding of the path we must follow. Gaining emphasis among the Sephardic Jews in Spain, it claimed roots going back to the Old Testament and beyond to primitive truths, which were set out in key books including the *Sepher Yetzirah*, the *Etz Chaim & the Eight Gates*, the *Bahir*, the *Zohar* and others providing the foundation of the Hebrew esoteric school known as the Kabbalah. It provides us with a limitless source of images and emblems which we can use to better understand the road we must travel; and finally, it even offers us an opportunity to experience the journey, not only in symbolic form, but experientially through meditation and active participation.

Now, I know it will be difficult to talk at a level which will satisfy all of you, since some of you are beginners on this path, while others are expert in the field. Nevertheless, I hope I will have something new for all of you to consider today, and to build into the lessons we will take away from this weekend.

All spiritual growth is a journey, as we learned in the talk I gave last year, and the Tree of Life is an image of the journey leading from God to Man, and from Man back to God. Essentially, this symbol provides us with a road map on how to navigate the Path of Return. But it also has a secondary function as a kind of celestial filing cabinet, as we shall see later.

However, this is not going to be a long repetition of the history and origin of the Tree of Life and long descriptions about what each element traditionally represents. You can get that in any book. Indeed, I will immediately plug one of the Chief Adepts in the S.R.I.C.F. by recommending the books of Chic and Tabby Cicero, which are splendid annotations of two of Israel Regardie's magna opera: *The Tree of Life* and *A Garden of Pomegranates*. Both are accessible and written in plain English. I would also be remiss not to mention Dion Fortune's classic, *The Mystical Kabbalah*, still a stalwart of her 'Society of Inner Light'. I intend to base this talk on Waite's Tree of Life, generally accepted in our Rosicrucian Societates, but which is slightly different to the traditional one used by most Western Mystery Schools. I also intend to present the Tree through the lens of our Christian Rosicrucian Societates, and hope that all will find something of interest to ponder and meditate upon long after I have finished talking!

I will state immediately that I will be talking about some aspects of our Grades as they are reflected on the Tree of Life. While I know there will be Fratres in the room at varying Grades in the Societas, I will not divulge any of the secrets of the Grades, other than what is generally known in association with the Tree of Life. Indeed, having a good overall understanding of the system can only enhance one's experience and understanding of this fascinating system. This is appropriate, since our entire Grade system is based on the Tree of Life. Just as God, in Kabbalistic and most other teachings created the Universe, so man, now finding himself fallen to the base of the Tree – whereas he was created by God to be in the middle as we shall see later – strives to ascend the Tree to reunite

The Kabbalistic Tree of Life

with his Creator. Symbolically, God created the Universe in a lightning flash, which man seeks to ascend once more by means of the Path of Return.

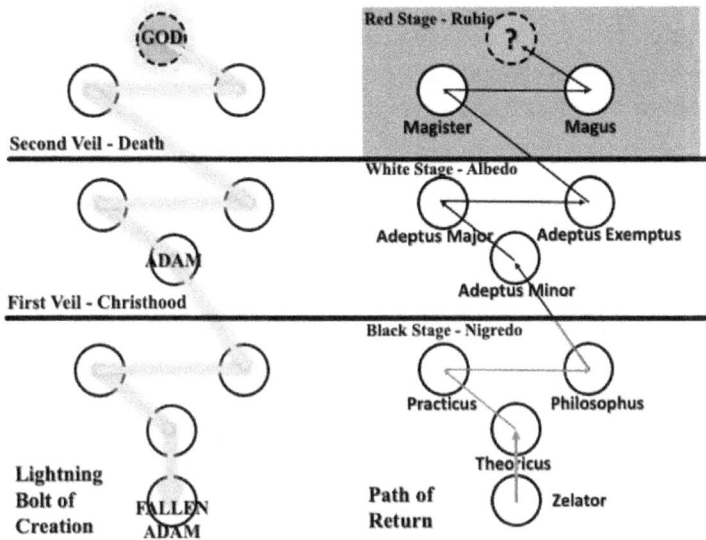

Figure 88: Creation (lightning bolt) and the Rosicrucian Grades (grades of ascent or Path of Return)

Of all the symbols, lectures and teachings revealed to you in the Grades of the Masonic Rosicrucians, none is more potent than that ultimate Kabbalistic emblem, the Tree of Life. In the First Order we experience the symbols in a passive sense, before we understand exactly what we are doing. When we enter the Grade of Zelator we experience the challenge of the four Elements, and hopefully begin to understand that our journey must start with a period of prayerful introspection, as we prepare ourselves for the Great Work. This phase of Spiritual Alchemy is intended to give us an opportunity to examine ourselves and to identify what we do well, and what we need to change. During this time we take ourselves apart, using the four classical elements as potent symbols, and examine our earthly, airy, liquid and fiery natures – or if you will, our sanguine, choleric, melancholic and phlegmatic identities – and learn to harmonize and balance them, so that it is a well-rounded and mature individual, confident and yet not arrogant who, having perfected his material self, now continues his journey by emulating Christ in the Adept Grades, who as an Adeptus Minor suffers and dies to the material, who rises a new man from the ashes of his former self as an Adeptus Major, and finally, as an Adeptus Exemptus, ascends to a sublime love of mankind, and an overwhelming desire to dispense mercy and assist his fellows in their own personal journeys.

It is appropriate, then, that at the Opening of the Vth Grade of Adeptus Minor, an Officer goes to the outer chamber where the Candidate is in waiting, unfurls a diagram of the Tree of Life, and says:

"Worthy Frater Philosophus, for four years and upwards you have been seeking the path of the return of the Soul to its Source. In the symbolism of the Kabbalistic Tree of Life, you started as a Zelator* in the Sephira of Malkuth* and, in subsequent Grades you have progressed to the Sephirah of Yesod*, Hod* and Netzach*. Thus prepared, you have returned to Yesod on the Middle Pillar but now you are looking upward towards the Supernals*. Before you is the Path of Ayin* which leads to the Sephira of Tiphareth*, the Christ-Center, while beyond is the hidden Sephira of Da'ath* where all things are dissolved into one.

"Across the Path of Ayin is the Veil of Paroketh*, but my Frater, this Veil has been rent asunder by the Redeemer of Mankind and the way laid open for all who follow Him. Are you, my Frater, in all humility, resolved to follow on that Path and dedicate yourself to the Christ-life?"

I wonder how many of you in the Adept Grades and above remember this explanation by the Inductor?

Now, in the text there is a rubric – a number of asterisks placed after all the key words. The rubric states: "the Inductor indicates with a pointer or by hand the points marked with an asterisk." I wonder how many of you would be able to point to each of the quoted Sephira and Paths on the Tree of Life without hesitation!

It is also interesting to note that most if not all of the earliest founders and ritualists in Freemasonry in England and continental Europe were familiar with the Kabbalah, either through their studies of Comparative Religion, Hermeticism, Alchemy or Theurgy, all of which require an encyclopedic knowledge of correspondences. By correspondences I mean the connections between archangels, their angelic throngs, the planets, plants, fragrances, Roman Gods, the sacraments, Words of Power – all of which would be used in the ceremonies accompanying the creation of an elixir or the summoning of an angelic power. Some of our founding ritualists, for example, Morin, Pasqually, Willermoz, and later Westcott, Mathers, Wentworth Little, Yarker, Pike and others were well-versed in these techniques, and used these correspondences openly in their rituals. Further, as we shall see, the Tree of Life is composed of ten Sephiroth or Centers, and twenty-two paths which connect them. This adds up to thirty-two. And even more curiously, there is a hidden, eleventh Sephira which Waite used in his version of the Tree of Life, making thirty-three in all. Now, I am sure I have no need to labor the importance of the numbers thirty-two and thirty-three in Rosicrucian teachings – and these numbers figure in many of our York Rite and Scottish Rite rituals, most usually in reference to the age of the Savior when He began his mission, and his age when He was revealed to be the Son of God through His Passion.

The Kabbalistic Tree of Life

For this reason, and for the fact that Christian mystics identified much of interest in the mystical teachings of Judaism, found in the Talmud, Mishnah and Kabbalah, the Tree of Life found a permanent home in the Christ-centric Western Mystery Traditions.

This talk will attempt to cover the basic elements of the Tree of Life. Now that is an optimistic claim, since one can make it a lifetime study! Evidently, I have two problems: time and expertise. Given the time allotted I will have to limit myself to some of the symbolism of Christian Kabbalah, omitting its rich history and many applications.; and for the more advanced reader, I can only hope that some of my more unorthodox viewpoints will provide food for thought, so that everyone will end this paper enriched to some extent.

Firstly, let's look at the diagram of the Tree of Life contained in the Vth Grade of the S.R.I.A. (*illustrated at the top of this paper*). Now, I must begin by alarming you in saying that it's not what might be called the 'normal' Tree of Life used in the Mystery Traditions. But this is not too important, since 95% of the elements are identical, and it is only at the top part of the diagram which differs slightly from the usual depiction. The 11th Sephira or circle – Da'ath – is featured, and some of the Paths, or lines joining the circles or Sephiroth are in different places to the more frequently seen version. By the end of this talk you should have a fair grasp of the diagram and what it stands for, and an understanding of its meaning. I can't promise you'll know everything about it: I don't think I can teach you Hebrew in 30 minutes! Your understanding will also only be at a superficial level. But that said, it will be enough for you to find it easy enough to follow most books on the subject you may decide to read. Of course, there is far more to the Kabbalah than the Tree of Life alone; but if you grasp the essentials of this seminal diagram, you will be able to follow most of the other teachings, all of which are to some extent predicated on this symbol. It is truly worth the effort: the symbolism of our *Societas* and much of Freemasonry is rooted in the Kabbalah and the Tree of Life!

The Hebrew alphabet, like the ancient Egyptian alphabet (and for that matter most early written languages) was made up of letters which had several meanings. A letter had a sound; a numerical value (in other words, they used letters to count); a name; a type; and a meaning, as well as many other associations. For now, let us simply look at this chart of the 22 letters, and draw some ideas from the alphabet.

Firstly, look for the letter 'Yod'. This looks like a tongue of fire, or a sperm. We can see it on the ring given out following the 14th Degree of the Ancient Accepted Scottish Rite. Indeed, it is considered to be the source of all the other letters, which are combinations of this basic form.

ENLIGHTENMENT MAN & MASON

Letter	English Name	Sound	Meaning in English	# Value
א	Aleph	'	Ox	1
ב	Beth	b (v)	House	2
ג	Gimel	g (g)	Camel	3
ד	Daleth	d (dh)	Door	4
ה	Heh	h	Window	5
ו	Vav	w	Nail / Hook	6
ז	Zain	z	Sword	7
ח	Cheth	h	Fence	8
ט	Teth	t	Serpent	9
י	Yod	y	Hand (open)	10
כ ך	Kaph	k (kh)	Hand (closed)	20
ל	Lamed	l	Ox Goad	30
מ ם	Mem	m	Water	40
נ ן	Nun	n	Fish	50
ס	Samekh	s	Prop	60
ע	Ayin	'	Eye	70
פ ף	Peh	p (ph)	Mouth	80
צ ץ	Tzaddi	s	Fishhook	90
ק	Qoph	q	Back of Head	100
ר	Resh	r	Head	200
ש	Shin	sh	Tooth	300
ת	Tav	t (th)	Mark	400

Figure 89: The Hebrew Alphabet

Hebrew has been called the 'language of the angels', and for this reason is considered to be an *heiratic* or *holy* language. The letters are considered to be sacred sounds and their combinations therefore have a power unto themselves. They were not seen as merely a means of attributing random noises to objects in order to communicate them between men: they were seen as a way of communicating with Higher Powers, and even as instruments of influence or change upon the world and the higher spheres.

Even until relatively modern times, learning the true name of someone or something gave one control over it. Think of every movie you've seen involving an exorcism: the main aim of the exorcist is to learn the possessing demon's name, for then he can compel it to depart.

Compare the following two phrases:

> "And God said, Let us make man in our own image, after our likeness: and let them have dominion over the fish of the sea, and over the fowl of the air, and over the cattle, and over all the earth...And out of the ground the Lord God formed every beast of the field, and every fowl of the air; and brought them unto Adam to see what he would call them."

...and...

"...For by names and images are all powers awakened and reawakened."

The first comes from Genesis, Ch. 1:26 and Ch. 2:19, allegedly written by Moses, although the version we now have comes from the work of Esdras during the Babylonian Captivity around 597 B.C. The second comes from the Opening of the Hall of Neophytes from the Hermetic Order of the Golden Dawn, founded by members of the S.R.I.A. in 1888 A.D.

In both cases the common theme is that, by naming something or knowing its name, one has dominion over that thing, be it animal, vegetable, mineral, demon or angel. This is the origin of the concept of the Logos, or Word, which is the word God spoke to bring the universe – and man – into existence. Those of you familiar with the works of C.S. Lewis, notably the Narnia series of books, may recall *The Magician's Nephew*, which is a retelling of the story of creation. Aslan the Lion literally sings the Universe into existence.

For those of you unfamiliar with his books, Aslan represents the Christ, and in his book *The Lion, The Witch & The Wardrobe*, willingly allows himself to be slain, only to be resurrected. Therefore, it is clear that having Aslan sing the worlds into existence closely identified him with the Logos. This is such a beautiful analogy, since the angelic language is a language of song, or vibration, rather than prosaic speech. This is why, even now, at all the important points of a Mass, the priest intones or sings the key phrases, and the choir sing the responses in Gregorian Chant. It is no coincidence that the term 'Cantor' for he who leads this intonation is common to both the Hebraic and the Christian traditions. In this we hope to hear an echo of the Harmony of the Spheres. But for now, let us simply reflect upon the beauty of God singing us into existence, and understand that the Christos, or Logos, is an eternal song.

Figure 90: Gregorian Chant

So, this Hebrew language, written in fire and song, was so much more than a way to verbalize *things*. But there were difficulties. You will perhaps have noticed that the language contains no true vowels. Like modern magical practice, the true pronunciation of the words was passed 'from mouth to ear'. Legend has it that only the High Priest knew the true pronunciation of God's name, which was uttered in the Sanctum Sanctorum but once a year, and since we know the consonants, the secret must have been in the vowels which linked them – an idea very familiar indeed to any Companions of the Holy Royal Arch Degree.

Figure 91: Elo Mikhael Gabriel ve-Raphael = 701

Now the fact that letters carried numerical values also led to the idea that words or phrases with an identical value were linked. This was called Gematria. To give an example, in Genesis 18:2 we read "Vehena Shalista", which is, in Hebrew, "and lo, three men", the three men who visit Abraham. Tradition tells us he was 'entertaining angels unawares'. The numerical value of these words is 701. This value also sums to the Hebrew words "Elo Mikhael Gabriel ve-Raphael' which, as you must have guessed, means the visitors were the three Archangels. There are two other similar practices, called Temurah and Notarikon, which either substitute a letter with another to obtain further insights, or take initial letters to create other words. So Temurah is a bit like creating a cipher, the most obvious in English being created by laying out A-Z against Z-A to create a code. Perhaps the most well-known example of Notarikon is the quasi-word 'AGLA', which is an acrostic of the Hebrew 'Atah Gibor le-Olahm Adonai', or 'Thou, O Lord, art mighty forever'. I know this is a whistle-stop tour of ideas, but you will have time to read this paper at leisure later, and then when some whippersnapper comes up to you and talks about Notarikon, at least you won't think he's trying to interest you in a Video Game!

So originally there were no vowels in Hebrew. Later, around the 6th Century A.D., the Masoretes created a system of suggesting vowels by using a series of dots and dashes above or below the letters called 'niqqud'. Note that the letters themselves were still considered too sacred to be interfered with, either by inserting new letters or by altering the letters themselves.

This is why, for example, you will come across so many different spellings of the word 'Kabbalah', including Cabala, Cabalah, Kabalah, Kabbala, and so forth, since the word is made up of four consonants: Qoph-Beth-Lamed-Heh or Q-B-L-H (קבלה), which means 'to receive' in Hebrew (remember Hebrew is written from right to left...).

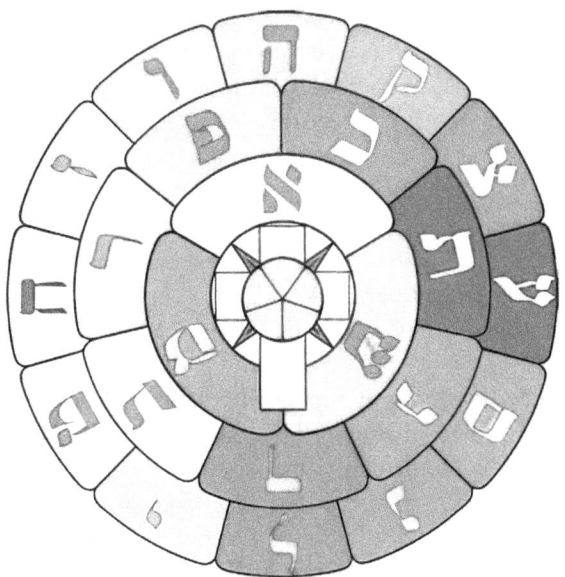

*Figure 92: Rose upon the Rosicrucian Cross.
Note there are 3 central petals, then 7, then 12.*

In perhaps the earliest extant book on the Kabbalah, the *Sepher Yetzirah* (or 'Book of Formation'), which tries to explain how the Universe came into existence, the Hebrew alphabet of 22 letters is divided into three groups: 3 'Mother' letters, 7 'Double' letters and 12 'Simple' letters. These 22 letters, together with the 10 Sephiroth, meaning emanations, add up to the 32 so-called 'Paths of Wisdom'. Without going into the significance of the Mother, Doubles or Simple letters in this talk, I hope you can see that these numbers reflecting 3, 4, 7, 10 and 12 reflect a number of ideas with which we are already familiar, including the 3 letters of God's name (Yod, Heh, Vav), the 4 ancient Elements, 7 Days of the week and the planets known to early man, the 10 directions, and the 12 Tribes of Israel assigned to the 12 constellations.

With regard to the 4 Elements, note that the 3 Mothers referred to Air, Water and Fire. Aleph, the first letter was assigned to Air, the breath of life, as it is an aspirate, which is like a breath. Water, or Mem, represents a mute, which has no sound in itself, but only relative to other letters. Finally Fire, or Shin, is a sibilant, which hisses. In this way the three letters are almost onomatopoeic, in that they make the sound they symbolize.

In the beginning the Ruach Elohim (or 'spirit' or 'air') moved upon the face of the waters and was itself was the genesis of fire. The water formed the earth, the fire the heavens, and air was the intermediary between them. This close connection again between the Word or the Logos, the breath of life, and creation shows how God created the Universe through His voice. We find it in our passwords: "And God said: 'Let there be Light'" – in Latin *'Fiat Lux!'*

According to the Zohar, which is a set of volumes dedicated to the study of the Torah, or interpreting the first 5 books of the Bible – the Pentateuch – in terms of Kabalistic symbolism, there are four ways the Torah can be studied:

- **P'shat**: the direct interpretation of its meaning;
- **Remez**: studying the allegorical meanings through allusion;
- **D'rash**: making comparison with other similar passages, and studying the context of Rabbinic teachings on the passage; and
- **Sod**: learning the esoteric, hidden meaning as revealed through Kabbalah.

Ironically – to me at least – many Christian theologians believe the same approach should be taken not only to what we call the Old Testament, but to the New Testament as well. This is why Fundamentalism has always been a bit of a mystery to me. Given it was the Jews who wrote the Old Testament, it strikes me as arrogant in the extreme that, several hundred years later, another religion usurped their religious books and told them to read them literally, when they had been reading them allegorically for centuries already. Let's not forget that the Babylonian Talmud, or *commentary* on the Torah, appeared around the same time that the Torah was initially set down in written form during the Babylonian Captivity! But what do I know…?

The initials of the four means of study, P-R-D-S form the Hebrew word 'Pardes', or 'Orchard' or even 'Garden', which is particularly pointed given that the Tree of Life was to be found alongside the Tree of Knowledge in the Garden of Eden. And 'orchard' suggests apples…

So why so many concepts thrown at you in a short space of time? Because much of the 'barrier to entry' in this area of study is in the language and the words used. By reading and rereading this paper, you will at least have access to a simple explanation of many of the key terms used, which will allow you to follow a person's conversation. And if you augment your understanding by reading books on the topic, you will readily be able to hold a conversation on these concepts.

If God created the Universe, it was certainly perfect. And if God created Man, then symbolically it was in Man's nature also to create. Whether this act of creation was for good or ill depends on the tradition. In most, however, it did not end well. One tradition, for example, has Adam attempting to emulate

Figure 93: Elohim creating Adam (Blake)

The Kabbalistic Tree of Life

God's act of creation by creating for himself a mate out of earth, but ends up becoming enmired in that same red earth, taking on a 'coat of flesh': that is, becoming mortal in the process.

Now, to create one must first conceive. This idea must take root in fertile soil to be nourished and to grow. Next, there must be the desire to manifest it. Finally, it must be fashioned or formed, and come to fruition in the physical world. Thought, will, action. As an example, a man may have decide to create a chair. But what kind? A sofa, a throne, a stool, an armchair? So, he must design it by creating a blueprint. This enables him to assemble the materials and cut them to the right size, finally assembling them into the chair he initially conceived. As man conceives his chair, so God conceives the universe. As above, so below. This gave rise to the idea of there being four worlds, in descending order:

- The World of Emanation, or **Aziluth**;
- The World of Creation, or **Briah**;
- The World of Formation, or **Yetzirah**;
- The World of Action, or **Assiah**.

So, we have looked at the Hebrew alphabet, its hieratic or holy nature, and its importance, both as a means to communicate with Higher Beings, and also as the manner by which God created the Universe. And we have considered the manner in which God has an idea and brought it to fruition, culminating in the creation of Man.

Let us now look at the Tree of Life, which from one perspective is a frozen image of this Act of Creation.

We won't go into the many theories about why God entered into an act of Creation, or how he became self-aware and wished to see Himself, or how, if He is omnipotent and omnipresent, how He created a place where he was not, in order to initiate the creation of something which was both part of Him and outside of Him. We would be here all day! So, let us start with the assumption that He initiates the Act of Creation. To accomplish this,

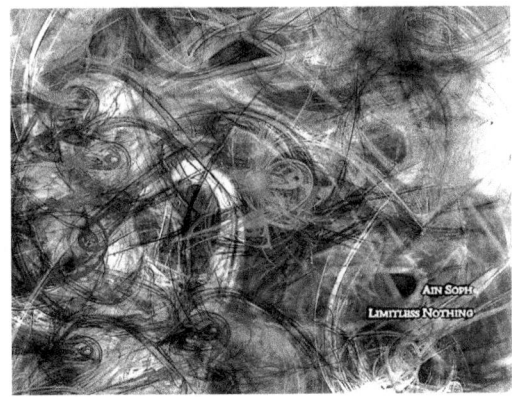

Figure 94: Ain Soph

from His position above the nascent Tree in Ain Soph, the Divine Infinite, he progressively reveals Himself through a series of emanations of Sephiroth, through a process often referred to as *tzimtzum*, or condensation, from the rarest spiritual manifestation down to the most physical, the tenth Sephira called Malkuth (note the plural of 'Sephira', or emanation is 'Sephiroth', and for this reason the Tree of Life is often referred to as the 'Sephirotic Tree').

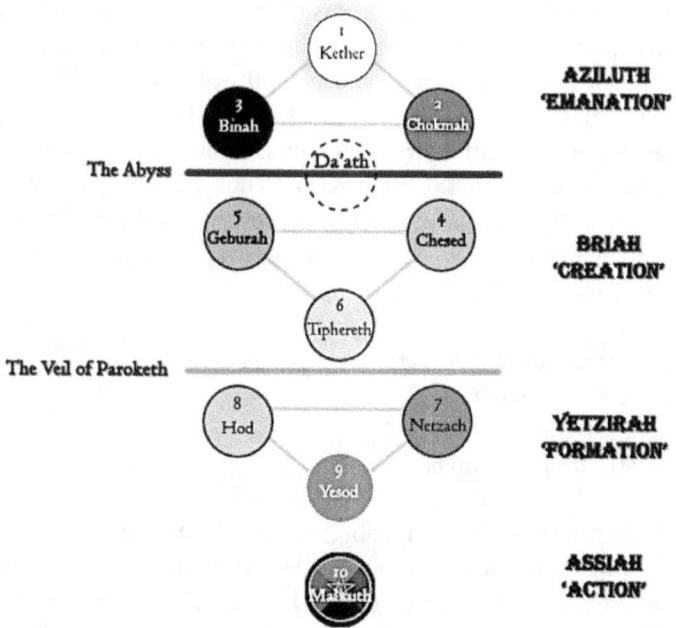

Figure 95: The Tree of Life

We can represent the initial condensation of the Divine Will as resulting in a sphere forming at the top of the tree. This Sephira is called '**Kether**', or 'Crown', and is assigned the number '1'. Now, this initial conceptual thought, as we saw earlier, needs to be created by an act of consciousness, and this is represented by Wisdom, or **Chokmah**, which forms the second Sephira. Wisdom must be balanced by Understanding, and so we find it balanced on the Tree by **Binah**, the third Sephira. While we need wisdom to contrive, we also need an understanding of how to bring this contrivance to fruition: as we said previously – thought, will, action. Let us recall Proverbs 3, which should be very familiar to anyone in the Ancient Accepted Scottish Rite (and let us note that is comes from the 18th, or Rosicrucian Grade): "Happy is the man that findeth wisdom, and the man that getteth understanding... she is more precious than rubies... her ways are ways of pleasantness, and all her paths are peace. She is a Tree of Life to them that lay hold upon her, and happy is everyone that retaineth her." But it continues: "The Lord by Wisdom hath founded the earth, by Understanding hath he established the heavens." (Prov 2:19-20). Note the references to Understanding make this Sephira feminine. So, we see one power divided into two, a male and female element. As a passage in the Golden Dawn Ritual of the Hall of the Neophytes: "Two contending forces and one which unites them eternally. Two basal angles of the triangle and one which forms the apex. Such is the origin of creation – it is the triad of life." This dividing of the unique force into two, or unity into duality, forms a triangle, again familiar to us in the Sacred Delta, which recognizes the striving of these two forces of Male and Female, Light and Dark, Life and Death, Peace and War, to reunite.

Here, in one interpretation, we have '*Aziluth*', or the 'Emanation' of the creative thought.

If this triad represents the entirety of the Godhead in itself as a manifestation of masculine and feminine properties, then since God does not interact directly and personally with His creation, but according to tradition through the action of intermediaries, called Archangels and Angels, and in our tradition the ultimate manifestation of His Son, Jesus, there is of necessity a separation between His Omnipotence and the rest of creation. This is referred to as the Abyss. Those seeking more light can read the works of Jakob Boehme, the German mystic, on the concept of *Byss and Abyss*. Some diagrams – including the one used in the S.R.I.A., show an eleventh, or 'hidden' Sephira on this barrier, called 'Da'ath' or 'Knowledge'. In some systems it represents all the Sephiroth combined into one; in others, a means by which mortal man, imbued with Knowledge, might bridge the Abyss to commune with the Godhead and return unscathed – and still alive, as did Enoch, Moses and Elijah.

As the manifestations descend, we find the two Spheres or Sephiroth of **Chesed**, meaning Mercy, or Grace; and **Geburah**, or Severity and Might. Chesed being the fourth Sephira is separated from the Godhead by the Abyss, and in a way is the first stirring into manifestation of the Divine Thought. Set against Chesed is the 5th Sephira of Geburah. If Chesed represents Mercy and Grace, this is counterbalanced by Justice, expressed through Might. These two manifested forces find their balance in the central Sephira of **Tiphareth**, or Beauty. We will come to see that this Sephira is placed in the center of the entire Tree of Life, and this is for a reason. At this point the concepts and balance meet in the next level of manifestation, and here we find the potential for manifestation of the power of God directly descending from the Crown of Kether. This is referred to in Christian symbolism as the Christ-Center, with the striking image of an emanation of God descending through the Abyss to become crystallized in the lower part of the Tree. These three Sephiroth form a descending triangle, reflecting the opposite polarity of the first, upward-pointing triangle. To many this represents the World of '*Briah*', or Creation, where the thought becomes idea, or the Word becomes flesh.

Below Tiphereth we find a veil which separates the Lower Tree from the upper, called the **Veil of Paroketh**. This is the veil which was symbolically rent in twain in the Temple when Christ died on the cross, which is actually a *good* thing, for it opens up the path to God which was closed to us at the instant of the

Fall. Unlike the Abyss, this is a veil which can be passed through by mortal man, if he works to perfect himself through the Great Work of Spiritual Alchemy.

As we continue to descend the Tree we arrive at the next condensation, called Netzach, or Victory. It bears the number '7' which is considered to be perfection, or completion. It is the love which binds all things together, and is often represented as the planet Venus and the color Green, both of which are associated with Divine Love. Set on the opposite side is Hod, Splendor or Glory, and reminds us that, although the Universe is held together by love, it is constantly excitable, in eternal movement, the mercurial quality of flux. Both rest upon the center Sephira of Yesod, or Foundation. This 9th Sephira contains within itself all the preceding numbers, and supports the Tree of Life. It is lunar in nature, and it often referred to as the Astral Plane. It supports and completes the third downward pointing triad upon the Tree, and represents for many the World of 'Yetzirah', where idea becomes form, or blueprint.

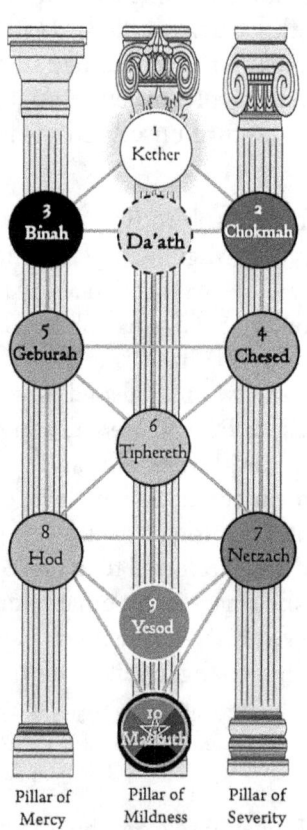

Figure 96: Wisdom, Strength and Beauty

Now let us move to the final manifestation of these Sephiroth, at the bottom. Here we find the 10th Sephira: **Malkuth**, or Kingdom. This is the physical world. This is where we live. Since the Sphere which lies symbolically above us is the Astral Plane, it is hard for rational people to believe in its existence. Therefore, as Saint-Martin said, most of humanity moves and lives in a 'Forest of Errors', living like automatons, with no concept of the immensity of teeming activity which interpenetrates the Sephira of Malkuth in which we live. Here form becomes matter, and the fourth World of **Assiah** is found. Some Christian Kabbalists note the similarity between Assiah and Asia as referenced by the great mystic St. John the Divine in his letters to the Seven Churches in Asia, or the lowest seven Sephiroth below the Abyss.

Of particular interest to Freemasons is the fact that these ten Sephiroth appear to lie on three vertical pillars. No doubt you will recognize the Pillars of Mercy and Severity as our own Jachin and Boaz. But now we see a Middle Pillar, a Pillar of Mildness, rising up between them: a direct path from Man in Malkuth to God in Kether through his Son in Tiphareth. To quote again from the Golden Dawn Ritual of the Hall of the Neophytes: "Unbalanced severity is but cruelty and oppression; unbalanced mercy is but weakness and would permit evil to exist unchecked…" And in the Zelator Grade: "Let the Neophyte enter the straight and narrow pathway which turns neither to the right hand nor to the left hand." It is our task to find that equilibrium, that balance within ourselves, in order to reconcile the opposing forces and seek reintegration with God.

So, we have learned that, in this order of symbolism, God created all things through ten emanations of Sephiroth, which forms the outline of a lightning bolt going through their centers.

Now, it all seems easy enough, doesn't it? We were created by God in the physical plane at the bottom of the Tree, and all we have to do to regain Paradise is go up the Middle Pillar.

Simple!

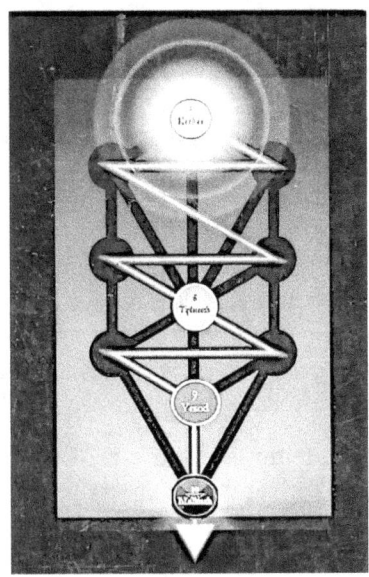

Figure 97: Lightning bolt descending the Tree of Life

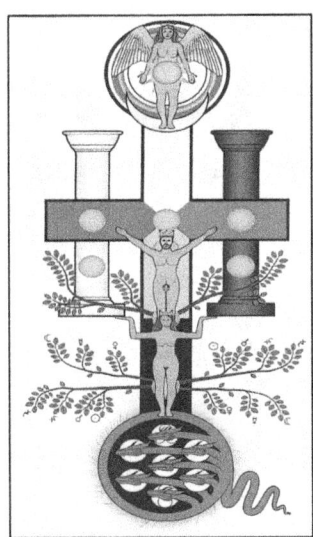

Figure 98: Before the Fall

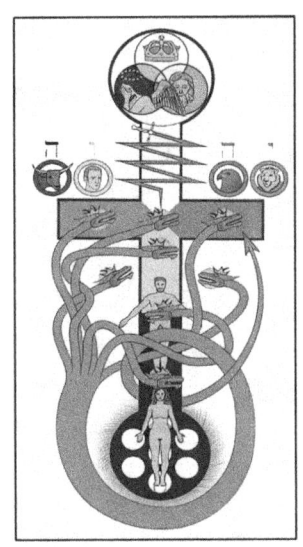

Figure 99: After the Fall

Firstly, we acknowledge that "there are more things in heaven and earth, Horatio, than are dreamt of in your philosophy" (Hamlet, 1:5). We breach the Astral Plane and see all the activity, all the vibration of the Harmony of the Spheres, before perfecting ourselves to cross the Veil of Paroketh and achieve union with Christ. From there it's just a 'little' matter of sacrificing ourselves in order to cross the Abyss and reunite with God.

At least that would have been possible before the Fall.

In this diagram we see the Godhead as a united being joined directly to Adam, who is stretched out upon the Tree at Tiphareth, while his consort, Eve, supports the two pillars, and the Tree of Knowledge grows out of Malkuth, the 10th Sephira. Below we see the infernal Sephira, the Qlippoth where Evil dwells in the symbolic form from the Apocalypse, of the seven-headed, ten-horned serpent (**Note:** both this and the following image are from the tradition of the Hermetic Order of the Golden Dawn).

But, tempted by the fruit of the Tree of Knowledge, Eve reached down into Malkuth and awakened the Serpent. In doing so she let fall the two great pillars, the vessels were shattered, and Adam fell into Malkuth, gaining his 'coat of skin'. Malkuth was cut off from the rest of the Tree by the enveloping coils of the Infernal Serpent, and to protect the Three Supernals, God placed a flaming sword, the one with which He had created the whole of the Tree of Life, between the lower 7 Sephiroth and the three Supernal Sephiroth, and placed the four faces of his Fourfold Name, the Cherubim (which is plural), set against the blasted Eden. Man was cut off from Redemption.

But this state is overcome by the coming of the Son descending down to Tiphareth, in order to atone for the Man's abomination or prevarication.

Figure 100: Wisdom upon a Tree...

Now for a moment, we are going to get a little Gnostic. To many sects, the Ophites and the Naassenes to mention but two, the Serpent in the Garden of Eden was not seen as an evil force, but rather one working for good. In this approach the Deity of the Old Testament, with his apparently insatiable appetite for blood and his all-too-human picking of favorites and taking sides was in fact a Demiurge, who visited hardship and suffering on mankind. Remember, for example, in Malachi 1:3, The Lord says: "And I hated Esau, and laid his mountains and his heritage waste for the dragons of the wilderness." That's very unpleasant thing to say about a human who had done nothing to offend you, and even had his father's blessing stolen from him by Jacob's subterfuge! The mission of the serpent was to open man's eyes to the true nature of this being, and in symbolically eating the flesh of the apple, this was accomplished. Enraged, the demiurge visited torment upon mankind for the knowledge it had acquired, and to keep it in subjugation. To them, the serpent represented and was the embodiment of Wisdom. To them, the serpent could be none other than the Logos, the Christ. Is this so far-fetched? Remember that even the Church Fathers saw a harbinger to Jesus in the Brazen Serpent raised high by Moses to cure the afflicted people of Israel, wandering in the desert, in Numbers 21: 6-9. The exegetes saw in this a link between the serpent on the Tree of Life, the saving faith of the Brazen Serpent on the Tau cross, and Christ on the Roman Cross atoning for our sins. In Chapter 3, verses 14 – 16, St. John the Evangelist writes: "And as Moses lifted up the serpent in the wilderness, even so must the Son of man be lifted up: that whosoever believeth in him should not perish but have eternal life."

But the 'Way of Return' to Kether, opened up for us by the sacrifice of Christ, is by no means a pleasant journey: for the Journey was never intended to be easy, but rather full of hardship; and that, like the phrase 'it is better to travel in hope than to arrive', it is the very journey itself which prepares us to face the conclusion with both Wisdom and Understanding, and makes us fit to pass by the Supernal Sephiroth and into the presence of God.

And now we come to the final, complete diagram of the Tree of Life. You will see that many of the Sephiroth are connected by Paths. It should come as no surprise that

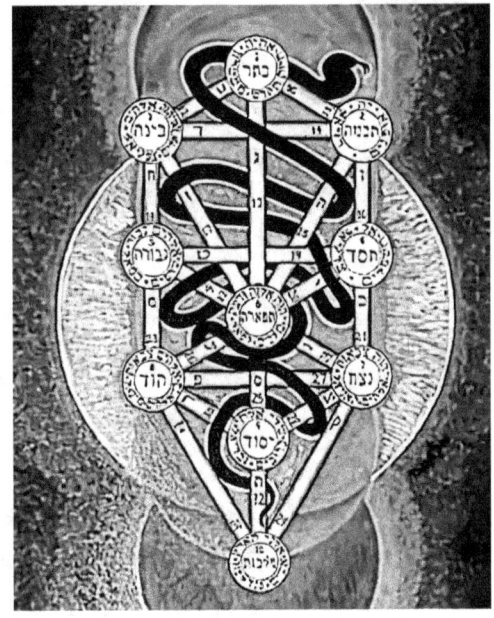

Figure 101: The Way of Return, or Way of the Serpent, from the Golden Dawn tradition.

there are twenty-two: the number of letters in the Hebrew alphabet. Also, for those who wish to read more on this topic later, there are twenty-two cards in the Major Arcana of the Book of Thoth, more commonly referred to at the Tarot. Many esotericists have discovered a close connection between the Paths and the Tarot cards, which for them symbolize the nature of each of these Paths.

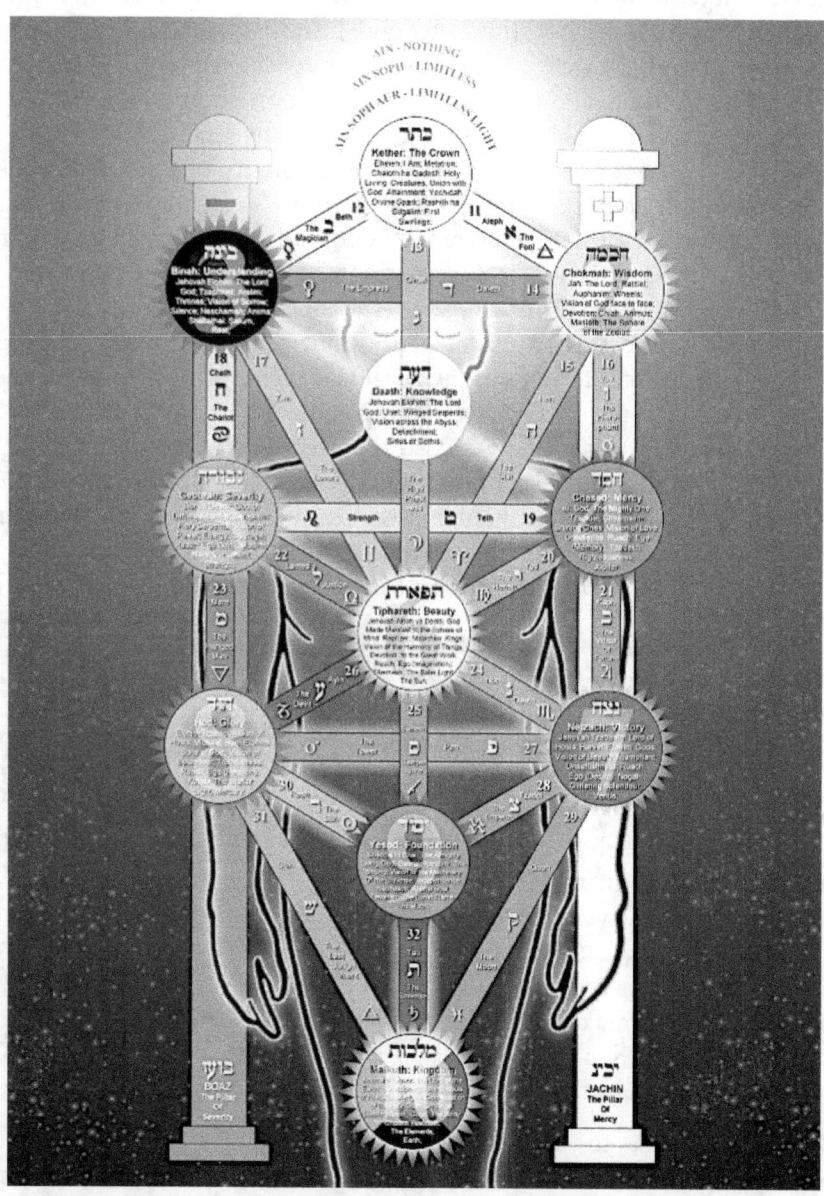

Figure 102: The Tree of Life showing some of its many correspondences
[Image from a purchased copy obtained from WallArtPrints4uUSA, etsy.com]

In one manifestation of the Path of Return, it is necessary for us to traverse each Path, for as God performed His act of Creation through a thunderbolt, condensing the 10 Sephiroth, so it is our duty to understand the interrelationships between the Sephiroth by traversing the Paths on our journey towards reintegration. And if we look at how this journey is to be accomplished, are we really surprised to discover that it assumes the shape of a Serpent, representing that Serpent of Wisdom which we need to acquire on the Path of Return?

As an aside, I also mentioned that the Tree of Life has a practical application. This can both be as a source of meditation and as a filing cabinet for rather more practical endeavors. As a vehicle for meditation, a common technique for experiencing the Tree in a practical sense, and one which we encourage is Pathworking. Visualization techniques such as this can provide a powerful means of exploring the Tree and better understanding ourselves as a result. However, each Sephiroth and Path can carry a multitude of associations which we can also use mnemonically, as it were, to create a practical ceremony based upon them. For example, a Sephira, as well as having a name, and attribute and a color, can be associated with a planet, an archangel, an angel, a planetary intelligence, a Tarot card, a geomantic figure, a rune, a perfume, an animal, a plant, a precious stone: the list goes on and on. From these associations one can create a magical ceremony which utilizes them to a common goal. At the highest, or theurgic level, one might use the associations to attempt communication with an angelic power. At a baser level one might attempt a love spell, for example, by using perfumes and herbs appropriate to Netzach, associated with Venus, and burn a green candle. The drawers of this cabinet are great indeed!

However, on a more appropriate level for our consideration, I would like to introduce two final aspects of the Tree of Life which are rather more relevant to us as seekers after the Rosicrucian mysteries.

The first introduces the symbolism of a sister organization which, while it is not Masonic, harmonizes very well with our Order. This is the Order of the Rosy Cross, or O.R.C. It provides the link we seek with the Christic interpretation of the Tree. If the four lower Sephiroth represent the trials of the Elements, known to us in the Grades of Zelator or Earth, Theoricus or Air, Practicus or Water, and Philosophus or Fire, so Christ had to perfect His human part before He could manifest the spirit. In the O.R.C. the explanation given by

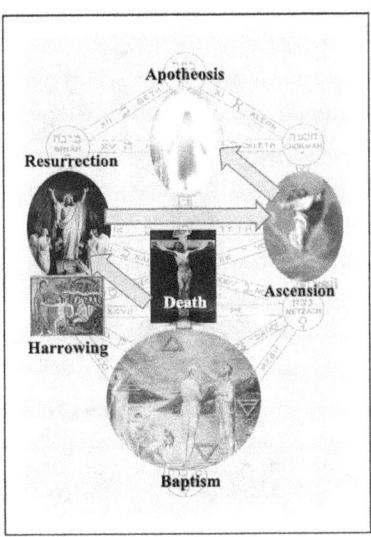

Figure 103: The Life of Christ Projected onto the Tree of Life

the Chaplain for the Trial by Water, similar to our Zelator challenge by the Third Ancient, combines the elements in a sublime manner, explaining the Baptism of Christ, representing the commencement of His ministry as follows:

"What Matthew describes in a mystery concerning the emancipation of the soul from the dross of the material world and all of its associations. Concerning this you should note that the waters from which Christ rises may be understood as a metaphor for the psychic realm. That He stepped from the Earth into Water and arose in Air, culminating in a descent of spiritual Fire in the form of a dove, is very suggestive and should form the basis of an ongoing meditation."

At this point many esoteric systems introduce the emblem for spirit, as a re-creation of bringing the inert body to life. Adam's body was lifeless until breath was introduced into it. This can be seen as the inflation of the body or, to use another symbol, the Hebrew letter Shin (ש), or spirit, which looks remarkably like triple tongues of fire. Thus, Spirit was introduced to the body in order to vivify it. In the image of the Baptism, the four elements come together in Jesus, while the Spirit in the form of a dove – and later seen as tongues of fire at Pentecost – descends. Now this becomes rather Gnostic again, and a number of schools, including that or Cerinthus, believed this was the point at which the Christos entered the man's body, and the ministry of Spirit-Man began. This is the dual being who is destined to be sacrificed, to Die, to be Resurrected and to Ascend, which is the message of the Adept Grades. I will leave it to those who possess these Grades to consider the implication of the Second Order telling us to identify with Christ in His life, sacrifice and ultimate triumph. This we see in his passing through Da'ath on His Ascension, rejoining the Three Supernals to take His rightful place through a mystical process of Apotheosis.

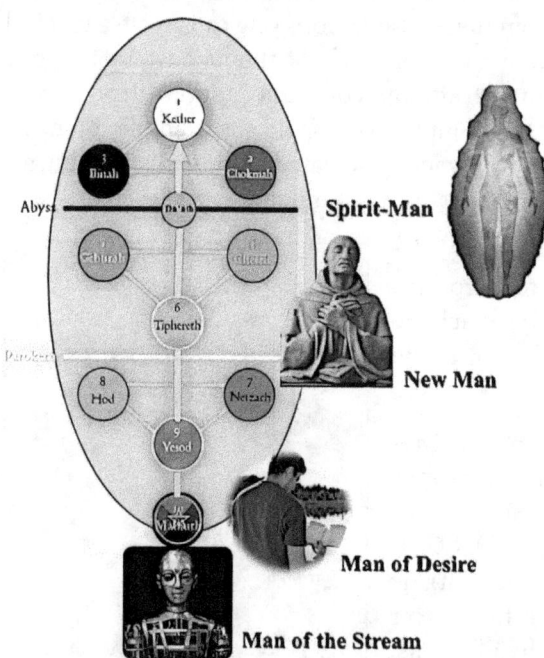

Figure 104: A Martinist Manifestation of the Tree of Life - Saint-Martin's 'Way of the Heart' or 'Cardiac Path'

The Kabbalistic Tree of Life

And Christ was the avatar, the pattern for all mankind. Man, once he has achieved a level of self-understanding, should begin to work on perfecting himself, and himself achieve reintegration with his Source.

This was the essence of the teachings of Martinez de Pasqually, made popular towards the end of the 18th Century by Louis-Claude de Saint-Martin. In his books, he described the original, glorious state of Man, his temptation by evil spirits into a solo act of creation, his fall and his ultimate work to accomplish his own Path of Return. Interestingly, while the fact that his book *Natural Table of the Correspondences Which Exist Between God, Man and Nature* has 22 Chapters, this is not, as some have suggested, because of the Tarot cards of the Major Arcana, but due to the 22 letters of the Hebrew alphabet, and the 22 paths on the Tree of Life, which would certainly have been known to him, especially noting Pasqually's access to the mystical teachings of the Sephardic Jews and the Lurianic Kabbalah.

And so, it is fitting to map Saint-Martin's Cardiac Path, or Way of the Heart, onto the Tree of Life. Saint-Martin referred to the unenlightened man, who was content to live like an automaton, never questioning anything or truly seeing the world around him as the 'Man of the Stream' (Malkuth), passively carried along through what he referred to as the 'Forest of Errors'. It normally takes an external stimulus, a shock or some sort of epiphany to shake him out of his complacency and realize that there is a lot more going on around him than he previously realized. At this stage he has the choice, like Neo in the movie *The Matrix*, to plug himself back in, tune out and go back to his state of vegetable somnambulism; or he can begin to try to make sense of what he now perceives around him. He now becomes a 'Man of Desire' (Yesod). This man will study books, seek teachers, exercise his brain, read the Bible, and try to understand his role in the Universe and his relationship with it and with God. As he does so, he realizes with horror the sad state into which he has fallen, and he will seek a way to raise himself up above the daily misery and strive to seek God. As he works to bring the dross of his form into a more perfect vibration, he aspires to become a 'New Man' (Tiphareth). Finally, seeing the Path of Return and following its direction, he may hope to finally be reinvested with what he has lost, to shed his physical body and be restored to his glorious one, and take once more his original place in the center of God's plans. He will finally have become, once more, the 'Spirit-Man' (Da'ath) he was originally created to be.

And surely this should be the true objective of any seeker after the Light!

This paper has taken us on a fast track through the nature of the 'Tree of Life'. It has introduced us to a lot of the jargon and terms used around the topic of the Kabbalah. It has of necessity left out very considerably more than it includes. For perhaps you are beginning to see, the Tree of Life is an astonishing glyph, reminiscent of the Art of Memory from which our Fellowcraft Lectures comes. It is the ultimate celestial filing cabinet, in whose Spheres one may store many different types of symbols, for example, planets, archangels, angels, herbs, incenses, virtues; and in using the Paths, discover previously unseen connections between them. It is a tool for trying to comprehend the incomprehensible. It is the story of Creation, of the Fall, of the Restoration and every man's personal journey of salvation. It is a manifestation of the Tomb of Christian Rosenkreutz, which if you remember, was a seven-sided vault (the seven lower Sephiroth), illuminated by a 'second sun' (the Three Supernals) and upon the altar was explicitly stated: "This compendium of the universe I made during my lifetime as a tomb for myself." The body was uncorrupted, almost as though it was left as a testament to the fact that Christian Rosenkreutz had been successful in his mission, and had been called forth, like Lazarus, from the tomb, while his body remained to show that he had conquered the burden of original sin and was therefore no longer subject to the laws of putrefaction, having accomplished the Great Work.

Louis-Claude de Saint-Martin

Did He Influence the Scottish Rectified Rite?

Did Louis-Claude de Saint-Martin Influence the Scottish Rectified Rite?

his talk was given on the occasion of my induction into the Society of Blue Friars, a prestigious American Masonic Order which admits Masonic authors of note. Membership is strictly restricted to one a year, so this event represented a highlight of my Masonic career, as you may imagine!

Introduction

In this paper I want to talk about Louis-Claude de Saint-Martin's influence on the Scottish Rectified Rite, sometimes referred to as the Knights Beneficent of the Holy City, developed by Jean-Baptiste Willermoz following the Convent of Wilhelmsbad in 1782.

There isn't time to introduce the whole tableau of French Freemasonry in the 18th Century, and I hope that most of you have some familiarity with the writings of Art de Hoyos, Brent Morris, Josef Wäges and others on the subject. All I can say here is that one of the many Orders founded at that time operated out of Bordeaux under the mastership of Martinez de Pasqually. Called 'The Order of Knight Elus or Elect Cohen of the Universe', it practiced a primitive form of Scottish Rite-type ritual mixed with personal work, which included strict fasting, diets and magical practices. Without going into its purpose in detail, the objective was to initiate communications with the higher realms, in order to understand one's personal path to Redemption. Two of his members were Louis-Claude de Saint-Martin, a minor aristocrat who became his secretary, and Jean-Baptiste Willermoz, a silk merchant and influential Mason from Lyon. Pasqually died shortly thereafter, and the Order quickly fell apart. But the teachings and theology behind the Order were considered so sublime and so important that both Saint-Martin and Willermoz attempted to preserve it: Saint-Martin through a series of books and solitary mystical Christian practice called the Way of the Heart, and Willermoz by embedding them in a Masonic Order he literally hijacked for the purpose, the Rite of Strict Observance. This Rectified version offered so much more than a series of nice plays: it claimed to present a blueprint for Salvation, or 'Reintegration' to use Pasqually's term.

Figure 105: Adhuc Stat - It still stands, it still endures

It is a testament to the Order that, despite the assaults against it from political, religious, and even rival Masonic organizations over the centuries, it has endured – *Adhuc Stat* to use one of its mottos – and is currently expanding across the world, being the fastest-growing forms of Freemasonry in France at the present time.

In another paper I refer to those three extraordinary Frenchmen and Masons who operated at the end of the 18th Century as the 'Magician, the Mystic and the Mason'. Perhaps here I might call them the Prophet, Priest and King, in that it takes the Prophet, Pasqually, to receive the divine inspiration and communication; the Priest, Saint-Martin, to interpret the messages and translate them into comprehensible messages; and finally, the King, Willermoz, to enact them into law. Pasqually provided the teachings, but he was not a good letter-writer or communicator, and it took his secretary, Saint-Martin, who had unlimited access to him to discuss his theology, clarify points, and write down his teachings as best he could. On Pasqually's death, Saint-Martin became the most reliable interpreter of Pasqually's teachings. But while Pasqually based his system predominantly on Judaic teachings, primarily the Talmud and Kabbalah together with other mystical and theurgic currents, Saint-Martin was raised a devout – if unorthodox – Christian who reinterpreted his Master's teachings in a new way. Meanwhile Willermoz, a true businessman and accomplished Mason, was a good organizer, politician and author of ritual. Yet he lacked what might be called that divine spark which would transform a Masonic ritual and raise it up above the morass of adequate historical and symbolic rituals being written throughout France at the time. It was the interactions between Saint-Martin and Willermoz which allowed an accomplished Mason to take a dying Order and rework it into one which went so far beyond being just another system of Degrees and offered the Illuminist of the time a means to transcend the material and seek the Path of Return.

Saint-Martin and the Scottish Rectified Rite

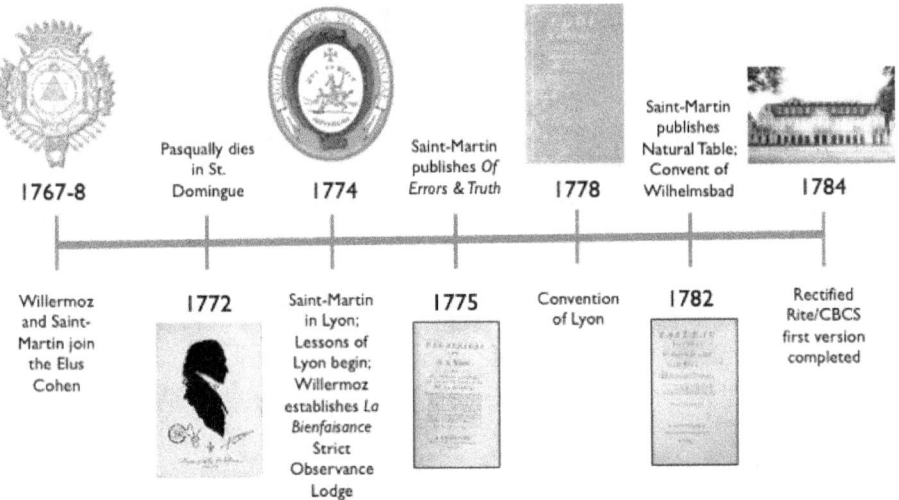

Figure 106: Timeline of key events

All this took place in a very short space of time. In 1768, both Willermoz and Saint-Martin independently joined the Order of Elus Cohen, one in Paris and the other in Bordeaux. Without this common bond neither would have had any reason to meet. In 1774, two years following the death of Pasqually in St. Domingue, Saint-Martin came to stay with Willermoz, and for two years he, Willermoz and Du Roy d'Hauterive met with the other local members of the Elus Cohen Temple while Saint-Martin taught them in a series of sessions which came to be called the Lessons of Lyon; and in 1775 he published his first book, *Of Errors & Truth*, immensely popular among Masons and the thinking classes, but vilified by the Rationalists is attacked. In 1782 he published his second book, *Natural Table*, while Willermoz engineered the Convent of Wilhelmsbad, at which the Rite of Strict Observance was effectively put to sleep and its skeleton used to create a new Rite, the Rectified Rite, which was heavily based on Pasqually's ideas as seen through the lens of Saint-Martin. By 1784 the definitive version of the new Rite had been published. In passing it should be noted that, far from simply tweaking the rituals, Willermoz overhauled them. For example, the Entered Apprentice Grade went from 19 pages to 122 pages, a more than six-fold increase!

Interestingly, for all his involvement with the formation of the Rectified Rite, Saint-Martin was only nominally a Mason, as we can see in his comment to Pasqually: "But Master, is all this truly necessary to know God?" And although he joined the Scottish Rectified Rite at the highest level – that of Grand Profès – in 1785, he asked for his name to be removed from all rolls in 1790, declaring a preference for personal development and growth over communal ritual. Yet we should also remember that, during this period, the symbolism of Freemasonry was certainly not lost on Saint-Martin, who used it to good effect in his early books.

As one example, consider the following extract from towards the end of Chapter 2 in *Natural Table*: "So, by what means could disorder and corruption come to Him (that is, God), seeing that in the Physical Order itself the powers of free and corrupt Beings, as well as all the rights pertaining to their corruption, only extend to secondary objects, and not to their originating Principles? Even the greatest disturbances they can bring to physical Nature cannot alter its fruits and its creations, and can never reach its supporting <u>columns</u>, which can only ever be shaken by the Hand which <u>established</u> them."

Unfortunately, current scholarship seems to fall into one of two camps. Some argue that Saint-Martin had no input whatsoever into the creation of the Rectified Rite Grades, since he was at best an occasional Mason, being far more focused on self-development and the solitary Cardiac Path for which he is most famous. Others make the case that he was very influential through his friendship with Willermoz, his regular visits to Lyon and stays at his home. However, little or no evidence is usually provided, and this area seems to have been left unexplored in any detail.

In the short time we have to explore this subject, I want to focus on three areas where I feel there is strong evidence to demonstrate Saint-Martin's influence over Willermoz' thinking as he developed the Rectified Rite rituals from the framework of the Strict Observance. These areas are Alchemy, Christianity, and his very public – if covert – statement of respect for Saint-Martin in his rituals.

Alchemy

Willermoz' "Instruction on the Antiquity and Purpose of Freemasonry" ends with an extraordinary injunction: "Admitted from this day into these Assemblies, my Dear Brother, you will hear the observations and research undertaken by your Brothers... But we should first warn you ... that initiations and Freemasonry have often been altered and corrupted by different Nations and in different ages; and that in many ways they have been perverted. That is what has induced them to warn you that you should be suspicious of those ... who apply the symbols of Freemasonry to the fruitless and illusory science of the Alchemists."

This reflects the teachings of Saint-Martin in Chapter 10 of his book *Natural Table*, in which he berates 'Hermetic Philosophers'. It is evident that he equates them with the Alchemists, as he says: "The purpose of the Hermetic Art, the one most widely known, never raises itself above matter. It is ordinarily confined to two objectives: the acquisition of wealth and the preservation and curing of disease which, in the minds of its disciples, removes all boundaries to man's desires and powers, and allow them to hope for jolly days of indefinite duration." Interestingly this is the only group he attacks in his early books other than his regular assaults on the 'Observers' or Rationalists.

Saint-Martin and the Scottish Rectified Rite

This seems to be a very specific attack, and quite out of keeping with the Illuminist tendencies of Willermoz and Saint-Martin. Indeed, Willermoz' brother, Dr. Pierre-Jacques Willermoz was a physician and chemist; and an alchemist who had studied in Marseilles, which was well-known at that time – as now – as a center of alchemical study. Willermoz wrote a number of alchemical-based rituals for his Masonic group in Lyon.

For example, the Rite of Knight of the Black Eagle Rose Croix includes a Lecture providing a description of the Alkahest as the *materia prima*, a spirit drawn from the four Elements extracted from the three Realms, being Animal, Vegetable and Mineral; and a Catechism which includes references to the 12 zodiacal signs, together with the 12 associated names of God and the Angels, the 7 Planets and their associated metals, and a number of sigils.

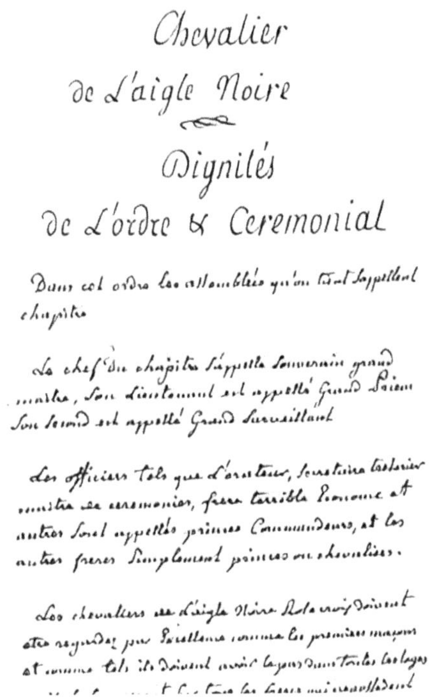

What makes Saint-Martin's – and therefore Willermoz' – dismissive attitude towards Alchemists in 1782 interesting, is that as recently as 1775, in *Of Errors and Truth*, he had little to say against them, and indeed according to Papus was himself an experimenter in alchemy in his earlier years. So why would a practitioner of alchemy come to be so hostile to it, and why would this attitude be taken up by Willermoz in his Rectified Rite?

Figure 107: Manuscript page in Willermoz' handwriting from Black Eagle Rose Croix

It appears that they weren't so much against Alchemy itself, but rather those charlatans who claimed to make gold from base material and to prolong life through expensive elixirs.

Instead, they adhered to the vision of the Rosicrucians, that alchemy should be seen and practiced through the lens of Spiritual Alchemy, and that it should be applied to man's process of spiritualization and reintegration rather than to make a quick buck and prolong life on a planet we should be doing everything in our power to leave. We can see this in the fact that Saint-Martin refers to the 'Great Work' only twice in passing in *Of Errors and Truth*; but by 1782 in *Natural Table* – published the same year as the Convent of Wilhelmsbad when Willermoz began work on the Rectified Rite – the term is used no less than twenty times. Saint-Martin may have given up practical alchemy, but he was still very enamored with its spiritual symbolism as an allegory for man's fall and his upward journey back to the Prime Cause; and Willermoz likewise incorporated this journey into his rites.

Figure 108: Saint-Martin's relationship with Willermoz?

Unfortunately, the subtlety of Saint-Martin's use of the term 'Hermetic Philosophers' to describe practitioners of physical alchemy appears to have been lost on Willermoz, who used the term 'Alchemists' in his warning to new Knights of the Holy City. Even so, Saint-Martin still had to caution his Brother Willermoz strongly against joining Dom Pernety's newly-minted Illuminés d'Avignon two years later in 1784, which based its alchemy on Masonic symbols: Strength being associated with black matter and Putrefaction, Wisdom with white matter and Purification, and Beauty with red matter and Perfection. I apologize for using a very modern image, but I often see the relationship between Saint-Martin and Willermoz as being something like the 'distracted boyfriend' meme!

Let us now turn our attention to Saint-Martin's unique Christian symbolism in the rituals.

Unique Christian perspective

We must remember that, while Willermoz was more traditionally Christian than Saint-Martin, the Rationalist legacy of distrust of established Religion was all-pervasive, and Pasqually's theosophy was far from orthodox. Despite the Christianization of his Master's heavily Judaeo-Mystical teachings, Saint-Martin's first book spent some time on the *Index Librorum Prohibitorum*, or list of books proscribed by the Catholic Church.

As Papus eloquently put it: "Willermozism, like Martinezism and Martinism, had always been exclusively Christian, but had never been clerical, and for good reason. It rendered unto Caesar that which was Caesar's and unto Christ that which was Christ's; but it didn't sell Christ to Caesar." Saint-Martin himself said: "It is truly the hypocrisy and ignorance of the priests which is one of the principal causes of the evil which has afflicted Europe for many centuries up to this day. I don't include the claimed transmission of the Church of Rome which, in my opinion, never transmitted anything as a Church, although some of its members could sometimes transmit it, either because of their personal virtue, or by the faith of their flock, or through a particular will to do good."

So, we shouldn't look to the rituals of the Rectified Rite to bolster traditional Catholic values, but rather to replace them with a unique theology which harkened back to the earliest times of Christianity. Joseph de Maistre tells us: "In the first place I am not saying that all Illuminists are Freemasons. I'm only saying that all those I have known, in France in particular, were. Their fundamental dogma was that Christianity, such as we know it today, is really like a veritable *Blue Lodge* created for regular men; but that the *Man of Desire* must raise himself from Grade to Grade up to the sublime knowledge such as the original Christians possessed, who were the true initiates."

Roger Dachez reminds us that in the Associate Grade the candidate is subjected to the Trial by the Elements, a not uncommon part of Illuminist rituals of the time, although in the original Strict Observance the only element used is fire, and that as a dramatic punctuation to the removal of the hoodwink. But the interesting point is that in the Rectified Rite only three Elements are used: Air is missing. This notion from Pasqually's *Treatise* that all things are bound in threes was taken up by Saint-Martin: in his three Elements and his belief that each of these was founded upon a combination of Salt, Sulfur and Mercury; and his explanation of this in the *Lessons of Lyon* clearly led directly to Willermoz including only three Elements in his First Grade without explanation or apology, yet implying that it was from these three Elements alone that physical man and the physical Universe had been created.

As another example of Christian and Masonic symbolism being reinterpreted, consider the popular high grade theme of the time which was centered around the Babylonian captivity, Zerubbabel, and the rebuilding of the City and Temple at Jerusalem.

In *Natural Table* Saint-Martin, linking the symbol of chains to the ideas of the Rationalist philosophers, says: "It is however in the heart of this privation that careless men let themselves conceive ideas which are so hazardous to their nature, and build blind systems upon the chains which we retain in our slavery; even persuading us that by suicide we can break them."

In his commentary on the Rectified Rite's origins and symbolism, Yves Saez focuses our attention on the imagery of bondage, and once again chains. In the Entered Apprentice Grade the Master says to the Candidate: "The man who wishes to find (truth) must break the chains which bind him, dismiss the illusions which deceive him, and conquer all obstacles with courage." Now this agrees with Saint-Martin's comment in the conclusion of his book *Of Errors and Truth*: "Is there a state more burdensome and at the same time more humiliating, than to be relegated to a Realm where man, chained in spite of himself to a body which possesses nothing more than any of Nature's other creations, drags around a Being with which he cannot even converse?" Yves Saez continues: "It is the need to 'break the chains' which the Candidate hears in the first moments of his entry into the Order. In the last symbolic Grade, the Green Grade of Scottish Master of St. Andrew, the Master of the Lodge instructs the Warden receiving the Candidate to '*Remove those chains!*'" And remember that the chains are triangular – symbol of the three – not four – elements introduced by Pasqually and discussed in great detailed by Saint-Martin in his early books.

Figure 109: Tracing Board depicting Hiram rising

The breaking of chains also accords with the transition from the Old to the New Testament, and the symbolism is compounded by the breaking of the chains of death, as seen in Hiram's resurrection, and the abrogation of the Old Law with the New Law of Love. Now, it is also important to note the emphasis on the resurrection of Hiram, who is after all a symbol of the Repairer – that is to say, the Christ – in those rituals.

It must have been quite a shock for those who joined both the Strict Observance and the Rectified Rite as experienced Masons to see the Tracing Board in the Grade of Scottish Master depicting Hiram Abif rising from the dead. For von Hund this represented the rebirth of the Order of the Temple; but to Willermoz it meant so much more, not least the beginning of our journey as Men of Desire. For Willermoz was adept at reusing the symbols of the Strict Observance to teach far more profound lessons. Here it represented the beginning the transition from the Old Testament to a series of images which ended with a Lion (the Lion of Judah?) toying aimlessly with Masonic instruments beneath a cliff, as if implying that from now onwards on the path, Freemasonry could no longer provide the answers, while the motto 'Meliora Præsumo' or 'I hope for better things', emphasized this transition into a new world of St. Andrew, the Holy City and Reintegration. If Saint-Martin was the major contributor to the Lessons of Lyon, and if he was able to fill in at least some of the gaps in

Figure 110: Meliora Præsumo

the instructions and the overall system which had so frustrated Willermoz, not least because their Master had now been dead for two years, would it be surprising that it was the vision of Saint-Martin which the religiously Christian Willermoz used to flesh out the Strict Observance rituals? After all, as Pasqually's secretary, Saint-Martin had constant access to a Master who wrote little and communicated less. It is only natural that Willermoz would rely on Saint-Martin to interpret Pasqually's teachings, and then incorporate them into his new Rectified Rite.

Respect for Erudition

In the 'Form of General Duties', given by the Dean in the C.B.C.S., these are expanded by several paragraphs specific to the Candidate's profession, be it that of a priest, farmer, businessman, soldier or man of letters. The duties imposed upon a Scholarly Knight closely reflect Saint-Martin's life and reflect the deep respect in which he was held by Willermoz. Keeping in mind that Saint-Martin was a man of unimpeachable reputation and high moral standards, well-respected, a notable author and mystic who believed strongly in education, and a man who was not afraid to take on the prevailing philosophical and scientific opinions of the time head-on, we should interpret the following paragraphs are being nothing less than a hagiography of Saint-Martin:

Figure 111: Image of Louis-Claude de Saint-Martin

1. The man of letters has more extensive connections with society: through his writings he communicates with all Nations. The Knight of this class should devote his efforts to seeking out truth, and his writings should encourage a love for virtue and lead men to the public good.

2. His writings should never express apology or indulgence for the corruption of the morals of his age. He should never soil his pen with licentious works or indulge those shameful vices which trouble the wellbeing of society with bass flattery. On the contrary, in his writings he should inspire a love of virtue and make use of his talents to extol good works.

3. He should seek the rights, duties and needs of man with courage, in his writings he should employ frequent objections to weaken the influence of prejudice which he should as soon uproot as overthrow. A zealous defender of truth, he should never fear making it public.

4. Above all he should concern himself with public and individual education, using all his powers to contribute to the care given by the Order to procure this inestimable gift for our youth, both physically and morally. If he cannot undertake this himself, he should use his words to enlighten those charged with this duty, providing them with the means, and encouraging with his counsel and his finances those whose talents should be developed. Finally, he should devote himself to the wellbeing of mankind, and above all to cultivating that portion of human knowledge which is most important: in a word, *to be a Christian philosopher*.

Conclusion

The 18th Century was one of upheaval, as philosophers moved away from religious dogma and found themselves questioning everything, from man's origin, how the world worked, how thoughts were transmitted, and even the need for a God. Most importantly, the new scientific approach had moved the current mindset from belief to empiricism, resulting in the ultimate statement of Helvetius, who proposed that man is a 'tabula rasa' or 'blank slate' upon which physical experience alone could write the individual's personality; while the Rationalists believed man could envisage everything within his mind, without resort to an external power – or even with reference to history. However, while most were carried along with this new tide, there were those who chose to swim against it, not because they blindly continued to follow Church dogma or old superstitions, but rather because they believed this new movement was in danger of discarding millennia of experiences and even observable data in support of an external Principle, and the operation of invisible forces. This is perhaps why Saint-Martin disparagingly called Rationalists 'Observers', in that they admitted to no inner experience, and were therefore reduced to merely obtaining all their information by means of their senses, unaffected by any inner impulsion or higher – and external – inspiration. He himself informs us that he was inspired to write a pamphlet when he became indignant after Boulanger wrote "that religions only came about as a result of fear occasioned by catastrophes of Nature." He read his pamphlet to the little group which met at Willermoz' house, and they encouraged him to write a complete book, *Of Errors & Truth*, disparaged by one Rationalist as being "the Koran of the Masons", thereby vilifying its content while grudgingly respecting its immense popularity.

If Willermoz had an ultimate purpose, perhaps it was to unite all of Continental Freemasonry into one Order which overtly practiced Illuminism, as a bulwark against the rising tide of Rationalism which brought with it a denial of thousands of years of philosophy, belief and practice. And what better body to attempt this than an Order which saw itself as the custodian of the earliest Mystery Schools, including Pre-Nicene Christianity? But while Willermoz was an accomplished Mason and adept at writing rituals, who had identified the Rite of Strict Observance as a stable vehicle in which to preserve his Master's teachings and to centralize anti-Rationalist forces, he lacked a deep appreciation for the nuances and overall vision of Pasqually, perhaps because he was so devout a traditional Christian, and perhaps because he lacked so much word-of-mouth instruction which only a personal assistant and companion to Pasqually could provide. Thus, through correspondence and particularly during the many times that Saint-Martin stayed in Lyon, their conversations and Saint-Martin's instructions to the members of the Elus Cohen, shaped his approach towards the content and the ultimate purpose of his Rectified Rite.

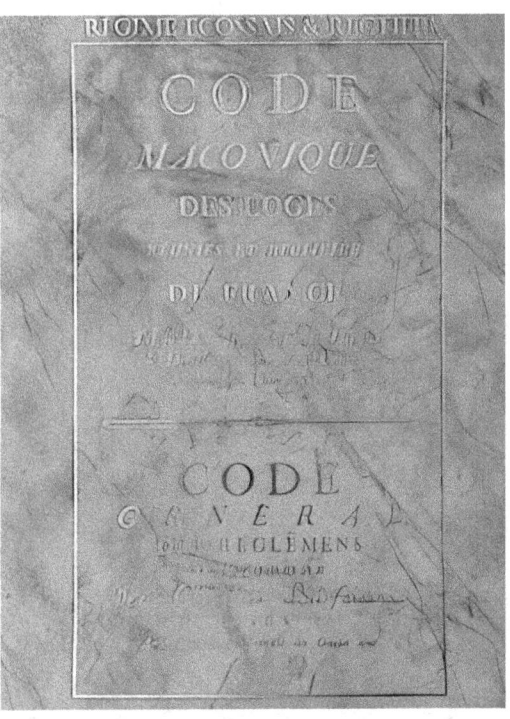

Figure 112: Willermoz' General & Masonic Code for Rectified Lodges

We will end this short paper with a quote from the 1928 book by the respected Masonic scholar René Le Forestier:

"But if the flirtation Écossais Freemasonry had with mysticism and occultism was not altogether central, it no less defines the role it played in the customs of all Freemasonry in the 18th Century. Lodges became the refuge of "men of desire"…if it is certain that many Brothers only knew the "High Sciences" by name, or through the more or less clear allusions within the rituals, and that they never considered studying them seriously, it is no less true that all the contemporary Occultists, whatever their nationality wore the symbolic apron, and that all the esoteric groups attracted their largest numbers of recruits from among the Masons, to whom they advertised themselves as the representatives of the true Masonic tradition and the custodians of its ultimate secret.

"Thus, Masonry shows us the other side of the façade by which we are accustomed to viewing the evolution of the 18th Century. Upon this scene flooded with light, before a room full of enthusiastic spectators, the first role-models of the new "philosophy" collected unanimous 'bravos'…

Figure 113: Behind the scenes…

"But if answering to the appeal which Écossais Masonry makes to us from behind the façade, we pass behind the scenes, and in the shadows, we perceive a completely new world. There we make out alchemists and theurgists, visionaries and casters of horoscopes, ecstatics and exorcists… If the mystique of feeling and imagination had to abandon the *public* battle against the mystique of reason, it never saw itself as completely vanquished, and its obstinate resistance earned it success which, while usually unknown, was no less important.

"From a completely different point of view, it took a path contrary to the ideas of the time. While… Rationalism claimed to be …following a method which could be called democratic… addressing themselves to the common man… (and) to give their doctrines the widest publicity (through) dialogues and philosophical debates, public letters, pamphlets, humorous or academic works, articles in dictionaries, all serving to work towards vulgarization; Masonry, on the other hand, distinguished between initiates and the profane. It worked to create an elite and measured out its revelations. It inspired itself with the idea that all men aren't indistinctly capable of extracting the most beneficent part of truth, and that the best endowed would themselves be dazzled by a light presented too quickly to eyes which till then had been covered with a blindfold…"

This is why I believe it took a mystic, Louis-Claude de Saint-Martin, with a unique insight into the issues of an established Church, the teachings of a Master steeped in gnostic knowledge, and the conviction to stand up against the currents of his time to ensure that the sublime teachings of Pasqually were worthily transmitted by Willermoz in his Rectified Rite, even if he personally believed that such a transmission should be conducted on a personal, rather than a Fraternal basis.

As a final personal aside, the motto and device of the Order is a phenix rising from the flames, with the words 'Perit ut vivat', or 'He dies in order that he may live'. When I attended School House in Brighton College as a school border, founded in the 1840s, the house had burned down a decade earlier and when it was rebuilt, the motto 'Ex igne resurgo', or 'I rise from the flames', was carved into the lintel above a main door. For some six years I passed under that lintel several times a day. Was that a harbinger of my unwavering interest in this Order…?

The Degrees of the Black Eagle Rose-Croix

Three Grades of the Aigle-Noir Rose-Croix

The Degrees of the Black Eagle Rose-Croix

veryone is aware of the great importance I attribute to education in a Mason's career, and recently the Northern Masonic Jurisdiction of the Scottish Rite has contributed magnificently to the cause. They have established a course called the 'Hauts Grades', which is freely available to all Scottish Rite Masons. This course takes a look at all the degrees of the system, from the 4th to the 32nd, before allowing the participant to focus in on several of them for a more in-depth analysis. The third level calls upon the participant to write a significant essay in academic format, which explores a hitherto unexplored area of the Scottish Rite. This truly creates a win-win situation, in that the participant learns how to examine and critique sources and develop a coherent argument; while the Scottish Rite opens up an ongoing source of new scholarship.

This paper gave them a challenge! While not strictly speaking a paper on the Scottish Rite grades, it was sufficiently allied to the Rite to allow it to be accepted. However, since it is a first translation of the Rite into English, it took them some time to find someone qualified enough to be able to mark it! I present it here as the final paper in this book, both as an academic conclusion to the papers, and as a resource for future scholars studying early French Masonic ritual.

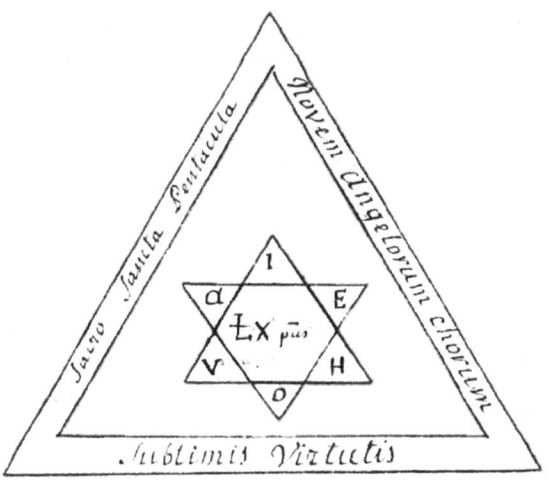

Figure 114: Image from Manuscript

Introduction

This paper explores one of the lesser-known creations of Jean-Baptiste Willermoz, the three grades of the Aigle-Noir Rose-Croix, or 'Black Eagle Rose Croix'. Heavily alchemical, and written for his younger brother, Pierre-Jacques, this was the last system written by Willermoz before his introduction to Martinèz de Pasqually and his subsequent involvement in the Order of Elus Cohen, and later his signal work on the development of the Scottish Rectified Rite.

The paper contains the first English translation of these rituals directly from Willermoz' own handwriting. It explores their possible origin and links to the almost identical ritual of Baron von Tschoudy. It also reviews some of the symbolism in the rituals and their place in the overall Lyon system of Grades, prior to the introduction of the Cohen Temple and subsequently the Rite of Strict Observance into Lyon. However, given the focus on Willermoz' rituals, it does not follow the development of the Grades after 1763, except to note the existence of some later variants.

Willermoz is mainly known for his work engineering the Convent of Gaules in 1778 and the Convent of Wilhelmsbad in 1782. This paper attempts to redress this emphasis by reminding the reader that Willermoz was both a prolific and an inspired ritualist, and considers some the themes in this early ritual which explain his lifelong interest in the spiritual side of Freemasonry, and his search for a path which would lead to a greater understanding of early Christianity and union with God

Jean-Baptiste Willermoz and the Historical Context of the Grades

Jean-Baptiste Willermoz was born on July 10th, 1730, to a moderately wealthy family in Saint-Claude, France. At the age of fifteen he moved to Lyon with his mother, remaining there for the rest of his life. He was apprenticed into the silk trade, and excelled in the business, becoming a silk trader for the rest of his life.[18] He had thirteen siblings, the most well-known of whom are the eldest child, Claudine-Thérèse (born 1729), who showed a great interest in Jean-Baptiste's spiritual pursuits; Dr. Pierre-Jacques (born 1735), who spent much of his youth studying alchemy in Marseille, Berlin and elsewhere, and who was guillotined following the Siege of Lyon during the French Revolution; and Antoine (born 1741), who was also a member of many of Jean-Baptiste's Lodges.

In 1750 Jean-Baptiste became a Freemason at the age of twenty, though we don't know in which Lodge. He rapidly rose through the ranks and became Master shortly thereafter. However, his initial impression of Freemasonry was not overwhelming. He wrote disdainfully that he soon became disgusted with

---

[18] Alice Joly, *Un Mystique Lyonnais et les Sécrets de la Franc-maçonnèrie*, (Éd. Maçon, Paris 1938), p. 2.

the frivolity and indiscipline which reigned in Freemasonry, and that, had it not been for the special care the Venerable Master took of him, he would probably have left then and there.[19] However, this may have been rather exaggerated: we know that joining the local Lodge was a shrewd business move on his part, since he was able to make new contacts and rub shoulders with the local aristocracy: something he craved and enjoyed throughout his life. However, even then we see an early longing for something more in life, a theme which was to direct his steps – and his friendships – throughout his many years. He and his family were devout Catholics, yet apparently even this wasn't sufficient for him. Indeed, in 1782, at the time he was putting the finishing touches to the famous Convent of Wilhelmsbad, he categorized alchemical Masons into three types, one of which was those who seek the knowledge of the 'Great Work', in which man would rediscover the wisdom and operations of early Christianity.[20]

His initial disappointment with Masonry might also explain why, early on, he founded his own lodges, filled them with like-minded friends, and embarked upon a career of writing Masonic Rituals. Dr. Gérard Encausse ('Papus') tells us that "In 1760 a first selection was made, and all the members appointed to the grade of Master have constituted a Grand Lodge of Masters of Lyon, with Willermoz as Grand Master. In 1765[21], a new selection was made, which saw the creation of a Chapter of Knights of the Black Eagle, placed under the management of Dr. Pierre-Jacques Willermoz, his younger brother."[22] Indeed, the eminent English Masonic scholar A.C.F. Jackson claimed that "the Rose-Croix degree was developed by a Frenchman, Jean-Baptiste Willermoz, a leading local mason."[23] He states that Willermoz included this ritual in a collection he was writing in 1761. This is only one year later than the earliest known example of this ritual

Prior to 1763, the year it is claimed that Willermoz began using the Grades of Black Eagle Rose Croix, he had assembled a series of Grades beyond the first three Blue Lodge Degrees, which are commonly called the 'High Grades'. These have luckily been preserved (this is indeed fortunate, since during the siege of

---

[19] Alice Joly, *Ibid.*, p. 3.

[20] Jean-Pierre Bayard, *Le symbolism maçonnique traditional: Tome 2*, (Éd. Maçonnique de France, 1981), pp. 245 – 248.

[21] However, despite the fact that Willermoz himself dated the founding of his Chapter from 1765, Alice Joy states that the Chapter already existed in 1763, citing the *Coste Manuscript* Nº 453, folio 97, V, dated December 10, 1763, in the Bibilothèque Municipal Lyonnais (Alice Joly, *Un Mystique Lyonnais*, p. 14).

[22] 'En 1760, une première selection avait été opérée et tous les members pourvus du grade de Maître avaient constituéune Grand Loge des Maîtres de Lyon avec Willermoz comme Grand Maître. En 1765, une nouvelle sélection fut opérée par la création d'un Chapitre des Chevaliers de l'Aigle Noir, placésous la direction du Dr. Jacques Willermoz, frère cadet du precedent.' Papus, *Martinèsisme, Willermosisme, Martinisme et France-Maçonnerie*, Chamuile, Paris, 1899, 13. Also, English version trans. Piers Vaughan (Rose Circle Publications, 2020), p. 21.

[23] Brig. A. C. F. Jackson, *Rose Croix, the History of the Ancient and Accepted Rite of England and Wales*, Lewis Masonic, 1980, p. 25.

Lyon in 1793, as the Lodge met in a building outside the city walls, Willermoz was forced to undertake a hazardous journey with a servant under cover of darkness to rescue as many of the Lodge rituals and archives as they could carry. Others were destroyed in the bombardment of the city by the Revolutionary Forces, so the remaining rituals, instructions and correspondence are indeed precious). The rituals comprising this series are listed as Fonds Willermoz Ms. 5457 in the Bibliothèque Municipal de Lyon, in the Part-Dieu building, as follows:

1. Apprentice
2. Companion
3. Master
4. Scottish Trinitarian – Apprentice, Companion, Master
5. Grand & Perfect Architect – Apprentice
6. Grand & Perfect Architect – Companion
7. Grand & Perfect Architect – Master
8. Perfect Architect
9. Founder or Sacrificer
10. Sovereign Commander of the Temple
11. Grand Elect Knight Templar
12. Elect Knight of Rose-Croix
13. Knight of the Sun
14. Black Eagle Rose Croix Apprentice / Knight
15. Black Eagle Rose Croix Companion / Commander
16. Black Eagle Rose Croix Master / Bailiff

However, Le Forestier suggests that the majority of these Grades were never worked (to begin with, as most of them required very elaborate costumes, props and *mises en scène*). He suggests that Candidates for the Black Eagle Rose Croix were handed folders containing the prior grades in order to familiarize themselves with them prior to receiving the *ne plus ultra*.[24] We should remember that Willermoz only invited close friends into the Order, so we may imagine these grades were nevertheless discussed in detail in order to extract the most important lessons from them. Indeed, we know that Willermoz invited Louis-Claude de Saint-Martin to stay as a house guest when he first visited Lyon, and that it was as a result of Saint-Martin reading some of his written thoughts about the problems with the Enlightenment that led to the masons assembled there encouraging him to write his first book, *Des Erreurs et de la Verité* ('Of Errors & Truth').[25] This was during the time that he and Roy d'Hauterive were instructing the Brothers of the Cohen Lodge in Lyon on the Elus Cohen.[26] Both are examples of how closely knit the circle of Initiés in Lyon was, and how they met frequently to discuss the intricacies of ritual and teaching at Willermoz' house.

What is particularly remarkable is the fact that J.-B. Willermoz selected an alchemical theme for the three highest grades in his overall system. While it is clear that he had a great fondness for his younger brother, Pierre-Jacques, this didn't extend to funding his alchemical adventures into foreign parts, and his pleas for money to fund a trip to Germany fell on deaf ears, Pierre-Jacques having to accept the protection

---

[24] René Le Forestier, *La Franc-maçonnerie templière et occultiste*, 2nd Ed. (Archè, Milan 2003), p. 282.
[25] A.E. Waite, *Saint-Martin the French Mystic*, (Rider & Con London, 1922), p. 38.
[26] Gilbert Tappa, *Instructions pour les Élus Cohens*, (Les Feuillets d'Hermopolis, Vol 2, Nice, 2000), p. 4.

of a person believed to be the monk and later alchemist Dom Pernety, in Berlin.[27] Yet Jean-Baptiste created a series of alchemical grades and put his brother in charge of them. Further, both Jean-Baptiste and his friend Louis-Claude de Saint-Martin, the 'Unknown Philosopher', both later expressed a distaste for alchemy and its practitioners, whom they referred to as 'Adepts' or 'Hermetic Philosophers'.

For example, in his Secret Instruction to the Profès in his monumental Scottish Rectified Rite system, in the seventh so-called 'Secret' Grade, he says: "Moreover, all that the most obstinate Alchemist, and the best versed in his Art can hope to obtain by his perseverance, is to penetrate only into the most elementary Principles of the corporeal entities submitted to his manipulations".[28] And in *Tableau Naturel*, Saint-Martin says: "The purpose of the Hermetic Art, the one most widely known, never raises itself above matter. It is ordinarily confined to two objectives: the acquisition of wealth; and preservation, and the curing of disease which, in the minds of its disciples, removes all boundaries to man's desires and powers, and allows him to hope for jolly days of indefinite duration."[29]

Nevertheless, it is important to point out that Saint-Martin uses the term 'Great Work', the goal of the alchemist, no less than twenty times in the same book! Earlier we saw that Willermoz also divided Masons interested into alchemy into

Figure 115: Examples of fonds Willermoz Manuscript covers

---

[27] Alice Joly, *Un Mystique Lyonnais*, p. 13.
[28] Paul Vulliaud, *Joseph de Maistre, Franc-Maçon*, 2nd Ed. (Archè, 1990 – orig. 1926), p. 246.
[29] Louis-Claude de Saint-Martin, *Tableau Naturel des rapports qui existent entre Dieu, l'homme et l'universe* (orig. 1782; English trans. by Piers Vaughan, Rose Circle Publications, 2018), p. 132.

three groups. While we mentioned the third category, the other two were: those who sought to make the Philosopher's Stone, and those who sought the panacea. In other words, to Willermoz the first two categories were mere 'puffers', while the third sought the inner work which leads to an understanding of the aims and wisdom of primitive Christianity. The phrase which both Willermoz and Saint-Martin were seeking is 'spiritual alchemy'; that work upon oneself which transforms the person, in Saint-Martin and Martinèz de Pasqually's – his Master's – words, from a 'Man of the Stream' into a 'Man of Desire', whether the path be through a spiritual Christian mysticism, or by the more robust path of active theurgy, which was more enthusiastically followed by Pasqually and Willermoz.

A short time later, Willermoz went on to seek a Charter to establish Baron von Hund's Rite of Strict Observance in Lyon, which he accomplished in 1774. Within four years he was revising and transforming the Rite into one which again contained the practical Spiritual Alchemy for which he yearned, by adding two 'secret' grades to the structure: that of Profès and Grand Profès, two grades which contained lectures paraphrasing the theosophical teachings of Martinès de Pasqually. By 1782 he had engineered the Convent of Wilhelmsbad, which saw both the birth of the Scottish Rectified Rite, or Chevaliers Bienfaisants de la Cité Sainte (C.B.C.S.) – 'Knights Beneficent of the Holy City' – a form of spiritual knighthood whose rituals, far from being a simple set of plays, claimed to provide a road map to Salvation. The Grand Plan was to come to a screeching halt due to the French Revolution which exploded onto the scene only a few years later.

Since Willermoz is mostly remembered for his participation in the now almost legendary Order of Elus Cohen and for his immense work on the Scottish Rectified Rite, which spanned several decades and occupied much of the remainder of his extraordinarily long life (he lived to the age of 94 and survived the Revolution, which his beloved Brother didn't), scholars have for the most part ignored or rushed through his earlier life. His earlier rituals remain curiosities for the most part. I reviewed the entire fifty-year Index of *Renaissance Traditionelle*, a highly regarded French quarterly magazine publish under the aegis of the *Institut Maçonnique de France,* and which focuses exclusively on this period in French masonic history, and found not a single reference to the Aigle Noir Rose Croix grades!

Having given some background – and while the rest of Willermoz' life and deeds have filled many books that is not part of this paper – we will now look in more detail at the rituals themselves.

Symbols Used in the Grades

Appendices D, E and F contain the English translations of the Apprentice or Knight, Companion or Commander, and Master or Bailiff grades respectively.[30] These have been included as the first instance that these grades are available in full in English, and as such are included in their entirety for future reference by any who wish to study them further and in more detail.

At this time, we will focus only on a few points in the rituals themselves, before comparing them to a contemporary ritual made available for Baron von Tschoudy in the next section, in order to attempt to determine the order in which these rituals appeared, and some of the key differences between them.

The symbolic content of the three grades clearly draws heavily from alchemical symbolism. However, there is a distinctly spiritual angle to their use in the rituals. It is quite clear that the symbolism would have come from Pierre-Jacques Willermoz – after all, he was the alchemist in the family, and he was put in charge of the Grades once they had been written. Nevertheless, the spiritual element was more likely Jean-Baptiste, and there is no denying that the rituals are in his handwriting. Therefore, he would have had editorial control over their contents. Nevertheless, if the Chapter which presided over all the other Masonic grades he wrote, and which was populated by family members and close friends, was his main Masonic outlet between 1763 and 1767, when he first met Pasqually and was initiated into the Elus Cohen in Versailles, we must believe that he was an active participant in these grades, particularly since he had not sought reappointment as Grand Master of the Grand Loge de Lyon in 1763 (thought he remained Guardian of the Seals and Archives until 1774).[31]

The content of the grades also reflects Willermoz' lifelong search for the 'true' secrets contained in Masonry. Here he searched in the ancient alchemical texts for an indication of these secrets, before being seduced by the theurgy of Pasqually and the Elus Cohen. Following this, he continued his search in the Strict Observance, and when he discovered there were no secret grades, he invented his own, and inserted them into the system at the Convent de Gaules. The Secret Instruction taught that there were secrets which went back to the beginning of time and the creation of Adam, which had been restored when Jesus (known to Martinists – or followers of Pasqually and Saint-Martin as the 'Repairer') had assumed human form and come to earth, and which he mentioned in his third category of alchemically-inclined Freemasons.

So, we are perhaps seeing the first fruits of Willermoz' search for real meaning in Masonic rituals, following his initial disappointment with the system and its members.

---

[30] These rituals, in J.-B. Willermoz' handwriting, were copied at the Bibliothèque Municipal de Lyon from the *Fonds Willermoz*, Manuscript 5457, Documents 14 – 16, and translated by the author.
[31] Le Forestier, *Franc-Maçonnerie*, p. 280.

However, we cannot completely rule out another motive. There was no doubt that Willermoz much enjoyed rubbing shoulders with the great and the good, and it was no coincidence that he engineered himself into a position where he was in regular communication with many of the aristocrats of Europe of the time (a trait also seen in the otherwise humble Saint-Martin). And the best way to engage a person is by letting them know you possess a 'secret', which is only to be shared with a very rare kind of mason, and that they have been selected to join! After all, it was a very successful approach for Weishaupt's Illuminati who were expanding across Germany and Austria at the time. Bearing both these points in mind, we will now look at the overall layout of the grades, then look more closely at a few specific symbols and ideas contained in them.

Perhaps the first question we should ask is: were these grades actually worked? Alice Joly leaves us in no doubt as to her opinion: "Jean-Baptiste Willermoz wrote in 1772 to Charles von Hund, describing the Chapter of the Black Eagle as a sort of conservatory of the High Grades, in which the worth of Masonic secrets were examined….which hid occupations which were more critical than practical".[32] I find myself disagreeing with her for three reasons.

Firstly, if the entire series of grades was never actually worked (other than the first three Blue grades of Apprentice, Companion and Master, without which experience one couldn't be considered to be a true mason), since the other grades offered every opportunity to be a place for discussion, why even bother to create three more grades? In any case, we know the number of members was relatively small, so the grades would not have been worked often, except possibly as exemplifications when there wasn't a worthy Candidate for initiation.

Secondly, seeing how both Willermoz and his friends were in constant search for the 'true' knowledge and the 'real' initiation of Freemasonry, and seeing how enthusiastically they successively signed up for the Order of Elus Cohen, the Rite of Strict Observance and the Scottish Rectified Rite, all of which had a series of worked degrees – and in the case of the Cohen at least, a significant amount of homework in the form of fasting, studying, praying and personal theurgical work – why would they content themselves with simply reading these grades? On a more mundane level the so-called High Grades were opportunities to meet in fabulously decorated halls, wear outlandish and extravagant clothes, knight one another and pretend to be nobility by vow and title. What use was a Chapter Room if devoid of fancy wall-hangings, a vast number of burning candles, trunks loaded with glittering regalia and the obligatory big chapeaux and shining swords? If nothing else, the High Grades were certainly theater.

---

[32] Alice Joly, *Un Mystique Lyonnais*, p. 14.

Thirdly, it would appear odd for Willermoz to devote his time and energy to create an alchemical-centric series of rituals for his brother and appoint him head of an Order which never met, and never conferred grades.

Nevertheless, I would state that it is my opinion that the first grade was not worked. Remember, in the Black Eagle Rose Croix the Masonic title conferred in each grade was Knight (for Apprentice), Chancellor (for Companion), and Bailiff (for Master). A reading of the grade of Knight/Apprentice will immediately show that it is very rudimentary. The Chapter Room, so carefully described in the subsequent two grades, is barely mentioned. There is no Chamber of Reflection – a standard requirement for the first grade of most Orders. The Sign, Grip, Word, Password, Coming to Order are all listed as 'as in the grade of Apprentice', by which it must be assumed Blue Lodge Apprentice, since there are no other instructions. Even the Explanation of the Tracing Board is given 'as in the Grade of Master' which makes little sense since Tracing Boards are normally cumulative in nature – each revealing more information than the previous one. Finally, the Catechism is very similar to that of Bailiff/Master, but without the detailed explanations in that one, contenting itself merely to list the various names of the months, zodiacal signs, Names of God and Angels associated with the Twelve Zodiacal Houses. Even an image of the Scales of Solomon (in fact taken from the Mystical Figure of Solomon, which in the McGregor Mathers translation[33] has been overly embellished with Hebrew names) is provided without explanation, followed by an apparently random list of Greek Philosophers, who again feature more prominently with more explanation in the Bailiff/Master grade. Finally, there are absolutely no rubrics in the entire ritual – no movements, and even the few salutes are cursory. The entire sense of the ritual is one which would be read rather than enacted.

In sum, the first grade has the feeling that it was added almost as an afterthought to what was truly a two-grade system, in order to provide the expected three grades. It is rushed, and borrows elements directly from the third grade without explanation. Indeed, later we shall briefly note that Baron von Tschoudy's version of Black Eagle Rose Croix used the second grade in Willermoz' system as the first grade, since it contains all the expected elements of an introductory grade, including a Chamber of Reflection and a serious trial prior to the Candidate's admission; while the second grade takes a tangent into the Rosicrucian history of Christian Rozenkreutz, before returning to the third grade which is remarkably similar to that of Willermoz.

---

[33] Samuel McGregor Mathers, annotated by Aleister Crowley, *The Greater and Lesser Keys of Solomon the King*, Mockingbird Press, 2016 (orig. 1888), p. 180.

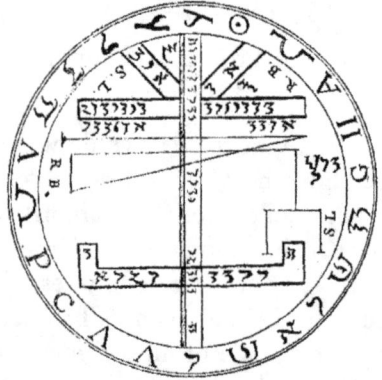
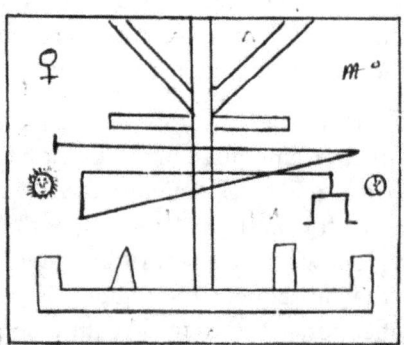

Figure 116: Mystical Figure of Solomon (McGregor Mathers' version).   *Figure 117: Scales of Solomon (Willermoz manuscript).*

With that in mind, the grade of Chancellor/Companion, is replete with detailed instructions on movements, salutes and words, and presents an altogether different form of ritual expression. The description of the Chapter room is far more detailed, and clearly lays out the twelve white marbles columns, representing the twelve Zodiacal Houses, interspersed with three-branched candelabra. There are also eight lights together, and a little apart a single light next to a representation of Hiram's tomb. In the West there is a large white marble board decorated with a golden triangle surrounded by a glory (oddly in Willermoz' drawing, the glory also contains six hearts), and in the center – as in the Master/Bailiff degree, a design which is barely explained, but which comes directly from the Heptameron, another earlier Grimoire attributed to Pietro d'Abano, and dated 1569 (since d'Abano died over two hundred years earlier, most scholars think this unlikely!).[34]

The unusual sigil in the center of Solomon's seal can be seen both in the Chancellor/Companion and the Bailiff/Master grades, firstly in a Sacred Delta in a glory, and finally in its full form in the full Pentacle of Solomon, this time going one further by adding the letters of JEHOVA to the six points. To further emphasize the importance of this seal, a second triangle surrounds it with the phrases 'Holy Sacred Pentacle', 'New Choir of Angels', and 'of Sublime Virtue' in what can best be described as substandard Latin.

This is also on one side of the two-sided jewel worn by the members, as imaged in the Knight/Apprentice Grade.

It is curious to note as an aside that, since the theurgists and magicians of old were forever working under the cloud of suspected heresy or even witchcraft, both of which carried extreme penalties, the practitioners of the Ancient Arts were careful to surround their magical practices with endless prayer to God,

---

[34] Image from http://www.esotericarchives.com/solomon/heptamer.htm on August 26th, 2020.

The Degrees of the Black Eagle Rose-Croix

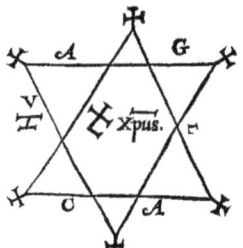
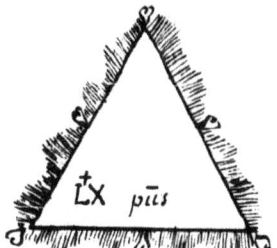
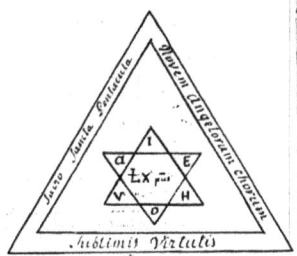

Figure 118: Seal of Solomon in Heptameron.

Figure 119: Sigil in Triangle from Chancellor/Companion grade.

Figure 120: Full sigil in Solomonic hexagram from Bailiff/Master grade.

Jesus, the Holy Spirit, Archangels, Angels and anyone or anything which would give their works the appearance of piety. Just as the early Christian exegetists sought justification for claiming Jesus to be the Messiah by raiding the Jewish Scriptures, and especially the Psalms, so the alchemists, mystics and theurgists of the Middle Ages and the Renaissance were not above melding old and new symbols. So here, in the Seal of Solomon we find two images: ·⟋ and X̄pus̄.·

The first is a variation on the famous formula LVX or 'Light' in Latin (if you look at the figure you can see the letters 'L', 'V' and 'X' contained within it). The second one is an abbreviation of *Christus*, Latin for Christ. The first two figures are in fact the Greek chi and rho (XP, or χρ) often used as an abbreviation of Chr(ist), followed by 'us' to complete the word. So, in the middle of the Pentacle of the Old Testament King we find the words LVX and Christus.

Now we have a problem. In both instances of the sigil in the two grade of Black Eagle Rose Croix we see a physical gap between the 'X' and the 'pus'. This can only mean one thing: the author – Willermoz – had no idea what he was writing! The Heptameron was used but the letters weren't placed in the correct positions. It is a little like writing JesusCh rist!

This issue continues into the Hebrew used. When one looks at the continual use of the twelve alleged 'Hebrew' letters composing the Most Great and Holy Name of God in the Bailiff/Master grade, we find an assortment of scratched letters which, while they have the decency to be consistent, bear no resemblance to any Hebrew letter I have ever encountered. This is truly both surprising and disappointing. While Hebrew may not exactly have been much more than a 'dead' language at that time (in that it wasn't the official language of a country and was probably only spoken in Synagogues and then with a significant possibility of mispronunciation), there were enough rabbis and rabbinical scholars available to make it relatively easy to verify the letters being used. The discrepancy between the letters even led the author to wonder if they weren't Hebrew at all, but rather one of the many esoteric alphabets available at the time (even most contemporary Masons are familiar with the so-called Pigpen alphabet used in the Royal Arch Degree). However, no alphabet was to be found which even vaguely resembled these scribbles. Another problem is the fact that even words beginning with the same letter have completely different signs associated with them. The following Table will perhaps demonstrate the problem.

Name of God	First Letter	'Hebrew' Letter in Notes	'Hebrew' Letter in Catechism
Agla	A		
Anasbona	A		
Eloyn	E		
Emmanuel	E		
Erigion	E		
Jehova	I, J		
Jesus	I, J		
Jessemon	I, J		
Melech	M		
Messiah	M		
Orpheton	O		
Tetragrammaton	T		

Table A: 'Hebrew' letters employed in Bailiff/Master grade of Willermoz' Black Eagle Rose Croix

Curiously, the only other place I can find similar writing is, of all places, on McGregor Mathers' seal of Solomon in Figure 124 above. Here we find a predominance of those vague '3s' and '7s' which seem to dominate Willermoz' so-called Hebrew. This is especially odd since McGregor Mathers was known to have a fine command of Hebrew! However, if he is in fact using an alphabet of which I am unaware, and Willermoz is tapping into the same obscure alphabet, I would be delighted to be set right!

In Table A above the twelve Names of God have been listed in alphabetical order for ease of comparison, with the 'Hebrew' letter associated with it in the Notes and later in the Catechism.

What is clear from the letters is that they are consistent in that, when repeated twice in the document – and in the names of God when spelled out in full – use the same characters. However, it cannot be denied that firstly, as can be seen from the table below, the same letter gives rise to different characters; and secondly, that Willermoz thought he was using Hebrew letters, since in the catechism he explicitly writes: "First the Grand Architect of the Universe with twelve Sacred Names, each taken from the twelve letters of the Great Name of God, written in Hebrew."

A final comment on specific symbols would be to draw attention to the seven Scales or Balances depicted in the Catechism of the Bailiff/Master grade. We have already seen that Solomon's Scales were introduced in the ritual as a variant on the Mystical Figure of Solomon depicted above and taken from the Greater Key of Solomon. Here we find seven more Scales, each associated with seven Ancient Greek Philosophers. The origin of these Scales seems obscure, but a little research has revealed that they are probably founded upon the Olympic Spirits found in several grimoires, including the Renaissance documents, the *Secret Grimoire of Turiel* and the *Arbatel de magia veterum*. This is certainly confirmed by the fact that each Greek Philosopher is associated with an Olympic Genius and his associated metal. However, it also appears that the seals of the Olympian Geniuses, as drawn in the *Arbatel*, are the basis for the Scales. Here is an example, using the Balance of the philosopher Thales.[35]

It is fairly easy to see that the Scales associated with Thales is an embellishment of the Sigil of Phul, the Olympian Genius associated with the Moon.

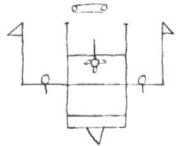

Figure 121: Scales of Thales from Willermoz Catechism.

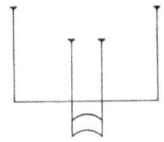

Figure 122: Sigil of Phul from Armadel.

---

[35] Samuel McGregor Mathers, *The Grimoire of Armadel*, (2nd Ed., Weiser, 1992), p. 55.

The final question is, if these Scales are included, why are they? In answer to this, we need to remember that the ritual continually emphasizes the need to weight the metals in order to create the Sun, the product of the six metals (for the text tells us that the Sun is not a metal, which probably introduces an element of Messianic symbolism into the ritual, where Sun = Son. The Orator tells us: "you will use the (Scales) in all your labors, which you will keep secret under your Key, in the impenetrable coffer of Prudence"; and "…who is fortunate to pronounce it with Cabalistic weight and measure…would possess all the virtues possible in man…". Finally: "How can one accomplish the alliance of the six metals to make only one…? By the Rule and the Scales left to us by Solomon in his Cabalistic Treatise of his Keys."

All of this refers to the great phrase in the Book of Wisdom 11:21, "Thou hast ordered all things in measure, and number, and weight." Clearly the alchemist belief that the correct proportion of metals would produce either the Alkahest, the 'universal solvent' capable of dissolving gold, or the *summum bonum*, a symbol for the Christ or Divine spark within us.

The purpose of this section is not to draw attention to the flaws in the ritual. They were written in the 1760s, when the concept of 'Spontaneous Generation', where the belief that breaking open a rock might discover a creature living within it still held sway.

Now we have considered some of the symbolism in the rituals and where they might have had their origin, let us now turn our attention to the overall form of the rituals, and what they were intended to accomplish.

The Overall Form of the Chancellor and Bailiff Grades

One of the greater surprises is finding that there is a particularly detailed – if not one hundred percent accurate – description of the grades in Arthur Edward Waite's A New Encyclopædia of Freemasonry.[36] The wording is clear enough to believe that he is speaking either of the Willermoz rituals or a close descendant. Seeing that Waite had had a relationship with Dr. Gérard Encausse (Papus), at least until 1902, and that Papus had acquired the archives then existing in Lyon concerning Willermoz, Pasqually and Saint-Martin, it would seem possible (if unprovable) that, knowing Waite's fascination with rituals, he would have shown him the Black Eagle Rose Croix and other rituals of Willermoz and at least afforded him to opportunity to read them while visiting. And we know that Waite could read French very well. Curiously, the rituals move the second grade to the position of the first and appear to split the third grade between the second and third. However, it also mentions the Scales or Balances. While the second grade becoming the first reflects their use by Tschoudy, the Scales are

---

[36] A.E. Waite, *A New Encyclopædia of Freemasonry*, Wings Books, 1994 (orig. published 1921), pp. 345 – 350.

The Degrees of the Black Eagle Rose-Croix

completely absent from his rituals. However, by the time the rituals found their way into the Rites of Memphis-Mizraïm, a hybrid version is seen, which both puts the Willermoz second grade as the first grade and retains the Scales and the names of the Greek Philosophers. However, again we encounter a problem, in that the second grade is closer to the Rosicrucian legend, which mentions Damcar, and introduces such exotic names into the Chapter as Isis, Zoroaster, Eleusis and Samothrace, thereby considerably muddying the waters since none of these are mentioned in the Waite description! This again seems to be a dead end: did Waite see the original Willermoz Rituals, and simply mis-describe them; or did he see yet another hybrid ritual which was neither Tschoudy's nor from Memphis-Mizraïm? That is beyond the scope of this paper, but I would suggest that he was probably looking at the Willermoz ones, and simply made a few errors from reading them quickly, confusing some elements of the Chancellor/Companion and Bailiff/Master grades.

Discounting the first grade, which we explained earlier is written in a manner which suggests it was never intended to be worked, let us turn to the subsequent two grades. Here will confine ourselves to three points. Firstly, we will look at the preparation of the Candidate and the trials undergone prior to being Initiated. Next, we will review the story contained in the grade of Chancellor/Companion and try to understand why such a jarring story which has no connection with alchemy might be included. Thirdly, we will take a step back and look at the rituals as a whole, seeking to determine whether the members were practicing alchemists and, if not, what the overall purpose of the grades was.

The key numbers featured in the grades are 1, 6, 7, 9 and 12. In most cases 1 refers to deity, and also to the sun which is created out of the six metals or planets which encircle it. 7 refers to the Ancient Greek solar system, as depicted in alchemy and magic as Solomon's seal, or the hexagram, with a point at its center representing the sun, the ruler or product of the six planets. The next number, 9, represents the nine Sages or Bailiffs who went in search of Hiram (or the sun), and 12 represents the 12 Houses, or planets through which the sun passes. The two sides of the pentacle worn by the members also reflect this notion. On one the six points of the hexagram replace the planets with the letters JEHOVA, its center containing the Heptameron's version of CHRISTUS LVX, implying the alchemical process of God becoming the Word. On the obverse side we find the six letters ADONAI or Lord transmuting to MESSIAH in the center. In both instances the 'Sun' becomes the 'Son', as we suggested earlier.

The overall setting is intended to impress. The room is surrounded by twelve white marble columns bearing shields or cartouches containing symbols and sigils related to one of the twelve Name of God in the ritual and to the relevant Zodiacal Sign. Between each is a three-branched candelabrum. All is white and gold, and the columns are further garnished with branches and leaves in appropriate correspondences with the zodiacal signs. This use of 'attributions' to indicate the Angel, Archangel, Name of God, Genius, perfume, animal, bird, fish, precious stone, time of day, month – indeed anything which comes in a variety of forms – is common to early alchemy and magical practices and is intended to attract the desired spirits or angels by providing a literal overload of correspondences to the entity being summoned.

In this case the overall effect is almost like stepping into Olympus, with a Zeus in seventeenth century attire sitting beneath a great canopy upon a throne in the East, and the other gods arranged at their stations. The layout accomplishes both the sense that one is in a great representation of the Universe, and at the same time satisfies the aesthetic and even snobbish expectations of the aristocrats they hoped would throng to this new Rite. 'If you build it they will come' might have been the motto even then. Indeed, the setting is also appropriate for a level of Mason – as described in the Privileges and Statutes – who can attend any meeting anywhere without invitation; require his reception to be by the Master of the Lodge; to be escorted by the Master with candlelight and an arch of steel to the throne, for the Master and senior officers to "kiss his heart", to give him the last word in everything, to keep his chapeau on, to sit during toasts – in fine, to act like royalty.

The form of the second grade follows that of a more traditional initiation. The Candidate is placed in a waiting room or Chamber of Reflection, stripped, and a blood-soaked shirt placed upon him. At this point all the knights file past him, glaring at him, followed by the three senior officers who accuse him of being guilty of an act for which an innocent has paid with his life. He is threatened: "Grand Prior, I deliver him to you, that he will not find death quickly, but will endure the cruelest tortures". He is blindfolded and led to another dark room, where he is strapped to a board next to a corpse. His blindfold is then removed.

Of course, those were different times, when most countries were in a near constant state of war, when plagues were rife, and babies often died in their first year. It was usual to carry a sword or pistol at all times, and a turn down the wrong street might lead to bloodshed. It is interesting to note, therefore, that now living in an age in which Freemasonry scrambles to remove the bloodthirsty penalties or add emasculating words to their delivery, just what terrors the Candidates of old endured in order to join. Having one's sword removed to prevent any possibility of defense, being tied down, blindfolded, stripped and suffering other indignities at the hands of strangers who then threatened your very life, must indeed have instilled a chill in most Candidates. And all through this, we are told, a huge black eagle made out of cardboard flies around the room and swoops over the corpse. While this may be necessary to the story being told, it can only be hoped that this was accomplished with a level of professionalism, to prevent the entire event from turning into a farce.

The trials continue. The Candidate, now blindfolded again, endures the return of the rabble (that is, the disapproving knights), and this time another 'co-conspirator' is captured and his ears hear that unworthy person try to escape, his capture and his bloody death, before again being left, now able to see with his blindfold removed once more, and with two corpses present, to contemplate his fate. At one point in the text the interesting rubric is added, that "the two Knights still remain outside the door of the Black Chamber, as much to offer assistance to the patient if needed, as to prevent him from leaving if he is able to loosen the ties". The use of the word 'patient' is indeed appropriate, perhaps…

Following a relatively short ceremony and obligation, after which the Candidate learns the usual steps, word, password, sign and form of Order, the key to the grade is then explained, along with a few alchemical formulae. The black eagle guarded Hiram's body while the search was going on, to prevent wild beasts from digging it up and devouring it. When the Bailiffs found the body, it swooped down and triumphantly took the sprig of acacia which marked the spot, flying up to the heavens in triumph. Nine Bailiffs were sent to find the body, and one succeeded (hence the eight plus one candles). Finally, the most fundamental phases of alchemy – black (*nigredo*), white (*albedo*) and red (*rubedo*) are turned into a cry of 'Vengeance!' with the following phrase: "The black signifies our mourning for the death of our assassinated Brother. The white is our innocence of the crime. The red is his blood which was spread." Are we talking about Hiram or Christ? Hiram or De Molay? Hiram or the Sun? Finally, do we speak of Hiram or the accomplishment of the Great Work? And who, for that matter, is the Black Eagle, the one who watches over the tomb? Is it Death? Is it Mercury, that strong messenger who carries communications from earth to the heavens? Is it the alchemical symbol of transmutation into a rarer substance? Or, in an age of religious warfare, is it even Frederick the Great?

But this is not a paeon to the noble innocent who died maintaining his integrity, whichever Exemplar we select. This grade is all about blood and revenge. Indeed, it is astonishing that Willermoz didn't completely rewrite it. However, he was compiling it at a time when he was in full communication with the Lodges of Metz, and his interest was already beginning to be piqued by the Rite of Strict Observance of Baron von Hund. Perhaps his strong views on the matter were beginning to give way to Masonic expediency?

However, the jewel in this Rite's crown is the third grade, which is nothing short of an alchemical world tour. Following a series of Privileges and Statutes & Regulation, all of which appear to serve the sole function of telling the new Knight how important he is, and going into great detail about the attire, jewels, sashes and other accoutrements to be worn, along with the elaborate decorations in the Chapter, we come across a series of 'Notes', which appear to the most part to duplicate what appears in the Ritual or the Catechism. However, the one exception, the list of Orders of Angels, followed by the name ADONAI in the faux Hebrew characters employed elsewhere, which is never developed in the rest of the Ritual, suggesting that these 'Notes' may have been for Willermoz' benefit, and that he either forgot to or decided not to elaborate on these symbols later in the text.

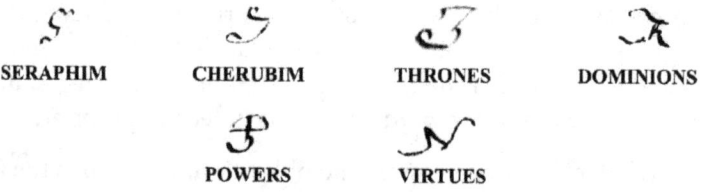

Figure 123: List of Angels and Sigils from Willermoz' third grade

A quick comparison with Table A above, which lists the faux Hebrew characters used in the ritual, will show that only two characters might possibly be similar: Thrones, which looks like a version of 'E', and Virtues, which looks like one of the manifestations of 'A'. All the rest of the characters or sigils are new.

Figure 124: 'Adonai' from the Willermoz ritual

Similarly, the word 'ADONAI' is rendered in letters which appear to bear no resemblance to real Hebrew letters. Compare the example above with the Hebrew of Adonai: אדני.

The key symbols of the Scales or Balance and the Key are explained in detail, and the Addresses of the Orator and the Grand Master, and the Catechism which follows certainly attracted the close attention of both René Le Forestier, who devotes seven long paragraphs to describing the third grade ritual, and Alice Joly, who discusses the contents in some detail. Indeed, Joly makes the important point that, after the heavily vengeance-oriented second grade, wholly in keeping with the burgeoning Templar-type grades, "The ritual preserved to us, and filled with alchemical, kabbalistic, astrological and arithmosophical designs makes no allusion to Jacques de Molay or to any other kind of Christian chivalry".[37]

---

[37] Alice Joly, *Un Mystique Lyonnais*, p. 14.

The Degrees of the Black Eagle Rose-Croix

In ending this brief review of the ritual contents, we will not go into great detail about everything mentioned in the third grade. Indeed, it is transparent enough that anyone with an interest can read it for themselves in Appendix F. Perhaps one important point, to which Le Forestier himself draws attention in his book, is the fact that its members were expected to report back on their findings to the group; a comment which suggests that they were expected to perform experiments at home and give an account of their results to the group in Chapter. This, as Le Forestier points out (on p. 285) comes from Article XXIII (which, in fact, he incorrectly calls 'article XXII').

The purpose of drawing attention to this small point is the fact that it would have been good practice for those same Brethren who were shortly going to become members of the Elus Cohen Temple in Lyon, when they would be expected to endure long fasts, regular prayer sessions, and perform theurgical operations in their own homes. Finally, we find an echo of the sentiments of Article XXIII in the Secret Instruction to a newly created Grand Profès in Willermoz' ultimate triumph: his Scottish Rectified Rite. This eighth and final grade ends with the admonition: "Collaborate with us through your *research* to increase what has been entrusted to us; do not forget that, as a Professed Knight, you have irrevocably devoted yourself to the service of mankind…"

Which takes us full circle from his first attempt to write and to work esoteric and spiritual grades.

Comparison with the Tschoudy Manuscripts

Although the Grades were probably no longer worked once Willermoz had found an exciting new series of rituals for his colleagues to practice in the Order of Elus Cohen, as late as 1772 he was still claiming to Baron von Hund and others that the Order of the Black Eagle Rose Croix was continuing to function well in Lyon.[38] The Black Eagle Rose Croix must have had a reputation, since it would be pointless citing it if the reference meant nothing to the people he was trying to impress. Whether the fame was from Willermoz' own Rite or that of Baron Tschoudy's remains unclear, though it is noticeable that both make strong mention of a connection with Frederick II, which would have impressed von Hund. Nevertheless, Willermoz' words are similar to Tschoudy's with one odd exception. Towards the end of the section in the Bailiff/Master grade on Ceremonial and Dignities, he added a paragraph which stated: "This Order is highly venerated in the Northern courts, among others in Prussia, where it has taken the name of Black Eagle, because the reigning King of Prussia was the first Grand Master, and because the Eagle is found in the Catechism." So far this follows Tschoudy,

---

[38] Le Forestier, *Franc-Maçonnerie*, p. 343.

but in Willermoz' case, after the words 'King of Prussia' there is an asterisk leading to a footnote which reads: "Frederic II, born 1712". Nevertheless, both also seem to focus on the Rose Croix link referring twice to Raymond Lully and his alchemical feats, which led the King of England to produce a coin or medal with an eagle on one side, and a pelican feeing its young on the other. It appears both wanted to have their cake and eat it, drawing lines both from a powerful political country and from the nebulous concept of the mysterious Order of the Rosy Cross which appeared on the European stage for a time during the previous century, and whose name was naturally associated with alchemically-leaning Orders, given the alchemical nature of the *Chymical Wedding*, and the reference to Rosenkreutz' uncorrupted body when his tomb was opened.

However, one of the most elusive facts about the Rite is its origins. Indeed, it is almost amusing to see how scholars such as Alice Joly and René Le Forestier avoid answering this question by focusing on Willermoz' ritual while barely mentioning any other manifestations. We know that Baron Tschoudy had a version which was almost identical to that of Willermoz. We have also discovered that another, almost identical, version existed as part of the Scottish Hermetic Rite, which we will examine later. Now, the latter is a classic example of an anti-Mason who includes a number of *exposés* of rituals to make his point and no doubt to tittivate the reader (although in this case there can't have been many readers, given that the initial edition was limited to 20 copies!). This is Gustave Bord, who wrote *La Franc-Maçonnerie en France – des origins à 1815*. An ardent royalist even in 1908 when the book was published, he wrote the book in the belief that the Freemasons had ruined everything, and that only a return to the golden age of monarchy would restore France to its greatness. Be that as it may, it contains a number of useful pieces of history and ritual. Interestingly, he adds a new angle to the symbolism of Hiram. We have seen Hiram as the good master, the avatar whom every good Mason should strive to emulate. However, in the rituals of that era which spoke of vengeance against those who brought about the demise of the Templars, such as the Rite of Strict Observance and, surprisingly, the second grade of the Black Eagle Rose Croix, which is all the more astonishing since Willermoz condemned the vengeance degrees as "contrary to the principles of morality",[39] Hiram was seen as a symbol for Jacques de Molay, the Grand Master of the Knights Templar who was burned at the stake on the Île des Javieaux in Paris in 1314, the vengeance mentioned being against the pope and the King of France who had presided over his fate. Bode adds: "and the execution of King Charles I", a fascinating link to the fact that the preponderance of French Lodges at the time were Jacobite; the Grand Lodge of England having only around five Lodges in France at that time. Later, we will see Hiram elevated further to the role of Christ in the Scottish Rectified Rite, his name eventually being associated

---

[39] Alice Joly, *Un Mystique Lyonnais*, p. 15.

with an acrostic which spells out *Homo Iesus Rex Altissimi Mundi*, or 'Jesus the Man, the Most High King of the World'.

So firstly, did Willermoz' rituals precede Baron von Tschoudy's or did the Tschoudy rituals precede the Willermoz ones?

Both Baron Tschoudy, and Dom Pernety, who we will meet later, had an advantage over Willermoz in the field of alchemy. Pernety was both an alchemist and a convert to Swedenborg, whose Illuminés d'Avignon is the stuff of myth, and his books *Les Fables égyptiennes et greque dévoilées* and the *Dictionnaire mytho-hermétique* were popular, with a Hermetic interpretation of early myths.[40] Similarly, Baron Tschoudy was renowned as an alchemist, whose work *l'Étoile Flamboyant* was held in high esteem and republished several times. Indeed, its catechism was later described by Eliphas Lévi, the great nineteenth century French occultist, as "the most luminous and unmistakable presentation of the alchemical mystery to have ever been put in words".[41] Against this, the middle-class silk merchant from Lyon would not appear to be a leading light in the world of alchemical writings and practice. This puts Willermoz at a disadvantage to begin with: how could Willermoz either have written or modified a Ritual brimming with alchemical notions if he hadn't purloined it from one of the 'great' alchemist Masons?

Unfortunately, I have been unable to find a single word connecting Jean-Baptiste Willermoz to Baron Tschoudy. There are evident peripheral connections, in that Willermoz was in contact from 1761 with the Master of *La Vertu* Lodge in Metz, Meunier de Précourt, a Lodge which was allied with that of *Parfait Amis*, and exchanged a number of rituals with them, though those of the Lodges in Metz were "less rich that those of Lyon in high mystical grades".[42] I also spoke with Ill… Pierre Noël, 33⁰, Sovereign Grand Commander of Belgium, former Great Prior of the Belgian Knights Beneficent of the Holy City (C.B.C.S.) and an acknowledged expert on this period in Freemasonry, as well as being a regular contributor to the most erudite Masonic journals in France, Holland and Belgium. He is convinced that Willermoz and Tschoudy never met, nor did they correspond directly.

Given this lack of information by the usual channels, my only recourse is that adopted by Theologians when they can no longer interview the authors or copyists of early Christian texts: exegesis. There are two general rules. The first is that the earliest texts are normally more confused and complex than later versions, since successive copyists attempt to clarify and simplify the obtuse points in the earlier writings. Secondly, it is a given fact that copyists tend to make errors when transcribing documents. This can take two forms. Either a copyist simply

---

[40] Joanny Bricaud, *Les Illuminés d'Avignon*, (2nd Ed. SEPP, Paris, 1995 – first edition 1927), pp. 12 – 13.

[41] https://freemasoninformation.com/masonic-education/esoterica/the-secret-tradition-in-freemasonry/masonic-systems-of-alchemical-degrees-and-the-hermetic-rite-of-baron-tschoudy/, as on August 20, 2020.

[42] Alice Joly, *Ibid.*, p. 10.

misses a line or misreads a word, particularly if translating from one language to another (which of course can drastically change the meaning of a passage) – a famous example of this would be in the interpretation of Mary, *virgo*, being a virgin, when *virgo* in Latin can also simply mean 'young woman' – or they can deliberately rewrite or add to a passage in order to reflect the changed dogma of the times in which they live. An example of the latter would be the addition of twelve verses to the end of the Gospel of Mark to include the resurrection scene, verses missing from the earliest copies.

Here I will give two examples.

The first comes from Willermoz' second grade and Tschoudy's first, which is almost identical. During the ritual a description of the Tracing Board is given. The sixth point of the description contains the following phrase in Willermoz: "Le triangle…et cette inscription **indicible** du milieu..". Now let's look at Tschoudy: "Le triangle…et cette inscription **invisible** du milieu…" The first phrase translates as: "The triangle…and this inexpressible inscription in the middle", while the second version says: "The triangle…and this invisible inscription in the middle…." Now, given that the inscription in the middle of the triangle is the "Grand and Ineffable Sacred and August Word", it would seem more logical that the correct word would be 'inexpressible' rather than 'invisible'. This looks like a transcription error and might suggest that someone made an error copying Willermoz' ritual.

A second example is as follows. In the same ritual, Willermoz' Catechism describes the work of the black eagle guarding Hiram's tomb as follows: "…et s'envola dans les airs triomphante du **précieux** depot qu'elle avoit gardé si **préciseusement**." Note that the word 'precious' has been used twice, which is an understandable error for a composer of a ritual who is writing quickly. In the same passage in Tschoudy we find: "…et s'envola dans les airs, triumphant du **précieux** dépôt qu'elle avoit gardé si **soigneusement**." Now the phrase says: of the eagle "…and flew up into the air triumphant, from the precious deposit which it had guarded so carefully". Here the change has been made by the transcriber to avoid using the same word twice in a sentence. This again is possible evidence that the Tschoudy version postdates the Willermoz one.

Now, I just immediately state in the interest of transparency that, while I was using Willermoz' original handwritten rituals, I had to rely on a French transcription for the Tschoudy version of the first Grade, since I only possess a handwritten version of the third grade (which as I mention later, is only *probably* a copy of Tschoudy's Ritual). Nevertheless, I find it hard to believe that an academic transcription of the Tschoudy Ritual would be so cavalier as to mis-transcribe it into French.

Therefore, in the absence of references to the relative dates of the Willermoz and Tschoudy versions, given the above exercise, I would state my opinion that the Willermoz version predates Tschoudy's; and secondly, that the Rituals may well have been forwarded to Metz in the apparent exchange of Rituals which took place between Willermoz and de Précourt.

Finally, as an example of the later version tidying up the complexities of the original, I would draw attention to the extraordinarily complex Scales created by Willermoz out of the sigils of the Olympian geniuses. I have given some examples of the original sigils from the Armadel, Willermoz' almost overly elaborate rendition and in between the Tschoudy attempt to be more in accord with the original without losing the Willermoz elaborations completely.

Philosopher	Sign	Genius	Armadel Sigil	Tschoudy Scales	Willermoz Scales
Albumasaris	♄	Aratron			
Pythagoras	♃	Bethor			
Plato	♀	Hagith			

Table B: Sample Scales from Tschoudy and Willermoz Rituals, compard to Armadel Sigils

Bode's book contains one of the most detailed reproductions of the Black Eagle Rose Croix third grade, describing his version as 'part of a collection of Rituals in use in the Lodges of the Scottish Philosophical Rite."[43] His Ritual is dated February 1784 and comes from the *Loge du Contrat social de Saint-Jean à l'Orient de Paris*. What follows are nineteen pages giving the entire ritual in precise detail (if not the images). With very few exceptions the grade is identical to that of Willermoz. One example of a fascinating detail which didn't exist in the original version is a glorious expansion of the aim of the grade:

---

[43] Gustave Bode, *La Franc-Maçonnerie en France – des origins à 1815*, Vol 1, (Nouvelle Librairie Nationale, Paris 1908, pp. 205 et seq.

"The purpose of this grade is the sublime science of understanding Nature and drawing from it work useful to an understanding of humankind, be it through the purification of imperfect metals in order to transmute them into gold, the only perfect creation of Nature and as such the emblem of Divinity which contains no impurity within Himself, nor beginning nor end; and gold is also found to be of the same weight and value in whatever fire you wish to put it; it is also the basis of the mystery of the salamander who lives in fire, and of the phenix who is reborn from his ashes. It is absolutely not included with the other six impure (metals) since physically it is all spirit and therefore incorruptible. From this pure metal, rendered potable, you can magnetically extract the universal medicine, whose existence cannot be denied, seeing all that is said about it in the Holy Scripture and in all the Hermetic Philosophies, and notably in the first aim of the Association of the Parisian Canons and other ecclesiastical officers who have come after the druids or priests of ancient Gaul, from whom they have obtained this knowledge through tradition, which can easily be founding he records of Paris."

It continues in this vein for another paragraph, naming locations in Paris where this mystical healing had been taking place. Apart from this whimsical late addition to the ritual, the rest is practically identical to its original from Lyon. This is important, since we will return to this point later in our search for the true origin of the Rite.

One last thing to take away from Bode's monumental book is his reference to Rabbi Neamuth, a mysterious Jew who is said to be the source of these rituals. We encounter him in both Willermoz' and Tschoudy's rituals: "This Grade, which composes an Order of Perfect Mason, was drawn from the Cabalistic treasure of Doctor and Rabbi Neamuth, Chief of the Synagogue at Leiden". This is reflected in Bode's book: "This grade, which includes the Order of Perfect Masons, was brought to light by Brother R.... who obtained if from the Kabbalistic treasure of Doctor and Rabbi Neamuth, head of the Synagogue of Leiden in Holland."[44]

However, another possibility is the comment made by Alain Guichard in an article for *Le Monde* (see footnote 73), in which he claims this transmission was conferred upon Dom Pernety. Pernety was known for starting the famous group Les Illuminés' d'Avignon, who were said to practice alchemy. The article states that: "Frederick II welcomed him (Pernety) to Prussia…An encounter with the doctor Neamuth, rabbi of the Synagogue of Leiden, in Holland, put him in contact with the high mystery of the Kabbalah." Dom Antoine-Joseph Pernety has therefore been proposed as the author of the Black Eagle Rose Croix, especially seeing that both the Willermoz and Tschoudy rituals mention that the teachings come from that venerable rabbi. This is not the place to go into a long explanation of the life of Pernety. Suffice it to say that the dates simply don't add up. According to Joanny Bricaud, Pernety was a Benedictine monk who studied esotericism as well as authoring a book on Egyptian and Greek fables which

---

[44] Gustave Bode, *Ibid*, p. 212.

discussed philosophy and Hermeticism. This was followed by a dictionary on Hermeticism and Myths. Now, from 1763 – 1767 his desire to expand his knowledge led him to volunteer as almoner on a voyage to the Falkland Islands from 1763 – 1764, and on his return he demitted from his monastery in 1765 and moved to Avignon, where in 1766 he founded the *Rite Hermétique or the Rite de Pernety*. At the time this Order consisted of 6 Grades, none of which included the Black Eagle.[45] In any case he was persecuted by the Roman Church and fled to Berlin, where Frederic II was sufficiently impressed to offer him a stipend, as well as the post of Conservator of the Library, and the income from the Abbey of Burgel in Thuringe. So, this is probably when he would have met Rabbi Neamuth (if this meeting indeed took place). He returned to the region of Avignon around 1770. Now, in 1770 he allegedly founded the Scottish Grand Lodge of Comtat-Venaissin, which was in fact the *Loge Saint-Lazare* in Paris, which became the *Loge Saint-Jean d'Écosse du Contrat Social* and which later became the Scottish Mother Grand Lodge of France. And we recognize this name from the section from Bode's book above! According to Bricaud, Brother Boileau, who was one of Pernety's most devoted followers, modified the grade system to include the Knight of the Black Eagle in 1778.[46]

Without wishing to pursue this line further, the importance of these dates concerning Pernety is the fact that he couldn't have met Rabbi Neamuth until 1770 at the earliest; and the Black Eagle wasn't associated with his (expanded) Order until 1778. Since Willermoz' system was in place in 1763, we need look no further at Pernety.

One final possibility arises, and this is the one which I favor the most. We should remember that Pierre-Jacques Willermoz was a dedicated alchemist, having been sponsored by his elder brother to study spagyrics, that branch of alchemy concerned with extracting elixirs from plant matter, before moving to Marseille in order to study medicine: at least that was his public claim and one which placated his concerned father.[47] He succeeded in his chosen career brilliantly, and was appointed Preparer and Demonstrator Royal at the famous School of Medicine. Interestingly Le Forestier adds the words "Intelligent et travailleur, déjà entrainé par ses travaux extra-universitaires…" (intelligent and a hard worker, already involved in his extra-university works), which leaves little doubt with what he was occupying himself outside of his formal studies. And as if to make this even more explicit, Le Forestier continues: "Mais il n'avait pas renoncé à ses premières amours et était resté un alchimiste impenitent, comme l'étaient alors nombre de ses confrères. Ses fonctions officielles ne l'empêchaient pas de continuer à collectionner documents et grades hermétiques." (But he hadn't renounced his first love and remained an impenitent alchimist, as did a number

---

[45] Joanny Bricaud, *Ibid.*, p. 32.
[46] Joanny Bricaud, *Ibid*, p. 42.
[47] R. Le Forestier, *La Franc-Maçonnerie Templière et Occultiste*, pp. 285 – 286.

of his associates. His official functions didn't prevent him from continuing to collect Hermetic documents and grades.) Le Forestier continues, regarding a letter the young alchemist wrote to his brother Jean-Baptiste: "Pierre-Jacques avait découvert une version hermétique du grade chevaleresque type et il n'était pas peu fier de sa découverte, car it ajoutait, sur un ton d'affectueuse taquinerie: 'Ce serait plaisant si votre élève devenait votre maître; méritez mes bontés.'"[48] (Pierre-Jacques had discovered a Hermetic version of a grade in the chivalric tradition, and he was not a little proud of his discovery, for he added in an affectionately teasing tone: 'It would be fun if your pupil were to become your master; prove you deserve my gifts!')

Although Le Forestier doesn't explicitly make the link, I will do so for him. If Pierre-Jacques was practicing Freemasonry in Marseille, and had come across a Rite which was both Chivalric and Hermetic in nature – and it should be borne in mind that the term 'Hermetic' was virtually synonymous with Alchemical at that time, as may be seen in the writings of J.-B. Willermoz and L.-C. de Saint-Martin mentioned earlier – which he and his associates had joined when not performing their usual duties at the School of Medicine, can we find a candidate for this exceptional Rite? Indeed, we can! As we saw above, Bode quoted a version of the Black Eagle Rose Croix which was almost identical to that of Jean-Baptiste Willermoz, which was printed in Paris in 1784, from the Scottish Hermetic Rite.

The reason this is so important is the fact that the Scottish Hermetic Rite was first practiced in Marseille in 1750! According to Folger, "the Scottish Philosophical Rite of the Scottish Mother Lodge is to be credited to the body established at Marseilles prior to 1750. It consisted of eighteen degrees, the first three being the symbolic degrees and the eighteenth the Knight of the Sun".[49]

If the Scottish Philosophical Rite existed in Marseilles from 1750, then it would almost certainly seem to be the one which Pierre-Jacques joined. While the other grades would have seemed similar to those he had already experienced in Lyon, surely the alchemical grade or grades of the Black Eagle Rose Croix (his 'Hermetic version of a grade in the chivalric tradition') would have strongly attracted the attention of this budding alchemist? His letter to his older brother makes it an absolute probability that he would have brought a copy of this degree to Lyon either before, or when he quit his post in Marseille and returned to Lyon permanently in 1763. There Jean-Baptiste, the consummate redactor, would have polished and improved on what he had received, and to honor his younger brother made it the *ne plus ultra* of his Masonic system, seating Pierre-Jacques at the head of this Rite.

---

[48] R. Le Forestier, *Ibid*, p. 287.
[49] Robert R Folger, *The Ancient and Accepted Scottish Rite in Thirty-Three Degrees*, (published by the author, New York 1862), p. 47.

In the interest of transparency, I must draw the reader's attention to one final anomaly in the papers I have managed to collect. The papers I have used pertaining to the Tschoudy rituals came from Latomia (latomia.org), a European source of many original Masonic rituals which is highly regarded by scholars as an excellent source. Among a number of rituals pertaining to the timeframe of the Black Eagle Rose Croix we have been studying, two are of immediate importance. One is from the Bibliotheca Esoterica, called *Tous les rituels alchemique du Baron de Tschoudy* (Latomia 152-t-f) from an unidentified 'Private Collection'. This contains French transcriptions of the three rituals, as well as others attributed to Tschoudy. It has been this document which I have used as my source for all quotations and comparisons, with one exception: for the passage on exegetics, where I had to compare original documents to one another, while I had the Willermoz manuscripts I only had the French transcription for Tschoudy. Therefore, I turned to a separate document in from Latomia (11-o-f) titled *Sublime Grade of True Rose-Croix of Germany or Knight Black Eagle or Unknown Philosopher* (a title worth a separate paper in itself!), from the Fonds Kloss XXXIV–5. The handwriting is completely different from that given as examples in the first document. However, a review showed that the handwritten document was identical to the French transcription in the first document, which also contained the same distorted words mentioned in the section of exegesis. I am therefore confident that, although the handwriting is different to that exemplified in the French transcription, both are from the same source – Baron von Tschoudy, probably copied out by two different people. It was common in those days for the newly initiated person to be given a copy of the Ritual to copy for his own use. For an example of the different handwritings look at Appendix C.

Conclusion

In this paper we have looked at a little-known Rite by Willermoz, which was nevertheless the *ne plus ultra* to his series of Grades before his involvement in the Order of Elus Cohen, then the Strict Observance and finally his dedicated work on the Scottish Rectified Rite. All of them reflect his endless search for meaning through Masonry for his Catholic beliefs, as he clearly saw the existing structure of the Catholic faith as not providing what he desired so earnestly: a return to a primitive and esoteric Christianity he envisaged, framed by esoteric belief and Ritual rather than conventional dogma.

While most scholars have paid little attention to it, this paper considers it as the precursor to the important lessons which his younger brother brought to his belief system and provides the first translation of these manuscripts into English for further study.

Willermoz was an expert administrator and a consummate editor of rituals. But he wasn't an innovator. He didn't deliver many lectures at his soirées called the 'Lectures of Lyon', leaving that task to Saint-Martin and d'Hauterive. He was not himself a true author, even though some of his extensive papers have come to us in French publications. He edited Pasqually's Treatise into two lectures in the Secret Instructions of the C.B.C.S. He used the Strict Observance as the foundation on which to build his Scottish Rectified Rite.

He needed a *basis*; not a blank sheet of paper.

In this paper I have, I believe, shown the Tschoudy rituals were either a parallel development to Willermoz or a successor. I tend to believe the latter, firstly because of the similarity of the grades; secondly because the second grade was rightly moved to the first, and a grade with a more 'Rosicrucian' feel was inserted as the second, and because of the exegetical examples in the Ritual which point to an order in their production.

While Dom Pernety has often been cited as a source, we saw he only possibly met Rabbi Neamuth much later in the story. Therefore, we can conclude that either his name was cited to lend credibility to the Order, or that Bode's comment about a Brother R… receiving the details was in fact likely. In any case Pernety was not the source.

So, discounting any vague references to the original Rosicrucians or Germanic Orders, otherwise mentioned in almost no sources except as the vaguest allusion, the most likely source seems to be from the Scottish Philosophical Rite of Marseille founded in 1750. This Rite, as we saw from Bode's writings (and isn't it interesting that it is often Masonry's detractors who provide the best information?), who told us that the Scottish Philosophical Rite ritual he obtained from 1784 might well be a reflection of the original rituals worked in Marseille; and would it have been Pierre-Jacques the younger masonic brother who might have come across these rituals – or even been invited into the Order – while he was studying in Marseille, and brought them back to his elder brother to develop and make a part of his Lyonnais system? Perhaps the Willermoz version, being better, was ultimately substituted in the Scottish Philosophical Rite as being an improvement on the original, which is why the Ritual quoted by Bode is so similar, with a few new extravagant accretions from the Parisians, who as usual, wanted to ensure that Paris was seen as the center of all things important, as the extended quotation above demonstrated?

I must conclude by saying that one single discovery can negate my hypothesis, and that the difficulty for anglophones to read, let alone locate, the appropriate French documents to support their theories is an ongoing challenge. Nevertheless, the fact that every scholar in the 20th century I have looked at has avoided this issue, from Joly, Le Forestier, to the prior Chair of Esoteric Studies at the Sorbonne, Antoine Faivre, and even the erudite publication on these matters, *Renaissance Traditionelle*, gives me hope that these are new ideas. My supporting documentation has been limited to what I have been able to find myself, and those books and papers which colleagues have suggested to me during my work on this paper. I therefore hope that I have included the majority of the key supporting documents for this paper.

The Degrees of the Black Eagle Rose-Croix

Bibliography

Manuscripts

Fonds Willermoz, Manuscript 5457, documents 14 (Apprentice), 15 (Companion) and 16 (Master), Bibliothèque Municipal de Lyon.

Kloss Ms., XXXIV 1 – 5, Tome VI, Tschoudy Black Eagle Third Grade Ritual, Latomia, 11-o-f.

French transcription of Tschoudy rituals, Collection Privée, Latomia, Document 152-t-f.

Books

Bayard, Jean-Pierre: *Le symbolism maçonnique traditional: Tome 2*, Éd., Maçonnique de France, 1981.

Bord, Gustave: *La Franc-Maçonnerie en France – des origins à 1815*, Vol. 1, Nouvelle Librairie Nationale, Paris 1908.

Bricaud, Joanny: *Les Illuminés d'Avignon*, 2nd Ed., SEPP, Paris, 1995 (orig. 1927).

Folger, Robert R.: *The Ancient and Accepted Scottish Rite in Thirty-Three Degrees*, published by the Author, New York, 1862.

Jackson, Brig. A. C. F.: *Rose Croix, the History of the Ancient and Accepted Rite of England and Wales*, Lewis Masonic, 1980.

Joly, Alice: *Un Mystique Lyonnais et les Sécrets de la Franc-maçonnérie*, Éd. Maçon, Paris 1938.

Le Forestier, René: *La Franc-maçonnerie templière et occultiste*, 2nd Ed., Archè, Milan 2003.

Papus (Dr. Gérard Encausse), *Martinèsisme, Willermosisme, Martinisme et France- Maçonnerie*, Chamuile, Paris, 1899; trans. Vaughan, Piers A., Rose Circle Publications, 2020.

McGregor Mathers, Samuel annotated by Aleister Crowley, *The Greater and Lesser Keys of Solomon the King*, Mockingbird Press, 2016 (orig. 1888).

McGregor Mathers, Samuel: *The Grimoire of Armadel*, 2nd Ed., Weiser, 1992.

Saint-Martin, Louis-Claude de: *Tableau Naturel des rapports qui existent entre Dieu, l'homme et l'universe* orig. 1782; English trans. by Piers Vaughan, Rose Circle Publications, 2018.

Tappa, Gilbert: *Instructions pour les Élus Cohens*, (Les Feuillets d'Hermopolis, Vol 2, Nice, 2000.

Thory, Claude-Antoine: *Acta Latomorum*, Dupart, Paris 1815.

Vulliaud, Paul: *Joseph de Maistre, Franc-Maçon*, 2nd Ed., Archè, 1990 – orig. 1926.

Waite, Arthur Edward: *A New Encyclopædia of Freemasonry*, Wings Books, 1994 (orig. 1921).

Waite, Arthur Edward: *Saint-Martin the French Mystic*, Rider & Con London, 1922.

THE DEGREES OF THE BLACK EAGLE ROSE-CROIX

APPENDICES

A. EXAMPLES OF THREE DIFFERENT HANDWRITINGS FOR THE INSTRUCTION TO THE THIRD GRADE

B. SAMPLE PAGES FROM THE WILLERMOZ MANUSCRIPT

C. COMPARISON OF HANDWRITING BETWEEN TWO TSCHOUDY RITUAL SOURCES

D. GRADE OF APPRENTICE / KNIGHT

E. GRADE OF COMPANION / CHANCELLOR

F. GRADE OF MASTER / BAILIFF

The Degrees of the Black Eagle Rose-Croix

Appendix A: Examples of Three Different Handwritings

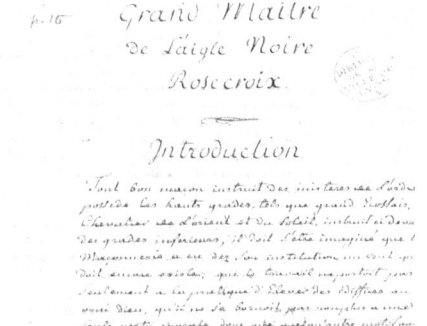

Figure 125: Instructions to the third grade - Willermoz MS

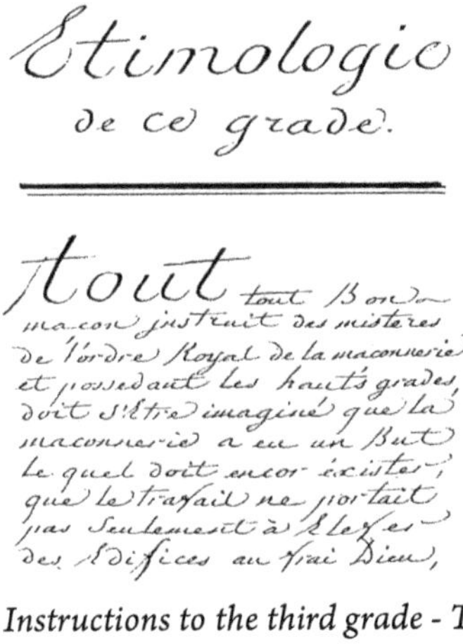

Figure 126: Instructions to the third grade - Tschoudy MS

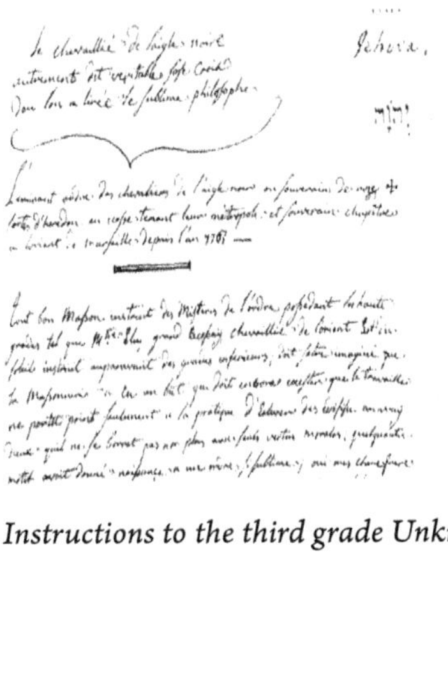

Figure 127: Instructions to the third grade Unknown MS

The Degrees of the Black Eagle Rose-Croix

Appendix B: Sample pages from Willermoz Manuscript

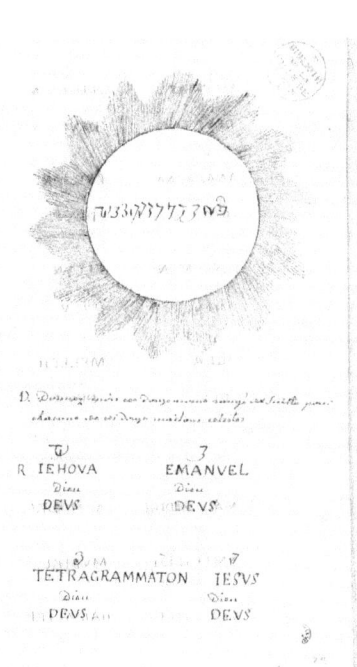

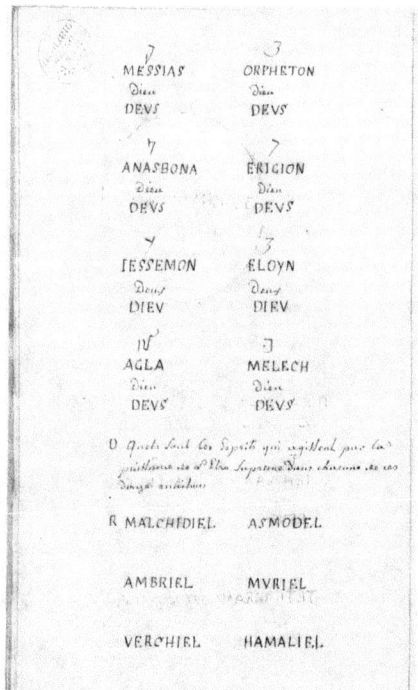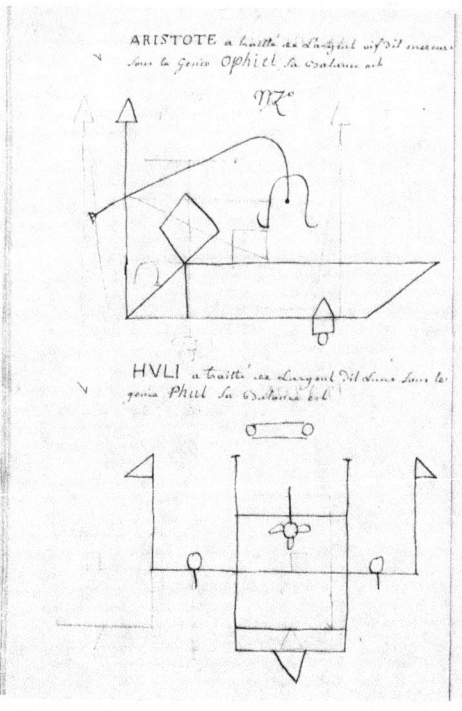

The Degrees of the Black Eagle Rose-Croix

Appendix C: Comparison of Handwriting Between two Tschoudy Ritual Sources

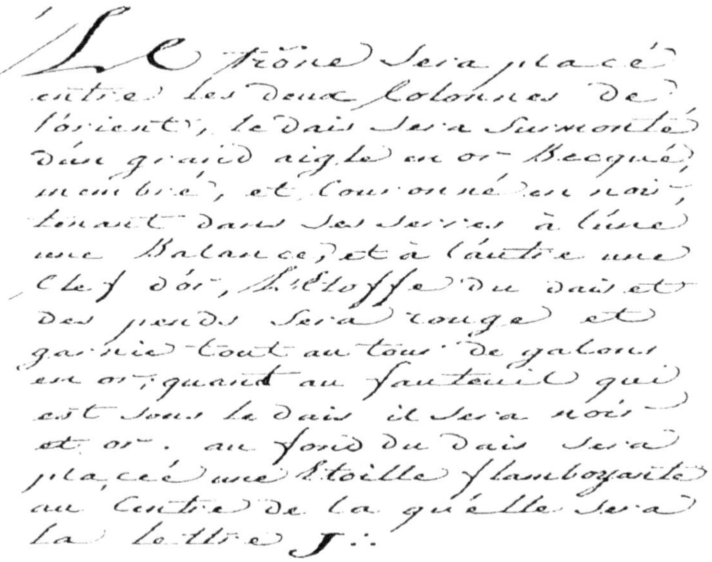

Figure 128: This example comes from the Fonds Kloss XXXIV - 5 (Latomia 11-o-f)

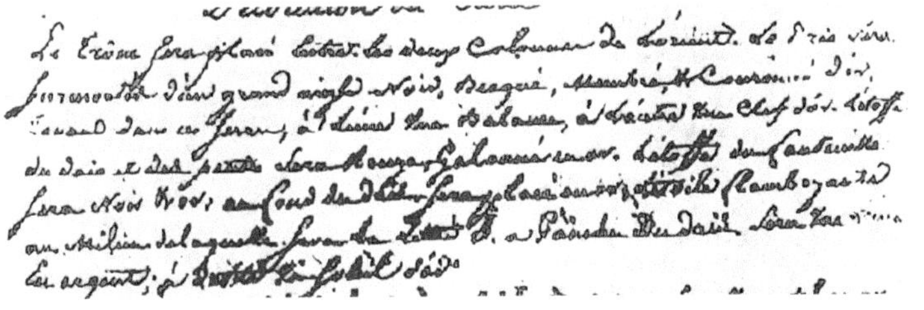

Figure 129: This example comes from the French transcription with a few pages of the original manuscript inserted as examples (Latomia 152-t-f).

The Degrees of the Black Eagle Rose-Croix

Appendix D: Grade of Apprentice or Knight of the Black Eagle Rose Croix

Dignities of the Order and Ceremonial

In this Order the Assemblies held are called Chapters.

The head of the Chapter is called the Sovereign Grand Master. His Lieutenant is called Grand Prior and his Second is called Grand Warden[50].

The Officers such as the Orator, Secretary, Treasurer, Master of Ceremonies, Frère Terrible, Almoner[51] and others are called Prince Commanders, and the other Brothers simply Princes or Knights.

Knights of the Black Eagle Rose-Croix should be regarded *par excellence* as preeminent Masons and as such they should have precedence in all the Lodges they attend, over all the Brothers who don't possess the aforesaid Grade. Their privileges are very extensive, as one can find detailed in the Grade of Master.

Origin of the Order of Knights of the Black Eagle

In the institution of Masonry, King Solomon divided the Order into three classes, Apprentice, Companion and Master.

The Masters weren't ordinary Master by any means, being enlightened men selected by the Prince and suitable to be initiated into the High Sciences called Kabbalistic Knowledge. Through this science they possessed all human knowledge, Hermetic knowledge was known to them, and the transmutation of metals was also known to them. Being of a small number, these Masters were distinguished by a jewel called the Pentacle, which they wore on their stomach.

On one side it had the following form:

---

[50] In French, *Surveillant*. This has been changed to 'Warden' throughout.
[51] Almost illegible. This is the best guess.

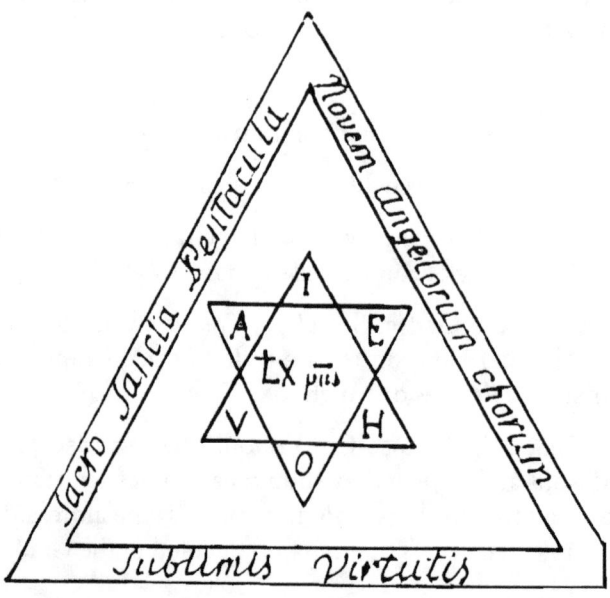

The letters of the double triangle make the sacred word **IEHOVA**. The other side has the following form:

The letters of the double triangle make the sacred word **ADONAI**.

The Degrees of the Black Eagle Rose-Croix

Decoration of the Chapter

The room in which the Chapter meeting is to be held will be hung in black, decorated by columns of white marble as described in the Grand of Master.

The Chapter will be lit by a 3-branched candelabra in the West, one in the center with one candle, and another in the East with two candles, and several 3-branched candelabras around the room, and at the throne. All the candles used must be of yellow wax (*i.e. beeswax, and not mixed in any way*).

Dress

On Reception days all the Knights will be dressed in black with a white feather in their hats, and all will have a sword embellished with a scarlet ribbon, removing their sash and collar, and at the end of the Reception they will put them back on.

Apron

They wear a white apron edged in red and in the middle of which there is a large Black Eagle. In their buttonhole they wear red-colored ribbon from which hangs a Black Eagle.

Jewel

The jewel consists of a crowned compass resting upon a quarter circle, supporting a cross at the feet of which is a pelican with its young[52], and on the other side an eagle, and between the two animals is a branch of acacia.

This jewel alludes to the three kingdoms of Nature, the Animal, the Vegetable and the Mineral used in the operation of the Great Work.

Gloves

The gloves are white embroidered and bordered with red.

Opening of the Chapter

The Chapter is opened with a blow of the gavel, given by the Sovereign Grand Master, to which blow the Grand Prior and the Grand Surveillant respond with another blow. Then the Sovereign Grand Master says:

Knight Princes, assist me to open the Chapter by saying these words.

---

[52] Pelican avec sa pitié.

He gives the Sign, to which all the Knights respond, and during this time the Grand Prior and the Grand Surveillant present the points of their swords to him. Then all the Princes come to Order. The Sovereign says:

Q. *Prince Grand Prior, what is the hour?*

A. *The day is preceded by the Morning Star, and work should be resumed.*

Q. *Prince Grand Surveillant, what is your duty?*

A. *To see if the Chapter is Hermetically sealed, if the materials are ready, if the Elements are ready, and if black makes way for white and white for red.*

Q. *See if all is ready.*

A. *All is ready, Sovereign Grand Master. You may begin the work. The Fire takes on color.*

Q. *Princes Grand Prior and Grand Surveillant, leave your places, take your gavel and dispose all the Princes each in their post.*

A. *The Grand Prior and the Grand Surveillant each announce the desire "to learn true the moral and physical significance of the signs, words and grips, furniture, jewels and ornaments which I have received or seen in the various Grades through which I have passed."*[53]

The Grand Master says to him:

My Brother, your patience will not be betrayed, and you will learn everything if you have made yourself worthy through your works. Tell me, what are the Grades you have received, for one must be in a state to reply to all the questions I shall ask of you.

Sovereign Grand Master, I will answer to the best of my ability concerning all the Grades I know which have been given to me in regular Lodge. I have arrived at the Grade of Knight of the East, also called of the Sword, which I was told was the final Grade.

Yes, my Brother, to be received as a Knight you must have passed through all the Grades which precede it up to Knight of the East and Knight of the Sun. The state in which you now present yourself before us is a guarantee of your fidelity by the trophy you hold among us as most certain proof.[54]

Prince Grand Prior, conduct the Brother to me to the foot of the throne.

---

[53] The fact that the replies are in quotation marks suggests the first grade was to be read, rather than enacted. This also makes sense from the point of view that the second grade contains the first Chamber of Reflection, and the first real trials for the Candidate. It is also noticeable that there are little or no rubrics in the first grade.

[54] This is further evidence that this Grade is simply a précis of the Master's grade, since it is in that grade that the Candidate enters the Chapter with a 'trophy' on the end of his sword.

The Degrees of the Black Eagle Rose-Croix

Steps

As in the Grade of Apprentice.

After the steps the Sovereign Grand Master has him take his Obligation.

Obligation

As in the Grade of Apprentice.

Once the Obligation has been taken, the Grand Prior raises the Candidate and presents him to the Sovereign Grand Master, who gives him the Sign, Sacred Word, Grip and Password.

Sign

As in the Grade of Apprentice.

Sacred Word

As in the Grade of Apprentice.

Password

As in the Grade of Apprentice.

Grip

As in the Grade of Apprentice.

Then the Grand Master invests him with the Apron, Gloves and Sash of Black Eagle, and gives him the Accolade, thereby constituting him a Knight.

Sash

As in the Grade of Apprentice.

Order

As in the Grade of Apprentice.

Following these Ceremonies, the Sovereign Grand Master tells the Prince Orator to explain to the newly received Brother Knight the images on the Knights Tracing Board.

Explanation of the Tracing Board

As in the Grade of Master.

After the Orator has given his explanation, the Grand Master says:

> *My dear Brother Knight Princes, let us work to instruct the new Knight, so that through his work he might come to discover the principle of life contained within the heart of the prima materia known by the name* **ALKAHEST**, *which is a spirit drawn from the four Elements extracted from the three Kingdoms of Nature: Animal, Vegetable and Mineral.*

To Close

The Sovereign Grand Master says:

Q. *Grand Prior, the work being done, matter takes form, and needs to rest.*

A. *The Elements have united the seven planets. They are enclosed within the Sanctuary, and a white veil covers them.*

The Sovereign Grand Master says:

> *Knight Princes, I am satisfied by your zeal. Be ever vigilant, that the night does not take you by surprise. Keep your lamp lit as best you can, according to the command I give you, until the moment that the Sun will come to the highest part of its zenith.*

The Grand Prior and the Grand Surveillant announce to the Princes by six blows of the gavel that the hour has come when the Evening Star is on the horizon and the Sun is beneath the waters.

Then the Sovereign Grand Master gives six blows, in groups of two, with his gavel, which are repeated by the Grand Prior and the Grand Surveillant, and says:

> *Princes, the Chapter is closed by the accustomed signs, and everyone gives claps three times saying:* **HOUZEL**.[55]

Catechism

Q. *Prince Grand Prior, what is the hour?*

A. *Sovereign Grand Master, the start of day.*

---

[55] This could be 'Huzzah!', or a variant to be used exclusively in this ritual.

The Degrees of the Black Eagle Rose-Croix

Q. *Prince Grand Surveillant, what is your duty?*

A. *To see if the Chapter is Hermetically sealed, if the materials are ready, if the Elements are ready, and if black makes way for white and white for red.*

Q. *Where is the Sovereign Grand Master?*

A. *In the East.*

Q. *Why?*

A. *To await the arrival of the Sun, and to accompany it in the twelve Celestial Houses.*

Q. *What are the names of these twelve Celestial Houses?*

A. | | |
|---|---|
| **Aries** | **Taurus** |
| **Gemini** | **Cancer** |
| **Leo** | **Virgo** |
| **Libra** | **Scorpio** |
| **Sagittarius** | **Capricorn** |
| **Aquarius** | **Pisces** |

Q. *What are the powers which preside and give honor to each of these twelve Houses?*

A. *Twelve sacred and primitive of the Grand and Supreme Architect of the Universe, drawn from a single one.*

Q. *Give me these twelve names arranged as follows for each House.*

A. | | |
|---|---|
| **Jehovah (Iehova)** | **Emmanuel** |
| **Tetragrammaton** | **Jesus (Iesus)** |
| **Messiah** | **Orpheton** |
| **Anasbona** | **Erigion** |
| **Jessemon** | **Eloyn** |
| **Agla** | **Melekh** |

Q. *What are the Spirits which act by the powers of the Supreme Being in each of these Houses?*

A. | | |
|---|---|
| **Machidiel**[56] | **Asmodel** |
| **Ambriel** | **Muriel** |
| **Verchiel** | **Hamaliel** |
| **Zuriel** | **Barbiel** |
| **Adnachiel** | **Hanael** |
| **Gabriel** | **Barchiel** |

---

[56] 'Marchidiel' in original manuscript.

Q. *What are the common names of these twelve Celestial Houses?*

A.
March	April
May	June
July	August
September	October
November	December
January	February

Q. *Which is the most powerful of the names of God inserted in the Pentacles?*

A. **...ADONAI!**

(Enclosed in the LX pus)

Q. *What is its almighty power?*

A. *To put the Universe in motion.*

Those of the Knights who are fortunate enough to pronounce them Cabalistically would have at their disposition the powers residing in the four Elements, and would possess all the virtues possible in man.

Q. *Are there any Knights who can attest to these powers and this knowledge?*

A. *Yes, many have had such powers, and several have learned them, but they only communicate it among the Knights whom they have tested and of whose discretion they are certain.*

Q. *Why are the Knights called Rose-Croix?*

A. *After our Respectable Master Brother Raymond Lully, Grand Mason and Hermetic Philosopher, who discovered through Cabalistic Science the true Sun of life by means of the marriage of six metals.*

He created a gold coin[57]*, and presented it to an English King who made him create medals*[58]*, where one side was a Cross and the other a Rose which is seen to this day on many cabinets. He was then made Knight Raymond Lully, and since then all those who have adopted the Cabalistic Sciences have called themselves Knight of the Rose-Croix.*

Q. *What is the philosophical name of these six metals?*

A. **Saturn**
Jupiter
Mars

---

[57] The words appear to be *appelle or* in French. It was evidently a gold coin, medal or token.
[58] The word in the manuscript is *monnoyes*.

The Degrees of the Black Eagle Rose-Croix

Venus
Mercury
Moon

Also called:

Lead
Iron
Copper
Tin
Quicksilver
Silver

Q. *How does one work the six metals to make them one?*

A. *By the Scales[59] of Solomon.*

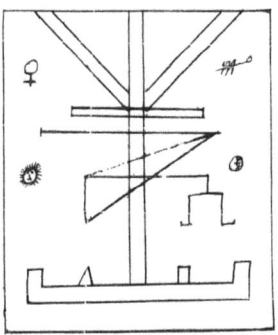

Q. *Nobody has explained the use of these Scales to me.*

A. *Allow me to name several Philosophers such as:*

Albumasaris
Pythagoras
Ptolemæus
Antidonis[60]
Plato
Aristotle
Thales[61]

---

[59] In French *balance*. The word 'scales' has been adopted throughout.
[60] No such name or anything similar is listed among the Greek philosophers.
[61] The name in the manuscript is *Huli*. The most likely is 'Thales' who was listed as one of the 'Seven Sophoi' or "Sages of 'Greece.'

Q.	What weights does Solomon make use of in the operations?
A.	The square of 5 which is 25. The square of 3 which is 9. The square of 2 which is 4, and its cube which is 8 and its cube which is 16.
Q.	Are all men in a state to work upon the Great Work?
A.	No, very few are able to do this, and only true Masons have the advantage of claiming it, but very few are worthy of accomplishing it.
Q.	What must one do to be initiated into the Cabalistic Art?
A.	One must become like our Master Hiram, who preferred to die than to reveal the secrets which had been confided to him.

The Catechism being ended, the Sovereign Grand Master says:

> My dear Brother Knight Princes, let us work to become worthy to possess such a treasure to know the prize. It is now time to retire.

The Signs, Words and Grips are the same as for an Apprentice.

The Degrees of the Black Eagle Rose-Croix

Appendix E: Grade of Companion or Commander of the Black Eagle Rose Croix

Decoration of the Chapter

The Chapter should be hung in black. The equally spaced columns at the various points are decorated with gold chapiters of the Corinthian Order, like the bases.

The number of columns is twelve, of which four are along the Northern wall, four along that of the South, two in the West and two in the East.

On each of these twelve columns are the twelve names of Divinity, written in gold letters. On the four in the North, on the first at the Eastern end is **JEHOVA**.

On the second **EMMANUEL**.

On the third **TETRAGRAMMATON**.

On the fourth **JESUS**.

On the four in the South, on the first at the Eastern end is **MESSIAH**.

On the second **ORPHETON**.

On the third **ANASBONA**.

On the fourth **ERIGION**.

On the two in the East, on the first on the Northern side is **JESSEMON**.

On the second in the South, **ELOYN**.

On the two in the East, on the first on the Northern side is **AGLA**.

On the second in the South, **ADONAI**.

On the Western wall between the two columns is a white marble board decorated with a gilded frame, on which is the following figure inside:

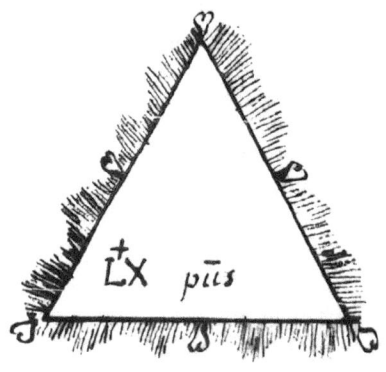

On the wall at the Eastern side, between the two columns is a large Black Eagle. On its right side is the Moon, on its left side is the Sun, and beneath it the Flaming Star with the letter 'J' above.[62]

Between each column is a golden three-branched candelabra, and in the East[63] and the West of the Chapter there are two three-branched candelabras, one at each end.

On the Eastern side of the South there is a two-branched candelabrum, and a little lower on the same side there is a single candlestick which is close to the Tomb.

All the wax used by the Knights of the Black Eagle must be yellow.[64]

The gavels are black, and the tables covered in black cloth; or they are painted black.

The Venerable Master is called Knight Grand Master, the Senior Warden is called Knight Grand Prior, and the Junior Warden is called Knight Grand Warden.

The other Brothers are called Brothers and Knights.

Attire

For dress a green coat is worn, long breeches, black shoes, black sword decorated with fire-colored ribbons, a black chapeau with a white plume.

Sash

The cord should be fire-colored, worn as a sash (passing from right to left). The is also another ribbon of the same color, passing from the buttonhole to the coat. On each is a jewel which hangs from its end.

Jewel

The jewel is an eagle, in gold or silver or metal, or brilliant, or black, ultimately what you will.

Gloves

The gloves are red edged with black.

---

[62] 'I' in French is represented as 'J' in English.
[63] In the original the manuscript says: 'in the middle'.
[64] It is assumed this means virgin beeswax, rather than yellow-colored candles.

The Degrees of the Black Eagle Rose-Croix

Apron

The apron is white and edged and lined with red. On the flap is a flaming star with the letter 'J' (or 'I'), and in the middle of the apron is a black eagle with nothing else.

Password

ELIAEL

Sacred Word

JABAMAIAH[65]

Sign

The Sign is made by extending the two hands, fingers touching the neck, kissing them in the same position, then lowering them to touch the two breasts[66], holding them there.

The response to the Sign is given by putting the right hand on the guard of the sword, and then bringing the same hand to the breast of the Knight who made the first Sign.

Grip

The first grip is given as Apprentice, saying: "Our Brother has been found." The second grip is given as Companion, saying:

ALPHA and OMEGA

Then the first gives the grip of Master and says: "A great eagle guards him."

The second turns his hands, gripping up from below, saying: "**KYRIE**", then they embrace.[67]

Order

To come to Order one closes the little finger and thumb of the right hand, with the three other fingers extended, and places them on the heart.

---

[65] Jabamiah, the 70th Genius or Angel of the Shemhamphorasch, is traditionally associated with alchemy and transformation.

[66] The original manuscript uses the word *tétons* or 'nipples' – not a word commonly found in Masonic ritual.

[67] Although this is the Companion Grade of the Black Eagle Rose Croix, the participants will have completed the three Blue Degrees a long time previously and will therefore be familiar with the Signs and Grips of the Master Masons Degree.

Enlightenment Man & Mason

Explanation of the Tracing Board

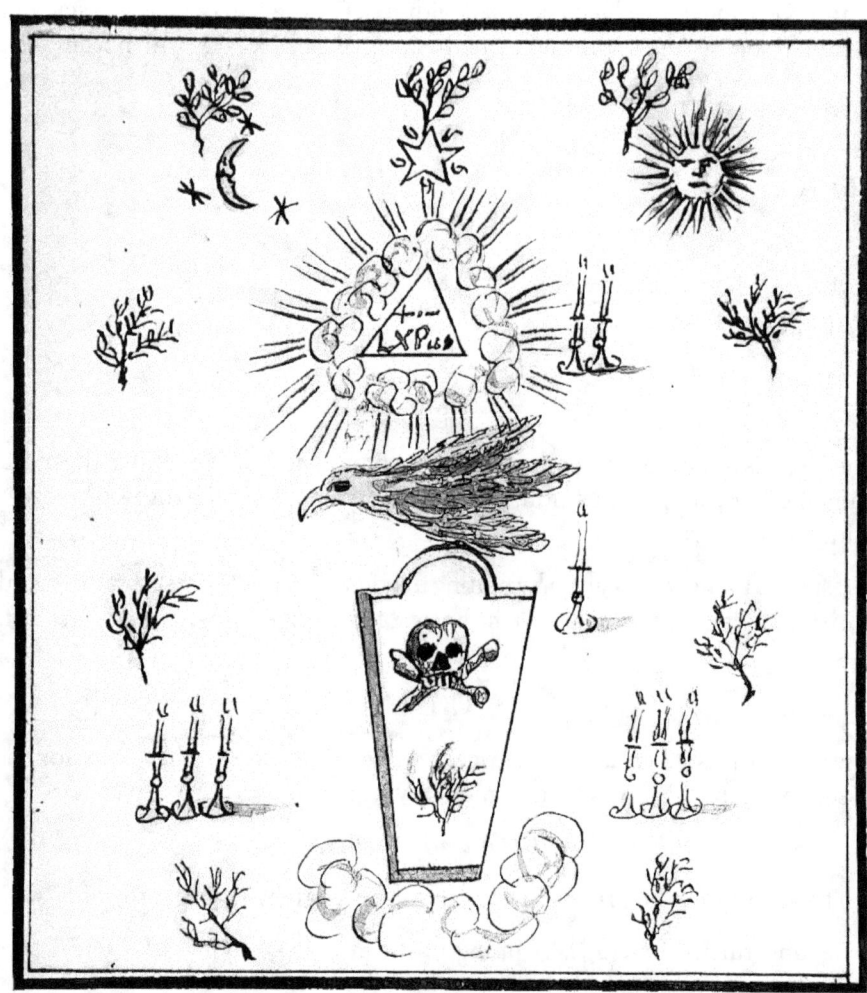

Figure 130: Kindly supplied by Dr. Oscar Alleyne. Taken from the Collection of 84 paintings by Bros. Löwen and Ducaten circa 1762.

1. The acacia[68] which was in the place where our Brother Hiram was placed after he had been assassinated, a branch of which was placed on the spot where he had been put, in order to recognize it.

2. A cloud which descended from the firmament to hide the place where our Brother Hiram had been placed, so that the assassins could no longer find him to remove him.

---

[68] In the Tracing Board image this is interpreted – as it is in some rituals – as an acacia tree grove.

The Degrees of the Black Eagle Rose-Croix

3. The candelabras represent the nine Masters who searched for our Brother; and the single candlestick represents the one who found him.
4. The Tomb of our Brother Hiram.
5. The Sun and the Moon which illuminated everything for the Brothers who participated in the search, without a cloud ever obscuring them.
6. The Flaming Star is the phenomenon observed by the Masters, and which was fixed over the tomb of our Brother, and the letter 'J' in the middle is the initial of the Redoubtable Name.[69]
7. The Triangle with the writing was another phenomenon which appeared when the body of our Brother was discovered, and this inexpressible[70] inscription in the middle is the Grand and Ineffable Sacred and August Word for which the flaming star was substituted.
8. The Eagle which faithfully guarded the grave in which our Brother laid for nine days, for fear that some beast would come to feed on him; and when Hiram was found the Eagle dived down on the tomb, took up the branch of acacia and flew into the air triumphant, having guarded the precious deposit, holding the branch of acacia in its talons.

Opening of the Chapter

The Chapter is opened by a loud blow of the gavel which the Knight Grand Master gives on the altar, to which the Grand Prior and the Grand Warden respond with another blow of the gavel. Then the Grand Master says:

> *Dear Knights Grand Prior and Grand Warden, assist me to open the Chapter of Knights of the Black Eagle.*

All immediately give the Sign, and while the hands are on the breasts, the Grand Prior and the Grand Warden present the point of their swords, then all the Knights come to Order, which is the three fingers on the heart, and all remain in that attitude. Then the Grand Master says:

Q. *Knight Grand Prior, what is the hour?*

A. *Sovereign Grand Master, the opening of day.*

---

[69] There is a striking similarity between this scene and that of the Epiphany with the three wise men, which is not surprising since Hiram was often seen as an archetype for Jesus in early rituals.

[70] This is another example of a transcription error which supports the evidence that the Willermoz Ritual predates the Tschoudy one. Here the word used is *indicible*, meaning 'ineffable, inexpressible'; in the Tschoudy ritual it is rendered as invisible or 'invisible'. The 'd' has been transposed to 'v', making for a meaningless expression ('invisible inscription', whereas the word in the center is also referred to as the Grand and Ineffable Sacred Word).

Q.	Knight Grand Warden, what is your duty?
A.	To see if the Chapter is tiled.
Q.	Assure yourself that it is.
A.	I answer for it with my head.
Q.	Brothers Grand Prior and Grand Warden, take up your gavels.
A.	*They incline their heads, replace their words in their scabbards and take up their gavels.*

Then the Knight Grand Master gives six blows in groups of two, with an interval after each second time, and announces to the Venerable Chapter that the work is open.

The Grand Prior and the Grand Warden repeat the blows, announcing to all the Knights that the work is open, and once this is done they go before the Knight Grand Master, all the Knight regarding at him in a pleasant manner, salute him and are then seated.

To Close the Chapter

The Chapter is closed by a loud blow of the gavel, which the Knight Grand Master gives on the altar, to which the Grand Prior and Grand Warden reply with another blow of the gavel. Then the Knight Grand Master says:

Dear Knights Grand Prior and Grand Warden, assist me to close the Chapter in Knight of the Black Eagle and give the Sign.

While the Knights' hands are on their breasts, the Grand Prior and the Grand Warden present the points of their swords, then all the Knights come to Order which is the three fingers on the heart, and all remains in this attitude. The Grand Master says:

Q.	Knight Grand Prior, what is the hour?
A.	Sovereign Grand Master, the beginning of night.
Q.	Brothers Grand Prior and Grand Warden, take up your gavels.
A.	*They incline their heads, replace their words in their scabbards and take up their gavels.*

Then the Knight Grand Master gives six blows in groups of two, with an interval after each second time, and announces to the Venerable Chapter that the work is closed.

The Grand Prior and the Grand Warden repeat the blows, announcing to all the Knights that the work is closed, and once this is done they go before the Knight Grand Master, who repeats the six blows of the gavel, and announces to the Venerable Chapter that the work is ended. They look at him in a pleasant manner, and the Chapter is closed, and all of them depart.

The Degrees of the Black Eagle Rose-Croix

Initiation

The Chamber of Reflection

This is a Black Chamber prepared in the following manner.

It is an apartment completely hung with black, lit by a single lamp, where sulfur and spirits of wine are burned to render the objects in the chamber even more hideous. At the side of the lamp is a real cadaver, if possible, or failing that a Knight who will act as one, completely naked except for his private parts, which are covered by an apron stained with blood.

If there isn't a real cadaver, the Knight who acts as one must not be known to the Candidate. The cadaver is painted with blood on each cheek, each breast, and in the hollow of his stomach.

A great eagle of cardboard will be made, attached by black threads so that they cannot be seen and operated by a Brother hidden behind the hangings who can make it move, going to and fro in the room and, at intervals, over the body of the cadaver by means of the attached threads.

There is a board of pinewood placed right against and beside the cadaver, with ten or more bands nailed to it, to which the Candidate will be attached in the manner to be explained.

Once the Black Chamber is prepared, the door is closed and the Candidate is made to enter a Chamber of Reflection containing only a table and candle and a cord.

When the Candidate has been in reflection for some time, the Grand Master dispatches two Knights to go to prepare the Candidate, and then to place him in the Black Chamber.

The Grand Prior goes at the head of the Knights and comprises the third Brother.

The door of the Chamber of Reflection having been opened, the three Brothers enter with swords drawn, wearing their full regalia, and the Grand Prior asks the Candidate if he feels strong enough to resist the Trials through which he must pass, and that he should take his time to think before saying "Yes", since once he says the word he will no longer be able to retreat, even if he must die.

If the Candidate replies "No", he is immediately made to leave and chased away; but if on the contrary he says "Yes", the Grand Prior tells the Knights to prepare him.

His attire is removed, his chapeau, his shirt, until finally all that remain are his shoes and breeches. Then he is dressed in a short shirt which only goes down to the top of his breeches.

This shirt is completely covered with blood, and he is left in that condition, being told to wait. The door is closed, and he is left in the Chamber once more.

When the Knights have closed the door, two remain outside with swords in hand, and the Grand Prior goes into the Chapter to announce that the Candidate is prepared.

Then the Grand Master says:

> Venerable Knights, all of you who compose this Chapter, let us go and see the Candidate, and regard him with a furious gaze.

Then they leave two by two, the door of the Chamber of Reflection where the Candidate is is opened, and all enter two by two with sword in hand and with eyes flashing with anger, each leaving in the same manner to resume their seats in the Chapter. The three who enter last are the Grand Master, Grand Prior and Grand Warden.

The Grand Master regards the Candidate with a terrible, menacing gaze, and says to him:

> We have been deceived! The innocent one has died while the guilty one still lives! We will ask mercy from the Supreme and Grand Architect of the Universe.

Then, addressing himself to the Grand Prior, he says to him:

> Grand Prior, I deliver him to you, that he will not find death too quickly, but will endure the cruelest tortures.

He then leaves with the Grand Warden.

As soon as the Grand Master has left with the Grand Warden, the Grand Prior says to the two Knights, who remain at the door with swords drawn, to enter and attend to their duties.

Then they blindfold him and bind his hands behind his back with a knot passing about his neck, and in that state, they lead him to the Black Chamber. As soon as he arrives, he is tied down on the pinewood board next to the cadaver; after which the two Knights leave and station themselves outside the dor.

Then the Grand Prior removes the blindfold of the Candidate, saying to him:

> See our scorn, you wretch! We put this innocent man to death on an unjust suspicion. Tremble, you unlucky one at the torments which await you. I leave you with this cadaver which makes me shudder with horror and fear. May you serve as food for the fiercest beasts!

He then goes to the Chapter to give an account of what he has done.

The Degrees of the Black Eagle Rose-Croix

However, the two Knight still remain outside the door of the Black Chamber, as much to offer assistance to the patient if needed, as to prevent him from leaving if he is able to loosen his bonds.

When the patient has been in the Black Chamber for a short time, the Grand Master says to the Chapter:

> *Venerable Knights and Brothers, let us go and see if the Candidate is worthy of being admitted in our August Chapter.*

Then the Grand Prior who is functioning as Master of Ceremonies goes first, the Grand Master next, and then the Grand Warden, as well as all the Knights one by one, and they go in procession with sword in hand to the Black Chamber where the Candidate is.

Having arrived at the door, the Grand Prior asks one of the two Knights who are acting as Sentinels if the Candidate is still strong and unshakeable.

After this information which by the response should be favorable to the patient, they all enter one after the other into the Chamber, coming to pass before the Candidate, and stand around the apartment walls except for the Grand Prior, who remains at the side of the Candidate. Once all are in place, the Grand Prior covers the face of the Candidate with a handkerchief, and the Grand Warden says:

> *Grand Master, this unfortunate who we hold here is not the only guilty one. We have discovered and arrested another of these wretched false Brothers, but who is, however less guilty then the one who is bound to this board.*

The Grand Master says:

> *So, let the other one be the first to be delivered to death.*

Then another Brother who is already prepared to pretend to be the man to be killed complains, sighs, and acts as if he is fighting. Finally, after some time in vain resistance, he acts as if he has succumbed.

There is a vessel full of lamb's blood which is spread in abundance on the floor.

Once this is done all the Knights go to resume their places in the Chapter. Only the two guards at the door remain, along with the Grand Prior who is inside. After everybody has left the Grand Prior, without saying a word, removes the handkerchief from the face of the Candidate and immediately leaves, leaving him with the two cadavers. He waits outside the Chamber with the two sentinels, and after leaving him for half an hour, he returns, blindfolds him, unbinds him and conducts him to the door of the Chapter, where he gives six knocks.

As soon as the Candidate has left the Black Chamber, the two Sentinels who were at the door tidy everything, and those who played the cadavers dress and go to resume their places in the Chapter.

The Grand Warden having repeated the knocks, the Grand Master orders to see who it is, and he is told it is the worthy Mason who asks to be received a Knight of the Black Eagle Rose Croix.

Once the Grand Master has ordered his admission, he is placed in the West between the Grand Prior and the Grand Warden. When he is there the Grand Prior gives an account of the courage of the Postulant Brother Mason to the Chapter.

Then the Grand Master says a few words about his courage. He then tells the Grand Prior to remove his blindfold; and that instant all the Knight come to order. The Grand Prior places the point of his sword to his cheek, and the Grand Warden does likewise, and the Grand Master comes forward and places the point of his sword on his stomach.

In this posture they have him advance to the foot of the throne, where they make him kneel in the usual manner. He then takes the following Obligation. Then the swords are raised, and those who held him return to their places.

Obligation

> *I, Name…… here present, promise and swear before the Grand and Supreme Architect of the Universe and in presence of this August Chapter, ever to conceal the secrets of the Knights of the Black Eagle Rose Croix. If I break my Obligation, I ask that three of my Brothers will plunge their swords into my cheeks and my breast, that my heart may be torn out, my body hung in the middle of this Venerable Chapter to serve as an example to all my Brothers. I also promise in the same Obligation to support our customs and privileges. May the Sovereign Architect of the Universe and His Holy Gospel assist me.*

Once the Obligation is ended, the Grand Master claps once, and all the Knights say: *We swear to punish him as he said, if he prevaricates in the least of things.*

The Candidate is dressed, and as soon as he is ready he is once more caused to kneel in the middle of the Tracing Board, and there the Grand Master receives him as a Knight, by attaching the belt from which hangs the scabbard of his sword. Then, taking the drawn sword, he has him kiss it, and with the flat a gives a light blow to his right cheek, then on the left cheek, then upon the shoulders.

The Grand Master has him put his sword in his scabbard and embraces him. All the Knights come and embrace him as well. Once this is done, the new Knight is placed in the West and made to advance to the throne with regular steps

The Degrees of the Black Eagle Rose-Croix

Steps

These Steps are made with the feet in a square. He begins in the West,

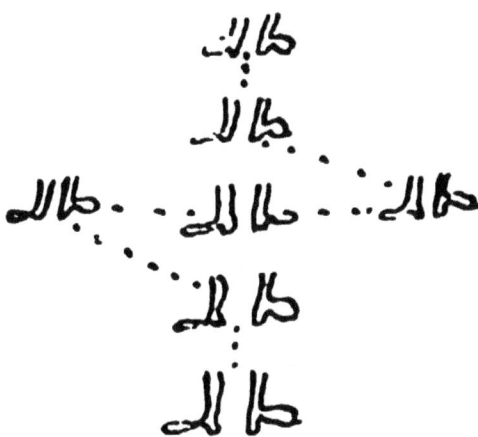

taking a step forward to the Northern side, another to the Center of the Tomb, another to the South, another on the Eagle, and another on the Luminous Triangle.

As soon as the new Knight arrives at the foot of the throne, the Grand Master gives him the Sign, Words and Grips, and tells him to repeat them with all of the Venerable Chapter, beginning with the Grand Prior and the Grand Warden, and then with all the Knights.

Once this has been done, the new Knight is seated on the right of the Grand Master, who decorates him with the sash, gloves and cords. Following this he has him sit and gives the following Instruction.

Instruction

Q. *Why is the Chapter hung with black?*

A. *To indicate that our secret must be held in the deepest obscurity with regard to Masons below our Sublime Grade as well as among the Profane.*

Q. *Why are the columns white?*

A. *To indicate the candor of the Knights.*

Q. *Why are the chapiters and bases gold?*

A. *To indicate the purity of the Knights.*

Q. *What do the twelve Names and the twelve columns in the Chapter signify?*

A. *The twelve columns are dedicated to the twelve Sacred and Mysterious Names which are written thereon. These are the Divine Names of the Great Pentacle of Solomon.*

Q. *Give me these twelve Names.*

A.
JEHOVA	**EMMANUEL**
TETRAGRAMMATON	**JESUS**
MESSIAH	**ORPHETON**
ANASBONA	**ERIGION**
JESSEMON	**ELOYN**
AGLA	**ADONAI**

Q. *What does the luminous triangle signify?*

A. *It is that marvel which suddenly appeared when the body of our Brother* **HIRAM** *was discovered.*

Q. *What does the star which is within signify?*

A. *It is the Great Name written Cabalistically, for which we have substituted another.*

Q. *What does the Eagle signify?*

A. *It represents the one which guarded the grave of our Brother Hiram, for fear that some beast would come to dig him up and feed on him; and when the Masters found him the Eagle, to mark its triumph, suddenly dived down on the tomb, took up the branch of acacia which the assassins had placed there, and flew into the air triumphant, from the precious deposit which it had guarded so preciously.*[71]

---

[71] This is another indication that this is the original version, since it would be easy to duplicate a word in this manner which could be corrected in a later version. For example, in the Tschoudy version this word is replaced by *soigneusement*, or 'carefully'.

The Degrees of the Black Eagle Rose-Croix

Q. *What do the Sun and the Moon represent?*

A. To remind us that the stars serve to illuminate the Masters, the sun during the day and the moon by night, when they were searching for our Brother, without which they would be forever in darkness.

Q. *What does the flaming star, with the letter 'J' in its center, signify?*

A. It represents that which was fixed over the grave of our Brother Hiram, and the letter in the center is the initial of the Sacred Word which has been substituted by that in the luminous triangle.

Q. *What do the nine luminaries signify?*

A. They represent the nine Master who went in search of our Brother Hiram, and the one near the Tomb is the Brother who drew him forth from his grave.

Q. *What are the candles yellow?*

A. To mark the grief of our Masters.

Q. *What does our dress in black, white and red signify?*

A. The black signifies our mourning for the death of our assassinated Brother. The white is for our innocence of the crime. The red is his blood which was shed.

Q. *What is our password?*

A. **ELIAEL**.

Q. *What property does this name have?*

A. When pronounced in a Cabalistic manner and combined in its forms, it makes the powers of darkness flee.

Q. *What is the Sacred Word?*

A. **JABAMIAH**.

Q. *What is it used for?*

A. To operate many things, this word must be pronounced Cabalistically.

Q. *What does our Sign signify?*

A. Having two cheeks and the stomach pierced if we prevaricate.

Q. *What does our grip signify?*

A. It makes us remember the Grades through which we have passed in order to reach the eminent Grade in which we find ourselves today in this Venerable Chapter.

Q. *What does coming to Order signify?*

A.	*That we have taken an Obligation to have our heart torn out if we prevaricate.*
Q.	*Why do we place three fingers on our heart, and not the entire hand?*
A.	*Those three fingers are symbolic of the mysterious triangular number.*
Q.	*What do the six steps of our march, and the six knocks given indicate?*
A.	*They represent the six Cabalistic pronunciations of our Sacred Word.*
Q.	*Can you explain these Cabalistic pronunciations as well as the Pentacle of our Brother Solomon?*
A.	*The Great and Supreme Architect of the Universe does not yet permit these sublime mysteries to be revealed, but I hope that my irreproachable conduct and my application to the Work will allow me to learn it one day.*

The Degrees of the Black Eagle Rose-Croix

Appendix F: Grade of Grand Master or Commander of the Black Eagle Rose Croix

Introduction

Every good Mason educated in the mysteries of the Order, possessing the High Grades such as Grand Écossais, Knight of the East and of the Sun, previously educated about the Inferior Grades, must imagine that, from its institution, Masonry has a goal which must still exist, that this work would not only lead to the erection of buildings for the True God, and that it would not be solely restricted to moral virtue, but that some other motive had to have given rise to the origin of such a Sublime Order. Yes, my Brothers, the true philosophy known and practiced by Solomon, the wisest of Kings of his time, is the basis on which Masonry is built. This wise King, being unable to work alone, chose a number of subjects in his states similar to his heart. He bound them with his kindness by regarding them as his Brethren, initiating them into the most hidden secrets of the Cabalistic Art.

It would be desirable, my dear Brothers, for this Art to have come to us in all its purity! But our old Masons, whether by prudence or due to other reasons, concealed from us the most important points of this Divine Art by means of threefold hieroglyphics, which only present enigmas to us. Happy is he among us, who will be laborious enough to discover by his research and his assiduity in working all these Sublime Truths! He will be assured of having found the true and pure happiness which a mortal might aspire to; his days will be lengthened; his morals will be exempt from being corrupted by the vices of indigence and infirmities towards which too many of the human species are led.

Consider, my Brother, all these objects which have struck you in the different grades through which you have passed, and you will see that they represent many signs and mysteries to which you will one day possess the key, which means, to truly learn to what they should apply them. The grade of Black Eagle includes them all; its analysis shows you the work to be undertaken. It is to you, my dear Brothers, to enter into this immense path of love for truth and perseverance, and to persevere on it.

This Grade, which composes an Order of Perfect Mason, was drawn from the Cabalistic treasure of Doctor and Rabbi Neamuth, Chief of the Synagogue at Leiden.[72]

---

[72] According to an article in the French newspaper *Le Monde* by Alain Guichard, dated June 7th, 1970, (https://www.lemonde.fr/archives/article/1970/06/02/de-dom-pernety-a-lord-chesterfield_2637917_1819218.html), in 1762 "Frederic II welcomed (Dom Pernety) into Prussia and provided him with the revenues of an Abbey in Thuringe. A meeting with Doctor Neamuth, rabbi of the Leiden Synagogue, put him in contact with the high mysticism of the Kabala. Thus, Dom Pernety found his definitive path and moved to Bédarrides, not far from Avignon, but outside of the papal frontiers." In fact, the date given in the article is ambiguous, and could be taken to be the year after 1761 or the year after 1767. However, the second gives rise to a date of 1768, which

Ceremonial & Dignities

In this Order the meetings held are called Chapters, the chief is Sovereign Grand Master, his First Lieutenant Prince is called Sovereign Grand Prior, his Second Lieutenant is called Sovereign Grand Warden, the other Officers have the titles of Sovereign.

Those who have the Third Grade are titled Bailiffs. Those who have the Second Grade bear the title of Commander, and those who have the First Grade are simply titled Knights.

This Order is highly recommended in the Northern courts, among others in Prussia, where it took the name of Black Eagle because the reigning King of Prussia[73] was its first Grand Master, and because the Eagle is found in the Catechism[74].

All these deliberations are titled from the Sovereign Chapter.

The Knights of the Black Eagle are regarded as First Masons *par excellence*, and as such they shall have precedence in all Lodges where they find themselves, over all the Brethren who do not possess this Grade. Their privileges are very extensive, and they should be due to the knowledge they possess.

Privileges

First Article

When a Knight visits a Lodge, the Venerable Master, accompanied by the two Wardens and the three other most qualified Brothers armed with drawn swords, goes to receive him at the door of the Lodge, hands over his gavel which he accepts, and with which he gives three gentle knocks on his forehead, and well as upon the two Wardens, and has them kiss his heart covered by his jewel[75]. After this ceremony is completed, he gives back to the Venerable Master his scepter and sword, which he carries crossed in his hands covered by his apron. At his sides he has the two Wardens each bearing a lighted candle. They walk one step in front of the Knight. When the Knight gives the order to proceed, two of the aforementioned Brothers will form an arch of steel with their swords, under which the Knight will stand, and the third Brother stands behind to complete the aforesaid arch. In this order they all advance towards the throne, and when they arrive, the Knight ascends the dais, takes the scepter and sword, places them upon the altar and salutes the Venerable Master, the Wardens and the other two Brothers, then seats the first on his right and the rest in their regular places.

---

seems highly unlikely, seeing that it was in 1766 that he founded his six-grade system, the *Rite Hermétique* or the *Rite de Pernety* (Joanny Bricaud, *Les Illuminés d'Avignon*, (2nd Ed., SEPP, Paris 1995, Orig. 1927), 32.

[73] Frederic II, Born 1712 (footnote in original text).

[74] or Instruction.

[75] *écusson* – lit. escutcheon, shield.

Article II

The Knights will have preference over other visitors in Lodge and at the banquet. They will be seated according to their Grade, and according to the date of their Initiation, that is so that that the oldest will be given preference. If the Venerable Master is a Knight, he will not cede his place nor his gavel to the visiting Knight, but he will place him at his right hand.

Article III

At whatever ceremony it may be, for an Initiation as well as for the entry of visitors, the Knights will always remain seated, just as for the Opening and Closing of Lodges they will always be covered.

Article IV

Whatever fault a Knight may make concerning his Lodge, it cannot be corrected by its leader. In every case, a process against him will be held before the Sovereign Chapter by means of a request justified by the leaders by whom he has been accused, because a Knight can only be judged by his peers; and if the case merits punishment, this will be done in the Chapter and not in presence of other Brothers.

Article V

During banquets the Knights will be seated as in Lodge. When a toast is proposed they always remain seated and covered They will always drink together without ceremony and when the King's health is proposed they will give thanks on his behalf, but always seated and covered. They will not give thanks for any other toast.

Article VI

Although they will be summoned to the Lodge meeting like the other Brethren, they will go when it suits them, and when they do not go then the Lodge cannot stamp the minutes or amend them to that effect. On their summons there will not be written 'by command of the Ven. Master' but 'Prince, you are informed, etc.'

They will all keep their armor in Lodge, and nobody can take the place of a Knight unless he occupies a function in Lodge. Moreover, they are exempted from the Catechism, and may leave and return without asking for permission of the Master. They will also visit all Lodges without permission.

Article VII

The Lodge will always be at Refreshment and observe the proprieties for them, so that they never have to ask for permission to speak and will always speak first.

Article VIII

The Knights will have three votes.

Article IX

When a Knight enters a Lodge, he shall have his hat on his head. All the Brothers will rise with their hats off. Only other Knights, if there are any, will remain seated, but they will take off their hats.

Article X

When a Knight enters the Lodge, he will be received by five Brothers, two of them bearing a lit candle, and the three others armed with their swords, as mentioned in the first Article.

Statutes & Regulations

First Article

The Knights shall never leave their collars in any Lodge they visit, under penalty of twenty- four livres.[76]

Article II

A Chapter will be held any time the Grand Master judges it appropriate.

Article III

There shall be no obligatory Chapter every month as with Lodges.

Article IV

All Knights not attending a Chapter after being summoned will be punished if they have no good reason.

Article V

From the seventh to the fifteenth day of the month all the Knights will be obliged to pay their fees to the Treasurer.

Article VI

The fees will be in proportion to the expenses incurred by the Chapter.

---

[76] Old French monetary system predating the Franc. *Livre* means 'pound'.

Article VII

Initiations of Apprentice will cost four Gold Louis, those of Companion one Gold Louis, and those of Master ten Gold Louis.

Article VIII

Every Knights will be provided with his Certificate of his privileges and his rules.

Article IX

The Knights, also called Apprentice, only wear one poppy-red ribbon in the buttonhole of their jacket, at the bottom of which is attached the jewel.

Article X

The Commanders, also called Companions, wear the great collar about their neck where the jewel will be attached to the bottom by a rosette of black ribbon.

Article XI

The Masters, also called Bailiffs, wear the sash and the plate over their clothes on the side of the heart. However, the Bailiffs may allow the Commanders and Knights to wear the sash and plate, and this permission will be registered.

Article XII

The Chapter is composed of a Grand Master, a Grand Prior, a Grand Warden, an Orator, a Chancellor, a Treasurer, a Master of Ceremony, a Terrible Brother and an Intendant, and in all there will not be more than eleven in the Chapter.

Article XIII

Chapter Elections take place every year on Trinity Sunday; only the Grand Master will remain for three successive years, and the Chancellor will remain in perpetuity.

Article XIV

The Chancellor is also the Archivist, the Guardian of the Seal, and takes care of the correspondence.

Article XV

The two great obligatory Banquets which all Knights are obliged to attend are held: the first on Epiphany, the second on the Sunday after Saint Louis.

Article XVI

The Bailiffs can make Masons up to and including Knight of the East, the Commanders up to and including Grand Écossais, and the Knights up to and including Écossais.

Article XVII

All Knights may visit any Lodges they wish to, and have the chair ceded to them.

Article XVIII

The assembled Chapter can constitute all authority when joined together in that Illustrious Assembly, provided that Frederic II, King of Prussia, their Grand Master General permits them.[77]

Article XIX

The Treasurer shall render his accounts every time the Grand Master wishes it and will write a profane note to the aforesaid Grand Master, or a person named by him, of the funds he has from the Chapter.

Article XX

When a Knight dies, the Chapter is obliged to have a Requiem Mass said for him within the octave[78] for the repose of his soul, which all the Brothers shall attend under a penalty of twelve livres which they will remit to the Treasurer.

Article XXI

All Knights are obliged to accompany the funeral cortege of their dead brethren up to the internment, all dressed in black, and they will have a Mass for the Dead said, which they will attend under penalty of twenty-four livres.

---

[77] Another fanciful reference to the King of Prussia being the head of the Order and his permission being required. Similar citations may be found in Scottish Rite documents, for example, in Thory's *Acta Latomorum* (Dupart, Paris 1815), 172, we read: "From the Golden Book of the Supreme Council of the 33° Degree in France, printed in 1807, p. 7, we read that on May 1st of this year, Frederic II, King of Prussia, had the High Grades and Masonic Constitutions of the Ancient Rite revised." Yet, Robert B. Folger, in his book *The Ancient and Accepted Scottish Rite in Thirty-Three Degrees*, (published by the Author, New York 1862), 63, stated that: "...in the official proceeding of the centennial celebration of the initiation of Frederick the Great, King of Prussia, into the fraternity of Masons, by the Grand National Mother Lodge of the Three Globes, Berlin, 1838, the Orator of the occasion endeavors to correct the assertion advanced in regard to Frederick by several French systems of Masonry, and positively declares that he never actively participated in any work except in that of the real Masonic Degrees, and that he was opposed to the High Degrees."

[78] An octave is a week following a feast Day in the Catholic calendar: in this case it means that the mass must be said within eight days of a deceased Knight's passing.

The Degrees of the Black Eagle Rose-Croix

Article XXII

At the requiem messes which the Chapter has said, three candles for the altar of half a livre each will be supplied, one of which is placed on each side of the altar and the other before the tabernacle, if there are only three lights upon the altar. These ceremonies are to be followed for all the Knights even if they no longer serve the Chapter, and even if proceedings were being brought against them, for all must be forgotten in death. And at the end of the year another Requiem Mass will be said, on the same day or within the octave of the time when the Knight died the previous year.

Article XXIII

The Knights, Commanders and Bailiffs are obliged to disclose their research and discoveries to the Chapter, so that they may be registered, as much regarding Cabalistic Knowledge as their physical experiences and their antipathetic and sympathetic efforts.

Notes

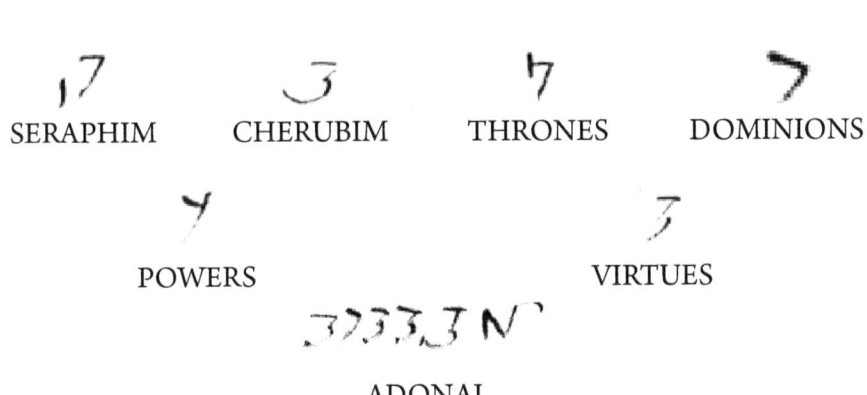

| SERAPHIM | CHERUBIM | THRONES | DOMINIONS |

POWERS · VIRTUES

ADONAI

by whose power we come to the discovery of the first of the metals which is the Sun, which arises from the intimate alliance between the 6 metals, of which each two furnish the seed.

♄	♃	♂
SATURN	JUPITER	MARS
Lead	Tin	Iron

♀	☿	☽
VENUS	MERCURY	MOON
Copper	Quicksilver	Silver

The Operation of this Great Work consists of knowing the perfect point of the alliance of these metals by the weight and measure contained in each of the six letters of the first name of God, which Solomon made known to his initiates as ADONAI, and for them he composed his Scales[79] – or the entire secret of the Great Work – enclosed within it.

There were seven sages who understood and used the Scales of Solomon, and who transmitted it in their works, as you will see in this Grade.

The Most Great and Holy Name of God composed of twelve letters, each containing a particular name which presides over the twelve months of the year, are indicated by the Signs of the Zodiac, and the Geniuses which guide them.

The Twelve Months of the Year

JEHOVA	EMMANUEL	TETRAGRAMMATON
♈	♉	♊
Aries	Taurus	Gemini
Ram	Bull	Twins
March	April	May
Machidiel[80]	Asmodel	Ambriel

JESUS	MESSIAH	ORPHETON
♋	♌	♍
Cancer	Leo	Virgo
Crayfish	Lion	Virgin
June	July	August
Muriel	Verchiel	Hamaliel

---

[79] The word in French is *Balance*, which can be translated as 'balance' or 'scales'. 'Scales' has been used throughout, naturally incorporating its allusion to the Zodiacal sign *Libra*.
[80] 'Malchidiel' in original manuscript.

The Degrees of the Black Eagle Rose-Croix

ז	ז	ך
ANASBONA	ERIGION	JESSEMON
♎	♏	♐
Libra	Scorpio	Sagittarius
Scales	Scorpion	Archer
September	October	November
Uriel[81]	Barbiel	Adnachiel

·ז	אך	·ך
ELION[82]	AGLA	MELECH
♑	♒	♓
Capricorn	Aquarius	Pisces
Sea-goat	Waterbearer	Fish
December	January	February
Hanael	Gabriel	Barchiel

To arrive at the great Cubic Stone, which contains within it all the gifts and virtues to make men perfectly happy in this world, one must work to find the Principle of Life which the Philosophers call **ALKAHEST**.

This spirit of virtue improves those vital elements of which man is composed, purifies them and by that prolongs life. It also has the property of transforming the six metals into a single one which is called *par excellence* the most perfect, which is fixed gold and potable gold.

ALKAHEST is drawn from the sublime and vivifying spirits of the three Kingdoms of Nature; that is to say, from the Animal, the Vegetable and the Mineral, by observing their month when drawing the spirits of each Kingdom and making it, outside of which they have no active power.

---

[81] 'Zuriel' in original manuscript.
[82] 'Eloyn' in the original manuscript.

Solar Year

MARCH
The goat, noctua[83] or owl, olive, amaranthus tricolor[84] or yellow amaranth, sardonyx.

APRIL
Hircus or he-goat, dove, myrtle, cupressus[85] or female cypress, sardius[86].

MAY
Taurus or bull, cock, laurel, cupressus or male cypress, topaz[87].

JUNE
Canis or dog, stork, corylus or hazel, symphytum or great comfrey, chalcedony.

JULY
Cervus or stag, eagle, æsculus, shalott, cyclamina or cyclamen, blood jasper.

AUGUST
Porcus or pig, sparrow, apple-tree, calamintus or calamint, smaragdus or emerald.

SEPTEMBER
Asinus or ass, anser or goose, buxus or boxwood or germantree, beryl.

OCTOBER
Lupus or wolf, picides or woodpecker, quince[88] or artemisia[89].

NOVEMBER
Cerva or hart[90], corvus or crow, palm-tree, anagallis (primrose), hyacinth[91].

DECEMBER
Leo or lion, ardea or heron, pine, mint[92] or morel, chrysoprasus or chrysoprase[93].

JANUARY
Agnus or lamb, peacock, laurus[94] or laurin, thyme[95], rock crystal.

FEBRUARY
Equus or horse, swan, elm or ulmaceae, Eastern sapphire, astrolochia.

The place in the Operations separately preserves each spirit drawn from each month, and all together compose the **AKAHEST** by means of the Scales of Solomon.

---

[83] Little owl (Athene noctua).

[84] *Elelisphatis* in original document. However, it is likely that many Latin names have changed over time as the relationship between different genuses has been established. The same goes for the rest of the footnotes below. Where a word is completely indecipherable, the words used in the Catechism of the Baron von Tschoudy version of the ritual have been used.

[85] *Peristerion* in original text.

[86] In the Catechism this is substituted by the topaz.

[87] In the Catechism at the end this is substituted by the agate.

[88] *Coznas* in the original text.

[89] *Cognafice arthemises* used in original text.

[90] This is listed as serpent in the Catechism.

[91] This is listed under October; Amethyst is given for November and Cornelian for December in the Catechism.

[92] *L'heatus* (?) in original text.

[93] *Crisolide* in original text.

[94] *Pehaminus* in original text.

[95] Dracantea or Ladragone in original text.

The Degrees of the Black Eagle Rose-Croix

Solomon, in the institution of Masonry created three Grades, as we know, the last being Master, and those who were initiated into it possessed like him the entire Cabalistic Knowledge. Over the Masters, they elected one *par excellence* who commanded all, and that was our Master **HIRAM**, whom all Masons know.

The honorific Emblem of his Grade was a triangular plate of gold called the Sacred Pentacle, by means of which all Science was known, even unto the most abstract things. On one side were the words:

Archangeli Sacris Inter; Archangeli, Minoriandis, Pon, Principat, Publicat, Curat

In the middle was a double delta, at each angle of which were the following letters

A, D, O, N, A, I

which joined together form the Sacred Word **ADONAI**; and in the center was the word **MESSIAH**.

On the other side were the words

Sacro Sancta Pentacula, Novem Angelorum Chorum, Sublimis Virtutis

And in each angle of the double delta were he following letters

J, E, H, O, V, A

which joined together form the Sacred Word **JEHOVA**; and in the center was

✝ ⅹ P̄V̄S .

This word expresses the Light of the Great Work accomplished.

When Hiram was discovered, they found upon his breast the aforesaid Pentacle suspended on a golden chain; they brought it to Solomon who having recompensed the Masters for finding the body of Hiram, and then his assassins, selected fifteen senior Masters and decorated them with the Pentacle, with the same power as Hiram.

The scapular worn in front of the stomach, attached by four poppy-red ribbons, is made of material of the same color, and is a white cross and an eagle.

Decoration of the Chapter

The Chapter Room should be hung with black stuff, and decorated with twelve white marble columns veined with black and red, of the Corinthian Order, the capitals and bases in gold, and placed:

{
- 2 in the East
- 2 in the West
- 4 in the South
- 4 in the North
}

In the middle of each column there will be suspended a shield[96] as a trophy and scalloped, composed of flowers and the leaves of trees, as will be explained.

As there are twelve columns or pilasters, for greater convenience there will be twelve shields, in each of which will be written in letters of gold one of the twelve Names of the Supreme Being Who presides over each month of the year, and in the same cartouche the month and the sign of the Zodiac will be recorded.

Order of the Shields[97]

In the East

On the column placed on the Northern side will be written and translated into Hebrew:

......**JEHOVA**
the month of
MARCH
His Sign ♈ of **ARIES**

On the column placed on the Southern side will be written and translated into Hebrew:

......**EMMANUEL**
the month of
APRIL
His Sign ♉ of **TAURUS**

---

[96] In French: *cartouche*.

[97] Interestingly, the order of these shields or cartouches is different in the Baron von Tschoudy version of the ritual.

The Degrees of the Black Eagle Rose-Croix

In the West

On the column placed on the Northern side will be written and translated into Hebrew:

......**TETRAGRAMMATON**
the month of
MAY

His Sign ♊ of **GEMINI**

On the column placed on the Southern side will be written and translated into Hebrew:

......**JESUS**
the month of
JUNE

His Sign ♋ of **CANCER**

In the South

On the first counting from the East will be written and translated into Hebrew:

......**MESSIAH**
the month of
JULY

His Sign ♌ of **LEO**

On the second to the Western side of the first will be written and translated into Hebrew:

......**ORPHETON**
the month of
AUGUST

His Sign ♍ of **VIRGO**

On the third still going to the West will be written and translated into Hebrew:

......**ANASBONA**
the month of
SEPTEMBER

His Sign ♎ of **LIBRA**

On the fourth and last in the West will be written and translated into Hebrew:

......**ERIGION**
the month of
OCTOBER
His Sign ♏ of **SCORPIO**

In the North

On the first counting from the East will be written and translated into Hebrew:

......**JESSEMON**
the month of
NOVEMBER
His Sign ♐ of **SAGITTARIUS**

On the second to the Western side of the first will be written and translated into Hebrew:

......**ELION**
the month of
DECEMBER
His Sign ♑ of **CAPRICORN**

On the third still going to the West will be written and translated into Hebrew:

......**AGLA**
the month of
JANUARY
His Sign ♒ of **AQUARIUS**

On the fourth and last in the West will be written and translated into Hebrew:

......**MELECH**
the month of
FEBRUARY
His Sign ♓ of **PISCES**

The Degrees of the Black Eagle Rose-Croix

Each shield will be ornamented and garlanded with flowers and leaves of the tree attributed to each month in the Great Work.

MARCH – leaves of olive and yellow amaranth.

APRIL – myrtle leaves.

MAY – laurel leaves.

JUNE – leaves of hazel and great comfrey.

JULY – leaves of shallot and cyclamen.

AUGUST – leaves of apple tree and calamint.

SEPTEMBER – box tree leaves.

OCTOBER – leaves of artemisia and hyacinth.

NOVEMBER – palm tree leaves.

DECEMBER – pine leaves.

JANUARY – leaves of laurin and thyme.

FEBRUARY – elm leaves.

The Throne

The throne shall be placed between the two columns in the East. Over the canopy will be a great black eagle, the beak, talons and crown in gold. The canopy is red bordered with golden fringes, the armchair black and gold. At the back of the canopy shall be the Blazing star in gold, in the center of which is an J.

On the left of the canopy shall be the moon in silver, at the right the sun in gold.

Before the throne, which should be elevated on three steps, shall be a golden altar with triangular form, on which are always placed the following four objects, namely:

**A BIBLE, AN URN,
A PAIR OF COMPASSES, A KEY,**

In the center of the room on the floor is painted the Scales of Solomon, and on top of it is placed a real set of scales.

Scales of Solomon

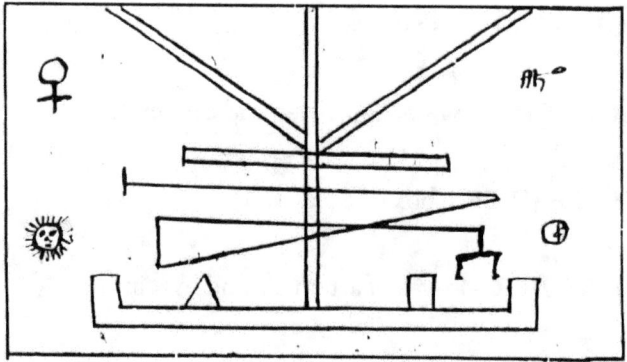

Illumination

The Chapter is illuminated on the four sides by ten gilded metal three-branched candelabra, placed in the four corners: two in the East, two in the West, three in the South and three in the North, making sure to place them between the columns. The Chapter floor is also illuminated by several candlesticks: a two-branched candelabra in the East on the Southern side; a candlestick with a single candle in the Center[98]; a three-branched candelabra in the West on the Southern side; a three-branched candelabra in the West on the Northern side.

All the candles used in the Chapter are yellow and made of virgin wax, called virginal, which alludes to the materials used for the Great Work, in which mixed ones are not admissible.

---

[98] Given the earlier instruction that the Scales of Solomon will be painted on the floor in the center of the room (au milieu du planché) with a real set of scales standing upon it, it must be assumed that the candlestick is placed slightly to one side.

For lighting the candles, tinder shall be set aflame using the rays of the sun; and if that is not possible by using a stone and iron, but never ordinary fire.[99]

Places

The Grand Master is seated in his armchair in the East.

The Grand Prior and Grand Warden will sit in the West in smaller black armchairs placed on a step. Opposite them is a small table for giving the knocks.

The Orator and the Secretary are seated in the same manner and have before them a table proportionate to their duties.

The tables are covered with a blue cloth adorned with gold.

All the Prince Knights are seated on uniformly blue chairs with black embroidery

Each of the Prince Knights' seats is decorated with the arms of the occupant and will not be occupied by anyone else except in case of necessity.

The gavels used by the Chapter will be black, decorated with yellow wood.

Attire

In the event of Initiations and Solemn Ceremonies there is an indispensable form of attire, and on other occasions they can wear ordinary dress.

Figure 131: Later image of apron, chronologically. Note the 'I' on the flap.

---

[99] This refers to 'new fire', which is not produced from another flame or by lighting a match which contains sulfur. This tradition of 'new fire' can be seen in the lighting of the Paschal Candle at the Paschal Vigil, lit from the brazier lit with 'new fire'; and it is also often used in theurgical operations.

For Initiations and Ceremonies, they will be clothed in black, with a chapeau with white plumes, and all have their swords decorated with a red knot of fire-colored ribbon, instead of wearing the sash which they remove until the Candidate has been received. They wear a white apron finished and bordered with red, in the center of which is a large black eagle holding a key in one talon and a balance in the other, and under the flap is the letter 'J'.

In their buttonhole they wear a rosette of fire-colored ribbon, from which hangs a black eagle with gold enamel, or completely made of gold or other metal.

The gloves have a fringe of gold or are bordered with black. On the upper side of one is a key and on the other a balance.

After the Initiation had ended the Candidate will wear this attire for one year, or as long as the Sovereign Chapter finds appropriate.

Figure 132: Collection of 84 pieces of paintings and clothes from different lodges done for the happiness of the Brothers by Bros. Löwen and Ducaten circa 1762. Kindly provided by Bro. Caleb W. Haines.

The Degrees of the Black Eagle Rose-Croix

The Initiation being finished, all the Princes will remove their regalia and their small sashes, with the exception of the Knights.

The Commanders will also remove their aprons, and put on the grand sash, and the Bailiffs will put on the grand scapular cord, and the sash with the great poppy-red cord which hangs at the bottom, the jewel attached by a rosette of black ribbon.

Jewels

There are three jewels.

Jewel I

The first jewel is composed of crowned compasses resting on a quarter circle, in the center of which is a cross bearing the Scales of Solomon, beneath which on one side there is a pelican feeding its young and on the other side an eagle. Between these animals is a branch of true acacia.

The composition of this jewel represents the symbol of the three kingdoms of Nature which enter into the Work of the true Philosophical Science: the **Animal**, the **Vegetable** and the **Mineral**.

Jewel II

The second jewel is the triangle, otherwise called the Pentacle of Solomon. This jewel comprises all Cabalistic Science, of which each letter composes a power acting in the Operation, as will be explained in the Instruction.

Jewel III

The third jewel is a crowned Black Eagle with golden beak and talons, which is worn in the buttonhole suspended by a red ribbon.

This jewel represents the Supreme Rank of the Grade[100] where it is used; just as the eagle is the king of the animals, so the Knights of the Rose Croix Black Eagle should be regarded as the Leaders and Sovereign of the Masonic Order, being in possession of the Scales and the mysterious Key to all the symbols, hieroglyphic enigmas of which all the inferior Grades are composed.

Sacred Word

MESSIAS, signifying treasure of the philosophers which is sought.

---

[100] In the original text: this should probably read 'Order' and not 'Grade', as in the Tschoudy version.

Password

OCH, signifying seed of all metals.

Sign

The Sign is given by placing the index finger on the nose, drawing it back across the cheek to the ear, then lowering it to the neck, thereby forming a Square.

The response is the same, except that if it is given with the right hand the reply is given with the left hand.

Grip

The Grip is given by embracing reciprocally, each bringing the right foot forward and then giving a reciprocal blow heel against heel.

Coming to Order

To come to Order bring the three middle fingers of the right hand to the area of the heart holding the thumb and little linger closed in the hollow of the hand.

Opening of the Chapter

The Chapter is opened by the Sovereign Grand Master with one loud knock of the gavel, which is repeated by the Grand Prior and the Grand Warden with the same knock. Then the Sovereign Grand Master says:

> Prince Knights Grand Prior and Grand Warden and Officers, assist me to open the Chapter.

While saying these words he gives the Sign, answered by all the Knights. Then the Grand Prior and the Grand Warden present the point of their sword to him, then all the Princes come to Order and the Sovereign Grand Master says:

Q. *Knight Grand Prior, what is the hour?*

A. *The day is announced by the morning star, the work must begin anew.*

Q. *Knight Grand Warden, what is your duty?*

A. *To see if the Chapter is Hermetically sealed, if the materials are ready, if the elements are distinguished, and if Black gives way to White and White to Red.*

Q. *See that everything is ready.*

The Degrees of the Black Eagle Rose-Croix

A. *Everything is ready. You can begin the Work, the fire takes on color.*

Q. *Knights Grand Prior and Grand Warden, leave the fire, take your gavels, arrange each Prince Knight at his post.*

A. *Prince Knights, who inhabit the Zodiac, observe precision in your work to procure for us the Animals, Vegetables and Minerals subordinate to each Sign of each month of the year. Enclose all these materials in the House of the Sun.*

Then the Grand Master says:

> *Knights, let the noise of your tools resound from one pole to the other, may the East and the West direct the course of the planets.*
>
> *He then gives six knocks, and groups of two.*
>
> *The Grand Prior and the Grand Warden repeat them, also in groups of two, leaving an interval between every two blows, after announcing[84] that the work is opened.*

To Close the Chapter

The Grand Master says:

Q. *Grand Prior, is the work advanced, has the matter taken form and does it have need to rest?*

A. *The elements are united, the seven planets are enclosed within the Sanctuary, and a white veil covers them.*

Then the Grand Master says:

> *I am content with your zeal, Prince Knights. Ever watch for that fear by which the night might take you by surprise, and keep your lamps lit though you are at the repose which I have ordered you to resume, until the moment when the sun arrives at the highest point of the Zenith.*

Addressing himself to the Grand Prior and Grand Warden he says to them:

> *Announce to all the Knights, Commanders and Bailiffs with six blows of the gavel in two by two, that the hour for repose has arrived, that the evening star appears on the horizon, and that the sun is below the waters.*

Then the Grand Master gives six blows, and says:

> *The Chapter is closed.*

Initiation of a Bailiff

When a Freemason is to be received a Black Eagle Rose Croix, the Grand Master nominates Commissioners to inquire about the life and morals of the Candidate, the manner in which he has carried himself in the Order up to that day, if he has any incorrigible faults, his current status, his talent or his employment, his abilities and his religion, because one can only admit men into that grade who have a good moral reputation, a gentle and pleasant character, even sociable. Moreover, he must have passed and have been initiated into all degrees of the Orders preceding the Black Eagle and the two first grades of this Order, that he must know the theory and practice of Freemasonry by heart, so that he can reply to any questions which may be asked concerning the different Grades, and if possible, that he confirms that he has meditated on and analyzed our most abstract mysteries, and that he wishes to receive the key to them.

After the Commissioners have fulfilled their mission, they make their reports to the assembled Sovereign Chapter, which decides whether they should admit or reject the Candidate.

Supposing that he will be admitted, the Sovereign Grand Master will nominate a Sponsor who will instruct him in all the duties he must fulfil in order to be Initiated.

When the day is fixed for him to be received, the Sponsor introduces him to the parvis of the Chapter, and from there he is taken into the Chamber of Reflection, where he remains for some time.

Decoration of the Chamber of Reflection

This Chamber is stripped of all wall-hangings and other furniture and is as dark as possible. It is only lit by one small, feeble light. There is a small table covered with a black cloth, on which are placed a jug of water, a piece of bread, salt, sulfur, and on the wall above the table is placed a picture on which is represented a cock, an hourglass, and the words 'Patience' and 'Perseverance'. Before the table is a triangular stool with a hole in the center for the Candidate to sit on.

After being received all the Emblems will be explained to him.

When the Chamber is thus prepared, the Aspirant will be left there as long as judged appropriate. Then his Sponsor, assisted by a Knight in the function of the Preparer go to see him. His Sponsor asks him if he has reflected well while left alone, and whether he is still prepared to be received as a Knight of the Black Eagle. If he answers 'Yes', the Knight Preparer bandages his eyes in such a manner that he cannot see anything. He takes him by the hand and conducts him to another room hung with black stuff, where there is a table on which there is a Knight lying on his back on the table, feigning death. The Knight Preparer has the Candidate travel around the room several times, then he leads him in front of the table and has him touch the body of the Knight lying there. Then he makes him circle the room once more, and during that time the Knight lying on the table gets up and in his place the heart of a cow or sheep is placed instead, and a skull and a lit candle.

Then the Preparer asks him whether he still has a desire to proceed, and whether he is still determined to pursue his course. If he answers 'Yes', he is furnished with a sword, and is brought close to the table, his sword being guided towards the heart; and his hand is held while the following is said to him: "**Strike! Do not hesitate, woe unto you if you tremble and if you would repent the blow you give!**"

The Candidate, prepared as just described, gives a strike with the sword and pierces the heart on the table with one blow, and holds the sword still plunged into it. The Knight Preparer asks him what he just did; he answers "*I don't know, but I have just stabbed a corpse, which I do not repent of, and which I am ready to repeat.*"

At these words, he is restored to light, and he sees that he just pierced a heart, and that close to it is a skull.[101]

The Knight Preparer tells him to take the skull in his hand, and the heart still pierced by the sword, and in this state, he introduces him to the Chapter.

Introduction into the Chapter

After the Candidate arrives at the door of the Chapter, he knocks with irregular blows. The Grand Warden reports them, saying:

> *Prince Grand Prior, someone knocks at the door of the Chapter as a profane, Alert the Sovereign Grand Master.*

The Prince Grand Prior says:

> *Sovereign Grand Master, someone knocks at the door of the Chapter as a profane.*

Thus alerted, the Sovereign Grand Master orders the Grand Warden to see who it is.

The Grand Warden opens the door slightly and asks the Sponsor who he led here to knock in this manner.

He replies:

> *I introduce a very worthy Mason who desires to be initiated a Knight of the Black Eagle Rose Croix.*

---

[101] A striking difference between this and the Tschoudy version is the fact that in the Tschoudy version there is no skull. On the other hand, it is even more dramatic, the Knight feigning death being naked except for a strategically placed cloth, and the blindfolded Candidate is explicitly told to touch the 'dead' Knight with both hands.

The Grand Warden goes to the foot of the throne of the Sovereign Grand Master to bring this answer to him.

The Grand Master tells him to ask the Knight Preparer if the Candidate has passed the trials, and if he can prove it.

The Grand Warden goes to the door of the Chapter and asks the Brother Preparer, who replies:

> Grand Warden, the trophy he presents to you and to the entire Sovereign Chapter is the clearest proof.

Then the Grand Warden asks the Sponsor for the name of the Candidate, his age, the grades he has passed through to come to be initiated a Knight of the Black Eagle Rose Croix. When the Sponsor has satisfied all the questions, then the Grand Warden goes to the foot of the throne of the Sovereign Grand Master and gives a report of his mission.

Then the Grand Master orders the Grand Warden to let the Candidate enter and to place him between himself and the Grand Prior, and at the same time the Sponsor and the Bailiff come to give an account to the Sovereign Grand Master of the commission given to them, and the manner in which they acquitted it up to the moment when the Candidate had been introduced into the Chapter, and for whom they will no longer be responsible. The Sovereign Grand Master thanks them both for their zeal and tells them to resume their places.

The Recipient, now placed in the West as said, the Sovereign Grand Master says to him:

Q. *What is the motive which brought you to be received as a Knight of the Black Eagle Rose Croix?*

A. *Sovereign Grand Master, the desire to learn the true moral and physical significance of the Signs, Words and Grips, Furniture, Jewels and Ornaments which I have received or seen in the different Grades through which I have passed.*

The Sovereign Grand Master answers him:

> *My Brother, your expectation will not be disappointed. The trophy which you hold in your hand is a proof to us of your fervor for Freemasonry. It is perhaps still an enigma to you, which can be easily explained.*
>
> *It is in the First Grade that the Solemn Obligation you took in becoming a Mason to have one's heart torn out, if one became a perjurer.*[102]

---

[102] This is incorrect, since the first grade appears to have been read rather than enacted, and there is no Obligation. The Obligation which mentions the heart being torn out is in the second grade.

The Degrees of the Black Eagle Rose-Croix

The Grade which you desire to attain, my Brother, being the most elevated of all, and at the same time the wisest of all, since it contains the key to all the others, it is proper that those who are initiated into it have been tested, that they are sufficiently educated in all the Grades which precede it, and that they are firm and can be counted upon when in need.

The strike you gave to that heart proves your courage, and you are such as must become our equal, forever ready to suffer everything, even death, or to inflict it rather than reveal any of our mysteries.

Q. Are you still intent, my dear Brother, on penetrating into our Sanctuary?

A. Very intent, Sovereign Grand Master. You have only to command me and I am ready to execute your orders, whatever nature they may be.

Then the Grand Master says:

Princes Knights, Prince Grand Prior and Grand Warden, you have seen him, you have heard him, let us make his happiness complete; it will be his fault if he renders himself unworthy. Conduct him to me by the steps of the four Elements.

Steps

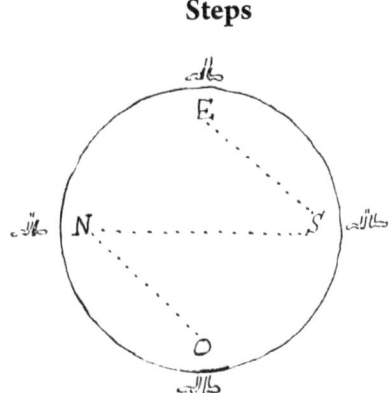

These steps are made by the four cardinal points of the sphere, leaving from the West, going to the North, traversing the center to go to the South., and from there to the East, at the foot of the throne, where the Aspirant is made to kneel.

When he is kneeling, the Sovereign Grand Master says to him:

> *My Brother, you are at the happy moment when you will be enlightened. A thick veil hides the true light from your eyes, thought they are open. In order to receive it, my dear Brother, you must bind yourself before the Sovereign King of Kings and before us by pronouncing a Solemn Obligation.*
>
> *Place this heart, legitimately pierced, at the foot of the altar, and pronounce with me:*

Obligation

> *I promise and vow before the Supreme Being and Grand Architect of the Universe, and in presence of this Sovereign Chapter to hele, conceal and never reveal the secrets of the Knights of the Black Eagle Rose Croix to a Mason of an inferior Grade, and even less to a Profane, under whatever pretext it might be, and only to speak of them in Chapter and when at Work. If I fail in my Obligation and perjure myself, I consent to losing my life in the most terrible torment, and I pardon those Knights who will bring me death in whatever manner it may be, whether by fire, or by sword, or by poison; that my memory may be held in horror among the Knights of the Black Eagle Rose Croix, and Freemasons spread throughout the entire World.*
>
> *Pray for me my dear Brothers, that God may aid me and His Holy Gospel and keep me from failing in my Obligation.*

Once the Obligation is finished the Grand Prior causes him to rise and presents him to the Sovereign Grand Master, who decorates him with the plate and sash, gives him the Words, Signs and Grips. Finally, he commands him to go to be recognized by all the Bailiffs, beginning with the Officers.

After they have recognized him, the Sovereign Grand Master gives him the Accolade[103] and says to him:

> *By the power which I have received from the Venerable Chapter, I make you Prince Mason by the most puissant Grade of Bailiff of the Black Eagle Rose Croix, with which you are clothed and of which you are now a member.*

Then the Grand Master says to the Orator:

> *Prince Orator, instruct the new Bailiff in the mysterious figures represented on the Lodge Tracing Board.*

---

[103] The Accolade is given by kissing the new Knight on both cheeks. Sometimes this is done three times, and sometimes on both cheeks and the forehead.

THE DEGREES OF THE BLACK EAGLE ROSE-CROIX

Figure 133: From the Kloss Archive XXXIV. Note: This is not in the Willermoz Ritual, but appears in what is believed to be the Tschoudy Rituals. Since it is an accurate portrayal of the description in the Willermoz Ritual it has been included for interest.

Address of the Orator

My Respectable Brother Bailiff, give your attention to what we are going to teach you and to everything you see.

The figure of this Tracing Board[104] is an oblong square, longer from the East to the West than from the South to the North, because the sun lights the terrestrial globe from East to West more than South to North since it never leaves one tropic or the other.

You see in the center a great circular space consisting of clouds which enclose circles, which form what is called the Zodiac, where are the twelve Houses of the Sun, each guarded by one of the Twelve months of the year. It is in each of these Houses that you should be prepared live during each month, working there in order to attract the beneficent celerity[105] of this Luminous Star which vivifies all matter prepared by these methods.

The Sun, entering into each of its Houses, must be received by the four Elements

AIR, FIRE, EARTH, & WATER

which you have to take care to invite to keep you company: for without them the House would be mournful. You will feast the Sun on matter drawn from animals and fruits nourished in the interior of each celestial month.

If you take care to observe all these things, be assured that when the Sun has lived in these twelve Houses, and it sees you have been attentive to serve him, you will become the most cherished of his favorites. He will share with you his most precious gifts. Death will no longer have empire over you. You will cease to live on earth, to which you render the material body it lent you, and which you borrowed, in order to possess a completely spiritual one.

In order to acquire all these things, during the course of your work you must regard matter as dead.

---

[104] This phrase in French is a little enigmatic: *Loge tracée*. This has been translated here as 'Tracing Board' a familiar object to Masons. It is interesting that, despite all the other diagrams Willermoz provides, there is no Tracing Board. However, that can be said for all his rituals, so we should not read anything particular into that. Indeed, the second grade has him being received by the Grand Master while standing on the Tracing Board.

The one included here is from the *Sublime Grade du Vrai Rose-Croix d'Allemagne ou Chevalier de l'Aigle Noir ou Philosophe Inconnu* ('Sublime Grade of True Rose Croix of Germany or Knight of the Black Eagle or Unknown Philosopher'), Kloss Archive XXXIV (see below. See also another interpretation in Figure 130).

[105] This is an instance where one can clearly see a transcription error. In a manner similar to the monks of old, while copying one handwritten ritual to another document in another hand, it is easy enough to misread words, thereby slightly altering the ritual. In this case the word in Willermoz' handwriting is clearly *vitesse*, or 'speed, celerity'; while in the Tschoudy manuscript the word is rendered as *visite* or 'visit', largely a transposition of the 't' and the 's'.

The Degrees of the Black Eagle Rose-Croix

The corpse of Hiram is its emblem. The evil workmen assassinated him. He must be vivified, made to be reborn from his ashes, which you can accomplish by the vegetation of the Tree of Life represented by the branch of acacia. But you will not be able to work with success if you deviate from the Square and the Compasses you should always have before you.

These jewels are not the only ones you should use. They are accompanied by two indispensable instruments. One is the Balance and the other is the Key. You will use the first one in all your labors, which you will keep secret under your Key in the impenetrable coffer of Prudence, which no Profane will ever penetrate.

A jewel still more valuable is required, which you cannot do without. That is the Cabalistic Pentacle, the precious jewel which contains all the celestial virtues in itself alone.[106]

This jewel is not of man's invention. It came from God Himself, and was given to King Solomon, from whom we have it.

The Pentacle carries within itself the power of commanding the Spirits inhabiting the four Elements. Therefore, my dear Brother, you must apply yourself to understanding its use, which you can do easily by working with perseverance.

In the Catechism you will learn the form and mysterious names of which the Pentacle is composed. It has the same virtue as those worn by Solomon, Hiram and all the true Master Masons who lived at the time of this wise king.

Let us leave the mystic center of our Lodge for a moment, dear Brother, and let us cross the cloud which must cover all our sacred mysteries, let us pass through the space surrounding it; there we find in

The West

a mountain called Mount Hebron. Every good Mason should know it. It was on this mountain that two great columns were erected.

The First called **JACHIN**

The Second called **BOAZ**

That is to say, Strength and Beauty, the first principles of the Great Work which you are going to undertake. Strength is represented by the materials which you must use, and Beauty the work which they will produce for you.

The Column **JACHIN** *was dedicated to God as everything comes from Him and used by the Apprentice to receive their salaries there, and to enclose their tools within it.*

---

[106] This is an intriguing reference to the Seal of Star of Solomon, the hexagram which, in many magical and alchemical systems, is symbolic of the planets (and therefore the metals), each point being one of the 6 traditional planets, with the Sun being in the center.

That is where you are presently, my Brother, since you are going to begin to work on the Great Work. You will become Companion when you begin to understand the beauty of Elemental[107] matter. Finally, you will become Master when you have drawn the path of the Sun upon the Tracing Board. But you must watch with ardor for all these things, you must feel yourself animated by an ever active and continual fire, which is represented to you by the cock beating its wings, and singing[108] on Mount Hebron, between the two columns. My Brother, let us now leave the West and pass to

The East

There we discover a great black eagle, the king of the animals of the air, the only one capable of fixing the radiant star, for the matter of Nature has no form, for it is form which develops color. Black is the foundational matter[109], change its color and it takes on a new form, a most brilliant Sun emerges.

But, my dear Brother, the birth of the Sun is announced by the morning star. It is this which represents the Blazing Star, which you know by its flaming redness followed on its course by the silver freshness of the Moon.

Follow me, my dear Brother, into that immense space which embraces the plan of our Lodge. There you will discover many tools which were placed into your hand when you were initiated in Masonry.

A Rough Ashlar, that is to say unformed matter, which must be prepared.

A Cubic Stone with pyramidal point, which is matter developed for the triangular form, such as Salt and Sulfur.

Implements such as a Square, a Level, a Plumb, a Gavel, implements necessary for the construction of the Houses through which you must have the material pass, Houses which must be built with rule and proportion, without which the Spirit of Life would not be able to inhabit.

With these implements you will construct the Great Altar on which will burn the fire drawn down from heaven, and the Great Laver will serve to purify your hands and body, and all that it touches.[110]

---

[107] Or 'elementary'.

[108] This is another example of a transcription error. The word in Willermoz' manuscript is *chantant*, or 'singing'; in Tschoudy's manuscript it is *cherchant*, or 'searching'. Incidentally the placing of the Cock at the entrance to the Temple (between the two pillars) also gives reference to its meaning of vigilance; and of the Cock which crowed thrice when Peter denied Jesus three times.

[109] *La matière hors d'œuvre*, lit. 'outside matter', perhaps more commonly known as *prima materia*.

[110] These reference the Altar of Holocausts and the Brazen Sea in the entrance to Solomon's Temple.

To operate with success, be as laborious as the beaver and conceal yourself like the barn-owl who only goes out at night.

That, my dear Brother, is in short what is represented on the image which you see. In time you will come to educate yourself more about our works, convinced as we are that you will become a new light which will help us to perfect the Great Work to which every good Mason has the right to aspire.

When the Orator concludes his Address, he says:

Sovereign Grand Master, it is now time for you to educate the new Bailiff on the work he must undertake.

Address of the Grand Master

Explanation of the Bread, the Water, the Salt, the Sulfur, and the Chamber of Reflection

Dear newly-initiated Prince, when you were asked to reflect, you saw Bread, Water, Salt, Sulfur, a Cock, an Hourglass, and the words 'Patience' and 'Perseverance', symbolic materials which are easy to explain.

The Bread and Water teaches you to maintain sobriety in your meals and cease all the debauchery which harms your health and your pocket.

The Salt leads you to understand the good morals you should continually preserve among men, just as salt preserves meats and liquids most subject to corruption.

The Sulfur marks the secret ardor you should bring to the Cabalistic Science by forming your spirit to promptly grasp all the moments of enlightenment, like sulfur, which the smallest spark sets aflame.

The Cock teaches you the vigilance you should have in all your works, accompanied by patience and perseverance.

The Hourglass indicates the time you should set aside for labor, which should be measured in hours.

This Address being ended, the Grand Master says:

My dear Brother Princes, let us work to instruct the new Bailiff, so that by his work he may come to discover the principles of life enclosed in the heart of the First Matter known by the name of **AKHAHEST**.

Catechism

Q. Prince Grand Prior, what is the hour?
A. The beginning of the day.
Q. Grand Warden, what is your duty?
A. To see that the Chapter is sealed and the materials are ready.
Q. What is the place of the Sovereign Grand Master?
A. In the East.
Q. Why?
A. To await the rising of the Sun to accompany it in the twelve celestial Houses.
Q. What are the names of these twelve Houses?
A.

♈ ARIES Ram	♉ TAURUS Bull
♊ GEMINI Twins	♋ CANCER Crayfish
♌ LEO Lion	♍ VIRGO Virgin
♎ LIBRA Scales	♏ SCORPIO Scorpion
♐ SAGITTARIUS Archer	♑ CAPRICORN Sea Goat
♒ AQUARIUS Water-bearer	♓ PISCES Fish

The Degrees of the Black Eagle Rose-Croix

Q. *Which are the presiding powers, and what do men do in these Houses?*

A. *First the Great Architect of the Universe with twelve Sacred Names, each taken from the twelve letters of the great name of God, written in Hebrew:*

IETIMOAEIEAM

The Hebrew characters are:

Q. Give me the twelve Names assigned to each of these twelve celestial Houses.

A.

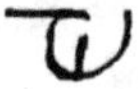

ש

JEHOVA
God
DEUS

ג

EMMANUEL
God
DEUS

ב

TETRAGRAMMATON
God
DEUS

ו

JESUS
God
DEUS

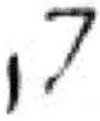

ז

MESSIAH
God
DEUS

ג

ORPHETON
God
DEUS

ח

ANASBONA
God
DEUS

ז

ERIGION
God
DEUS

י

JESSEMON
God
DEUS

ג

ELION
God
DEUS

שׁ

AGLA
God
DEUS

ן

MELECH
God
DEUS

Q. Which are the spirits acting by the power of the Supreme Being in each of the twelve houses?

The Degrees of the Black Eagle Rose-Croix

A. | MACHIDIEL | ASMODEL |
|---|---|
| AMBRIEL | MURIEL |
| VERCHIEL | HAMALIEL |
| URIEL | BARBIEL |
| ADNACHIEL | HANAEL |
| GABRIEL | BARCHIEL |

Q. What is the common name of each of these twelve Houses, and the Order the occupy in the Universe?

A. | MARCH | 31 days |
|---|---|
| APRIL | 30 days |
| MAY | 31 days |
| JUNE | 30 days |
| JULY | 31 days |
| AUGUST | 31 days |
| SEPTEMBER | 30 days |
| OCTOBER | 31 days |
| NOVEMBER | 30 days |
| DECEMBER | 31 days |
| JANUARY | 31 days |
| FEBRUARY | 28 days |

In the month of February, one distinguishes between the years of grace and the bissextile year. There are ordinarily four[111] years which follow which are called years of grace, then the month has 28 days; and the year which follows is called the bissextile year when the month has 29 days.

Q. What is the most puissant Name of God in the Pentacle?

A.

---

[111] This should be three, since the fourth year is the leap year.

271

Enlightenment Man & Mason

Q. *What is His Almighty power?*

A. *To set the Universe in motion.*

The Bailiff who is fortunate enough to be able to pronounce it with Cabalistic weight and measure, would have at his disposition those powers which inhabit the four Elements, and the celestial spirits, and would possess all the virtues possible in man.

Q. *What use would he make of them?*

A. *Through their powers he would acquire the discovery of the first of the metals being the Sun, which comes from the intimate alliance of the six metals, each of which contains the seed, and supplies it in the nuptial bed.*

Q. *What are those metals?*

A.

♄	♃
SATURN	**JUPITER**
♂	♀
MARS	**VENUS**
☿	☾
MERCURY	**MOON**

Q. Do they not have other names among the vulgar?

A.

LEAD	**TIN**
IRON	**COPPER**
QUICKSILVER	**SILVER**

Q. *Why is gold not included?*

A. *A. Gold is physically not a metal; it is all spirit and therefore incorruptible, whereas the other metals are corruptible Therefore gold is the emblem of Divinity, which has neither beginning nor end.*

Q. *How can one accomplish the alliance of the six metals to make only one, and whichis not a metal?*

The Degrees of the Black Eagle Rose-Croix

A.   *By the Rule and the Scales left to us by Solomon in his Cabalistic Treatise of his Keys.*[112]

Q.   *How are these Scales made?*

A.   *Here is the design.*

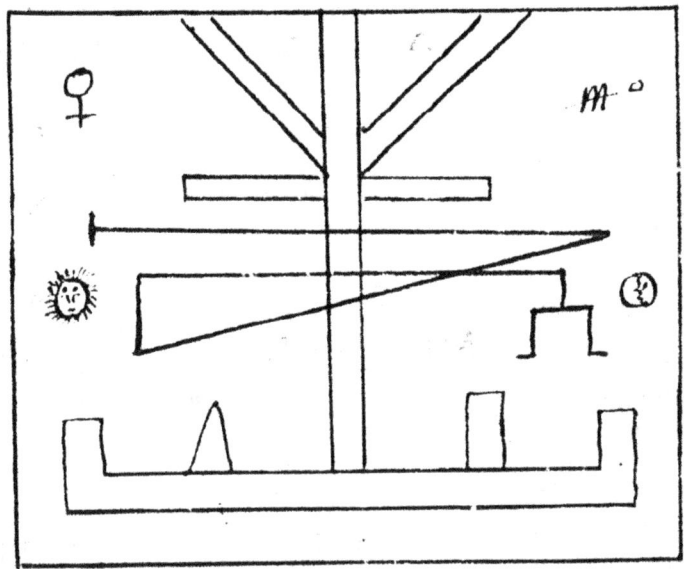

Q.   *Which weights*[113] *did Solomon use with these Scales?*

A.   *Cabalistic weights containing 25 numbers.*

Q.   *Which were the divisions of these weights?*

A.   *1, 2, 3, 4, 5 which contain 25 times Unity,*

       12 times 2,

       8 times 3,

       6 times 4,

       5 times 5.

---

[112] Here the other implement held in the talons of the Black Eagle – which represents the *prima materia* from which the gold is ultimately refined – along with the Scales is the Key, and here it is pivoted nicely to mention the two great Grimoires, the Greater and Lesser Keys of Solomon.

[113] Again, this is a powerful allusion to the important phrase in the Old Testament from Wisdom 11:21: "Thou hast ordered all things in measure, and number, and weight." This phrase focused the minds of most of the alchemists and magicians, including Newton who spent much of his life attempting to determine the true proportions of Solomon's Temple; and even including Willermoz himself, who only a few short years later would encounter Martinez de Pasqually and Louis-Claude de Saint-Martin, both of whom were equally preoccupied with the idea that, if God created the Universe by measure, by number, and by weight, it should be possible to understand how it was created and how it functions by means of a thorough understanding of numerology.

Q. What Cabalistic meaning do these numbers contain?

A. The square of 5, the square of 2, its cube and its square of square produces 16. The square of 3 which is 9.[114]

Q. Are there no Philosophers who could have given us the key to these Scales?

A. There are indeed seven.

Q. What are their names?

A. **ALBUMASARIS**   **PYTHAGORAS**
PTOLEMÆUS   **ĀTIDONIS**[115]
PLATO   **ARISTOTLE**
THALES[116]

Q. What are the explanations they gave?

A. Each of them was connected to a metal. They made a study of it, and gave its measure, rule and scale to put it to labor. Each book is under the dominion of an Elemental Genius who assists in the Work.

Q. Explain to us these authors by their works?

A. **ALBUMASARIS** studied Lead, called Saturn, under the Genius **Aratron**[117], and under the form of his Scales drawn below:

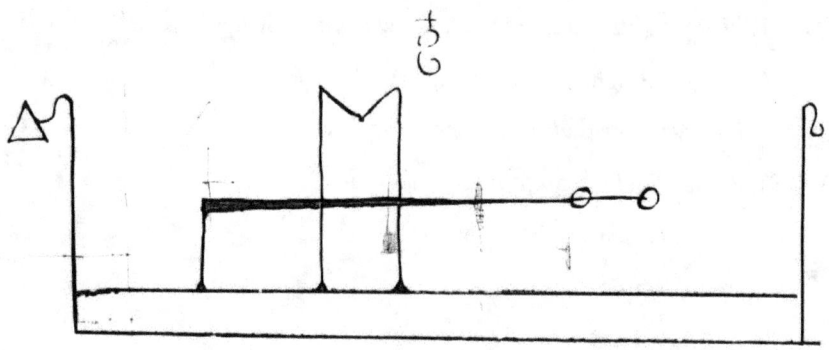

---

[114] 5 squared = 25; 2 x 2 = 4; 2 x 4 = 8 (cube of 2); 2 x 8 + 16; 3 x 3 = 9; 16 + 9 = 25.

[115] Unable to find any Greek Philosopher on French pages with this name, including the later spelling in the text of Anthidonis, or Antidonis. This is surprising since he is attributed to the Sun, the most important of the planets, and to gold.

[116] This was given as 'Huli'. There is no clear Greek Philosopher with a name which is close to this. However, Thales is listed as one of the 'Seven Sophoi' or 'Sages of Greece', and his axiom, 'Know Thyself' was engraved on the Temple of Apollo at Delphi, so he would appear to be a good contender.

[117] The names of the Olympian Geniuses, their attributions (metal, planet) as well as their sigils (which here have been elaborated to form the Scales), are from the *Arbatel of Magic*, an early Grimoire.

The Degrees of the Black Eagle Rose-Croix

PYTHAGORAS studied Tin, called Jupiter, under the Genius **Bethor**. His Scales are:

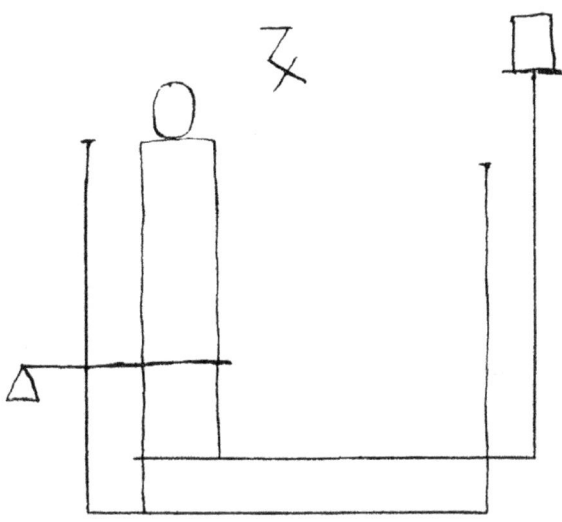

PTOLOMÆUS studied Iron, called Mars, under the Genius **Phaleg**. His Scales are:

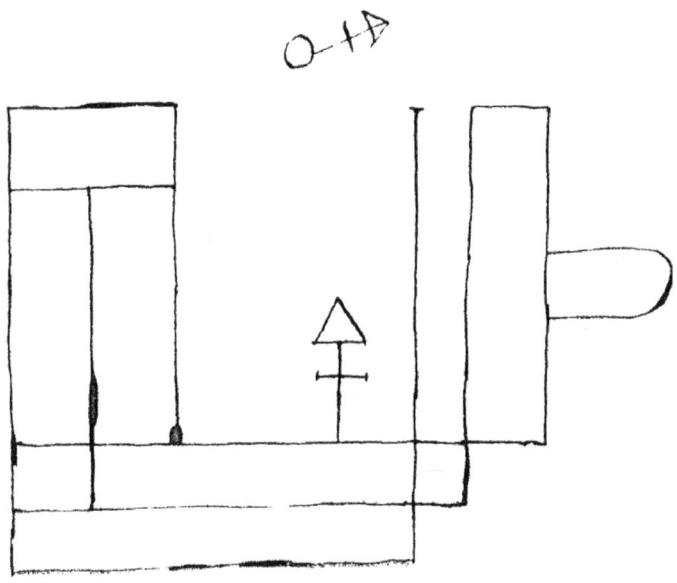

ANTHIDONIS *studied the Sun, called Gold, under the Genius* **Och**. *His Scales are:*

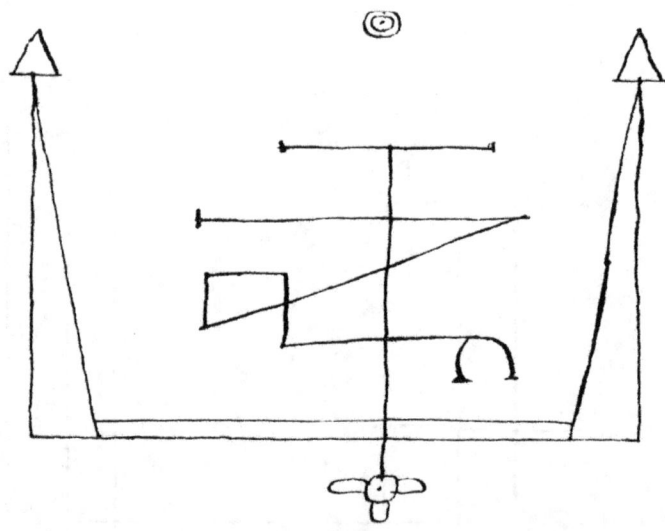

PLATO *studied Copper, called Venus, under the Genius* **Hagith**. *His Scales are:*

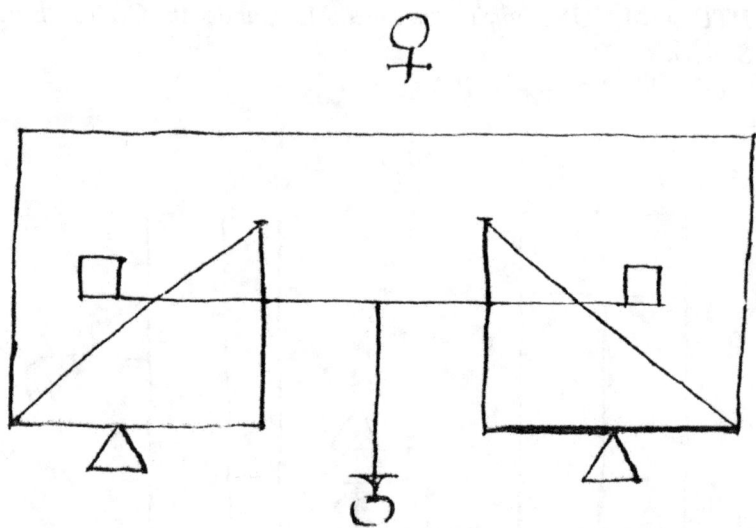

The Degrees of the Black Eagle Rose-Croix

ARISTOTLE studied Quicksilver, called Mercury, under the Genius **Ophiel**. His Scales are:

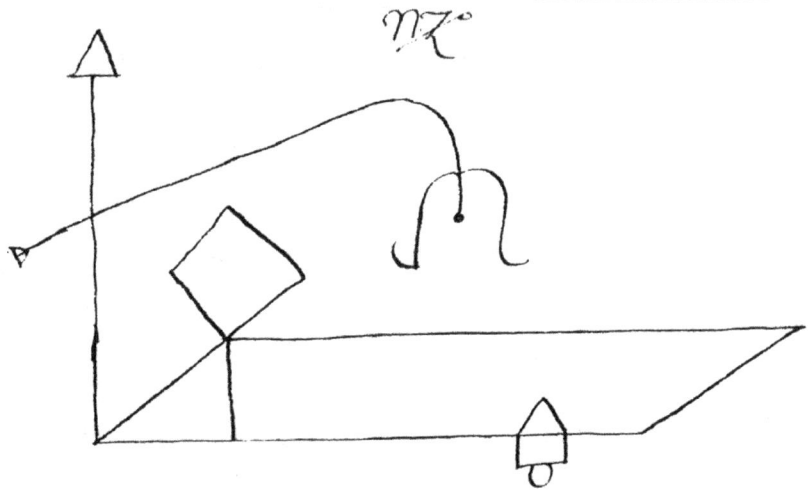

THALES studied Silver, called the Moon, under the Genius **Phul**. His Scales are:

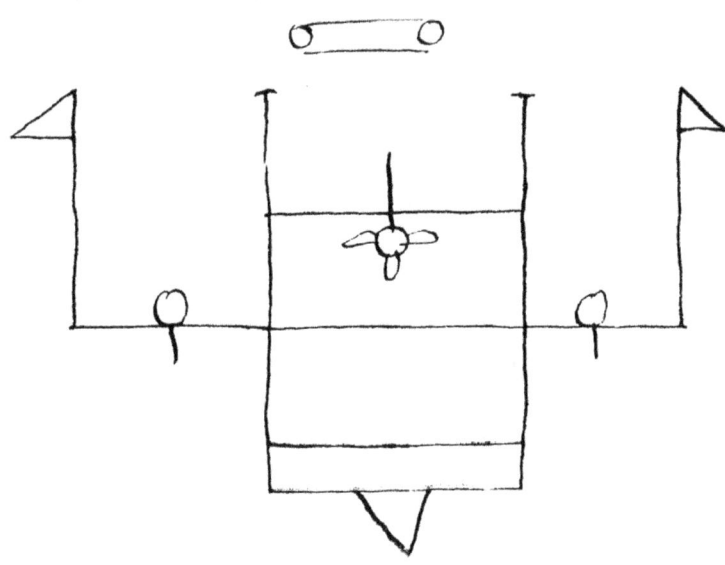

Q. *Name the four elements.*

A. **AIR**   **FIRE**
     EARTH   **WATER**

Q. *You heard that I spoke to you about a vivifying spirit called* **ALKAHEST**, *which has alone the generative virtues for producing the great cubic stone with the pyramidal top, which encloses in itself all the gifts and virtues to render men happy in this world and in the other, when good use is made of it. Could you give us an idea of the means to succeed in composing this* **ALKAHEST**?

A. *Yes, Sovereign Grand Master. One has to start by working on joining together the four simple Elements of which men are composed. These Elements are drawn from the three Kingdoms of Nature, that is the Animal, the Vegetable, and the Mineral.*

Q. *Which order do you observe for this labor?*

A. *The Rule, the Measure, the Weight, and the Balance of which each is a key.*

Q. *What else?*

A. *To employ in that labor the Animals, the Vegetables and the Minerals, each in their season, each enclosed in one of the Houses of the Sun, a time when they gave all their virtues, and not otherwise.*

Q. *Which are these Animals, Vegetables and Minerals proper to be used*[118] *on the celestial table of each House of the Sun. Explain each to us in their Places and Ranks.*

A. **MARCH**[119]

In the House of March one uses:

     The goat   The yellow amaranth
     The owl   The sardonyx
     The olive tree

APRIL

In the House of April one uses:

     The He-goat   The male cypress
     The dove   The topaz
     The myrtle

---

[118] Or 'served': *servir* can mean either.

[119] Some of the animals and stones are different from their first appearance in the text. These are listed in footnotes 9, 10, 13 and 14.

The Degrees of the Black Eagle Rose-Croix

MAY

In the House of May one uses:

The bull
The cock
The laurel

The female cypress
The agate

JUNE

In the House of June one uses:

The dog[120]
The stork
The hazel tree

The great comfrey
The chalcedony

JULY

In the House of July one uses:

The stag
The eagle
The shallot

The plant called cyclamen
The blood jasper

AUGUST

In the House of August one uses:

The pig
The sparrow
The apple tree

The calamint
The emerald

SEPTEMBER

In the House of September one uses:

The full moon[121]
The goose
The boxwood

The germantree
The beryl

---

[120] This is actually listed in the original manuscript as *barbet*, or 'poodle'. We have substituted the generic term 'dog' as used earlier in the text. It would seem odd to be so specific, going so far as to single out the French poodle for sacrifice. Did somebody Willermoz didn't like own a poodle....?

[121] This appears out of place. The earlier list for September listed this as the ass.

OCTOBER

In the House of October one uses:

    The wolf   The artemisia
    The woodpecker   The hyacinth
    The quince

NOVEMBER

In the House of November one uses:

    The serpent   The primrose
    The crow   The amethyst
    The palm tree

DECEMBER

In the House of December one uses:

    The lion   The morel
    The heron   The cornelian
    The pine tree

JANUARY

In the House of January one uses:

    The sheep   The thyme
    The peacock   The rock crystal
    The laurel

FEBRUARY

In the House of February one uses:

    The Barbary horse[122]   The astrolochia
    The swan   The Eastern sapphire
    The elm tree

---

[122] *Le cheval barbé entier*, lit. 'entirely Barbary horse', probably a thoroughbred Barbary. However, like the poodle above, this seems quite specific, and the original mention earlier in the text only calls for a generic 'horse'.

The Degrees of the Black Eagle Rose-Croix

Q. *Why did you begin this arrangement of the celestial Houses with that of March?*

A. *Because in Hermetic Philosophy and Astronomy sun years are counted beginning with March.*

Q. *How are the three creations of Nature prepared for use in each celestial House?*

A. *They are prepared very mysteriously without common fire, but an Elemental Fire taken from primary matter, by attracting sextruple[123] mixtures placed in digestion in the Philosophical bed, lighted by the four Major Winds.*

Q. *Name these four Major Winds.*

A. **NORTH   SOUTH**
EAST   WEST

Q. *How is the meat served on the table of the Spouse with six Virgins?*

A. *They are each served separately:*

Some in Salt   Others in Sulfur
Others in Spirit   Others in Oil

Q. *What do the newlyweds do with all these courses[124]?*

A. *Each month he takes a sufficient quantity to compose the* **Alkahest** *by means of the Scales of Solomon to serve for the newlyweds when they are placed on the nuptial bed.*

Q. *What does this alliance create for humankind?*

A. *Immense treasures which will last as long as the World.*

Q. *Are all men capable of laboring on the Great Work?*

A. *No, very few are capable. It is only true Masons who can claim this right, but very few are worthy of attaining it.*

Q. *What must one do in order to be initiated into the Cabalistic Art?*

A. *One must be like our Master Hiram, who preferred to suffer death than to reveal the secret entrusted to him.*

---

[123]The word used, which looks like *sextripette*, doesn't exist. However, following the previous logic, one would expect the six metals to be put in this 'Philosophical bed'.

[124]The word used is *mets*, literally 'cooked food' or 'prepared food'.

Q. *From where did he receive these secrets?*

A. *From King Solomon, who in his Cabala instituted an order which he called Masons, divided into three Grades, the last being that of Master. Those who were initiated possessed all of the Science like this King, instilled by virtue of a plate of gold called a Pentacle, by means of which the whole Science was known to them, and nothing was kept hidden.*

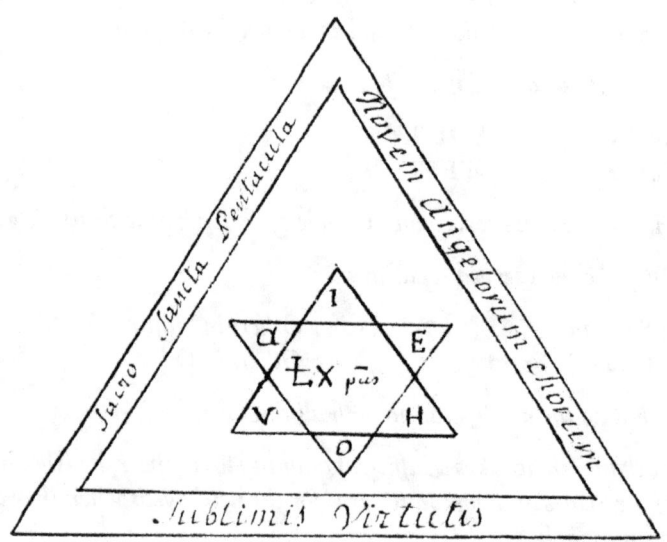

Figure of the Pentacle

Such is the image of the Sacred Pentacle which is triangular, where many thing are written on each side which are not revealed to the Profane, and which bring misfortune to those who abuse it.

The Degrees of the Black Eagle Rose-Croix

The Instruction being finished, the Grand Master says:

> My Dear Bailiffs, let us work to make ourselves worthy to possess such a jewel, knowing its full power. Let us be zealous for our Order in general, and in particular for the Sovereign and Most Serene Order of Knights of the Black Eagle Rose Croix.
>
> After the Grand Master has finished, the Grand Prior addresses the Grand Master and says:

Q. *Why are the Knights called Rose Croix?*

A. *A. Raymond Lully, a famous Mason and a great Hermetic Philosopher accomplished the celestial marriage of the Spouse with six Virgins, from this was born the* **MESSIAH**[125] *which he was expecting. He presented it to a King of England who caused medals[126] to be made, on one side of which was represented a Rose and on the other a Cross, and the abbreviated name of their author whom the King made a Knight.*

> *That is why all Philosophers who apply themselves to the Great Work, and who have knowledge of the Cabalistic Science are called Rose Croix, whose number is very small.*

After this response the Grand Master continues:

> *My dear Prince Bailiffs Rose Croix, it is time for us to rest.*

He Closes the Chapter as described earlier.

END

---

[125] To be understood as the Philosopher's Stone, and not the actual Messiah!
[126] The word in the manuscript is *monnoyes*.